Historicizing Theories, Identities, and Nations

Histories of Anthropology Annual

Historicizing Theories, Identities, and Nations

Histories of Anthropology Annual, Volume 11

EDITED BY REGNA DARNELL
AND FREDERIC W. GLEACH

University of Nebraska Press | Lincoln and London

CONTENTS

EDITORS' INTRODUCTION

This is our fourth volume since *Histories of Anthropology Annual* returned from the journals to the book division at the University of Nebraska Press. This may seem nothing but a structural question of production, but there are real distinctions between journals and books that are quite significant to the ways we conceived and continue to produce *HoAA*. After more than a decade we find ourselves reflecting on the peculiarities of an annual cycle of publication geared to professional colleagues in anthropology and history (broadly defined to include ethnohistory and history of science) and in Native studies and other specific cultural studies, as well as to a more generalist audience. On the one hand, the book division attracts readers whose curiosity about ideas, cultural communities, and those who study them leads them to explore the wide variety of topics and themes in each issue. On the other hand, we have developed a fairly specialized audience whose members look to our regular publication to keep them in touch with the emergence of new ideas about the discipline and where its ideas come from and how their continuities are shaped. *HoAA* has become for many a reflexive practice within their understanding of the discipline(s); it functions like a journal to reflect current research.

Reading a journal is a very different experience from reading a single-authored book or an integrated series of topical essays in which multiple authors have coproduced the work. The book format allows the author to develop the ramifications of an argument and to present detailed evidence in its support. The book composed of essays also imposes an order in advance. A journal issue does not stand alone in the same way. Even though many of its articles may eventually become books, ideas in a journal are presented in a framework of the ideas that surround them. Very few academics write papers without thinking about what journal they might fit, where they might attract an audience that will articulate their work within larger disciplinary frames. *HoAA* strives to merge the best features of both book and journal. Our rule of thumb is no more than three articles from the same conference or session, prepared as a set. Nonetheless, the cumulative quality emphasized above gives a book-like flavor because of how the papers in each volume resonate with previous ones, unique but also drawing on and recombining ideas and themes. Serendipity perhaps, or perhaps an editorial imposition of overarching strands onto the individual contributions, but also perhaps reflecting an inherent coherence of anthropology and the process of anthropologists and others toward historicizing it. We believe that this is an ideal model of knowledge production—always a work in progress with unanticipated offshoots and cross-overs.

There is a cumulative quality to all scholarship that is enhanced by the annual cycle of our volumes. Journals that appear multiple times in a year have a continuous flow that does not readily pause for periodic reflection. Each year, however, *HoAA* produces a new series of papers, and we as editors attempt to interrelate them around themes of import to contemporary anthropology. Both editors are anthropologists, so we begin from the assumptions of our training, remembering that anthropology itself is always already interdisciplinary and connected by our ethnographic commitments to what is happening in the world beyond the ivory tower.

Increasingly, each volume displays an intertextuality with those that have preceded it. Biography, national tradition, schools of thought, genres of writing for different audiences, relationship of anthropological research (both archival and ethnographic) to communities studied, and autoethnography drawing on the background of the author are some of the recurrent themes that cross volumes and authors. The title is almost always the last thing to fall into place. This time, "historicizing" stresses the process of scholarly understanding the history of anthropology. Theories are implicit in the contexts and biographies (aka identities) of research subjects, and nations are the counters of context within which ideas develop and scholars do their work.

Much of this volume appears to focus around a single figure from different angles, that of Franz Boas, founder of Americanist anthropology. But the resonances of the papers and their interconnections are complex and rhizomatic. Regna Darnell calls for a revisionist revisiting that debunks presentist (i.e., nonhistoricist) readings of Boas and what he actually said and did. Her paper traces the theoretical intertwining of Boas's seminal work on physical anthropology, largely anthropometric, and his cultural and linguistic studies of Native Americans. He emerges as a thinker far ahead of his time, his views of plasticity foreshadowing contemporary epigenetic and biocultural paradigms. Independently, James M. Nyce and Evelyn J. Bowers explore how A. Irving Hallowell implicitly integrated his views of human evolution with those of human nature and cross-cultural variability. Both Hallowell and Boas have been remembered for a retrospectively perceived dichotomy in their thinking that the biological is relegated to a residual position not influencing the cultural. The four-field approach to anthropology in North America would seem to promise more flexibility across subdisciplines, but perhaps we have not heard the messages of our forebears and need to reexamine our methodological and theoretical roadblocks.

The question of cultural relativism, often associated rather narrowly with the Boasian paradigm, proves more complex across articles in this volume. Andrew P. Lyons elegantly explores the work of Edvard Westermarck, not usually remembered as an important source for Americanist anthropology but whose explorations broaden the origins and scope of relativist principles—despite other aspects of Westermarck's thought that are less palatable to many today. The Germanic roots of cultural relativism in the inseparability of language and culture are emphasized in Robert C. Ulin's characterization of changing ideas about the history of anthropology itself. He sees "history of anthropology" as an anthropological question to be approached with our discipline's established ethnographic techniques, deeply grounded in the study of language and the relativity of conceptual thought to its use. These are Boasian (and Hallowellian) ideas, but their instantiation in the global and interdisciplinary study of language surpasses that context. Relativism also underlies Michael E. Harkin's speculative essay on what Boas might have made out of 9/11. Boas's principled pacifism and valorization of science over nationalism gave way at the end of his life to a passionate critique of Nazi Germany, a movement toward engagement in moral debates as a public intellectual. Hitler became the ground zero for relativism debates in anthropology. Frank A. Salamone explores how Ruth Benedict, a core Boas student, drew on the psychology of Maslow and then-emerging cybernetic models of social process to talk about a synergy that might transcend the nihilistic failure of judgment that potentially plagued some relativist arguments.

Two more papers directly frame Boas in relation to the larger intellectual milieu of his mature career. In a second contribution—we felt the two papers worked well together but as separate works, and so we bent our policy regarding multiple submissions by a single author—Michael E. Harkin finds limitations of the pragmatist philosophy of John Dewey reflected in his correspondence with Boas that led the former to the roots of contemporary neoliberalism. Pragmatism as social engineering might be expected to have unexpected consequences. Both Harkin and David W. Dinwoodie are intrigued by the figure of Randolph Bourne and the circle of "young intellectuals" that briefly coalesced around him in interwar New York, where Boas—though hardly a young intellectual in that period—drew on their energy and access to a larger public than his own discipline to push his version of relativism and cultural tolerance. Boas's textbook *Anthropology and Modern Life* (1928) was geared to this elite public audience and drew on its fascination with modernity.

Cultural analysis and ethnographic research are standpoint-based practices grounded in the position of the observer. The three papers on Vietnam add a new geographic site to the *HoAA* corpus, but the question of national tradition proves more complex. In this sense, each of these papers explores different aspects of the question of observer and observed. Nguyen Phuong Ngoc documents how scholars socialized to professional practices during the French colonial era in Vietnam adopted a standpoint fundamentally external to a slowly emerging indigenous national identity. The issues are global, the details local. What Audre Lourde called "the language of the enemy" was the language available, and scholarly credibility depended on using it effectively. (Ashis Nandy's *The Intimate Enemy: Loss and Recovery of Self under Colonialism* [1983] similarly responds to the internalized values and perspectives of empire.) Nguyen Van Huy provides a dramatic contrast by focusing on his own experiences as an administrator and intellectual. The term "reminiscences" in his title is somewhat disingenuous, because the standpoint is so clearly systemic, searching for forms of expression and social criticism that arise from within both the self and the social and cultural context. In this context, Bradley Camp Davis argues from a more characteristic social science standpoint that is informed by time perspective and response to emergent social movements in Vietnam. By juxtaposing these perspectives, the reader is encouraged to develop a more rounded vision than could be derived from any one of the papers in isolation.

Representing another world region, Olga Glinskii's analysis of ethnonationalism in Ukraine also draws heavily on the analytic effectiveness of standpoint. She argues that before World War I, in a tradition evocative of the Brothers Grimm in Germany, Ukrainian intellectuals turned to the peasant as the figure of their own particularity. An absorbing analysis in itself, this contribution also may be read productively alongside several in recent *HoAA* volumes focusing on literary connections, on peasantry in anthropology, or on national and regional traditions.

The final paper in this volume is a new genre for *HoAA* but a long-established one in anthropology: the obituary of the "informant," consultant, collaborator. The names of such individuals are as well known among areal specialists as those of academic colleagues. Thomas McIlwraith, who writes for a dual audience, was invited to prepare a eulogy for Tahltan elder Arthur Nole, but he also shares (after being given permission by the family) his memories of a beloved teacher who spoke in the oral formats of traditional knowledge with an expertise no outsider could duplicate. McIlwraith renders that knowledge accessible to readers who did not know Nole and do not know Tahltan peoples. There is a powerful cross-cultural synergy that is at the heart of the genre and indeed of anthropology itself, and manuscript reviewers described the piece as "beautiful," an epithet rarely applied to academic writing.

We remain excited by this project to bring together such explorations in disciplinary history, relishing the surprise that comes with each new submission. We hope that readers will also find here surprise, fascination, and ideas and aspects of the discipline's history that will prove novel, productive, and useful for teaching. As always, we encourage readers to also become contributors—*HoAA* cannot continue without both!

REGNA DARNELL
FREDERIC W. GLEACH

Historicizing Theories, Identities, and Nations

1

Franz Boas as Theorist

A Mentalist Paradigm for the Study of Mind, Body, Environment, and Culture

Franz Boas is uniformly credited as the dominant figure of American anthropology from the late nineteenth century to the Second World War. His stature as a public intellectual is acknowledged to have extended far beyond the borders of the discipline he established. Nonetheless, few contemporary anthropologists actually read Boas or have a clear sense of what he wrote or thought. Sadly, little of the enormous Boas scholarship is based on historicist engagement with his work. In the seven decades since his death, the theoretical preoccupations of anthropologists have shifted more than once. Furthermore, the world itself has changed such that the context of Boas's work now requires historicist reconstruction of his professional, personal, and culture-historical milieu.

The centennial of *The Mind of Primitive Man* (MPM) in 2011 brought renewed attention to Boas's theoretical position.[1] But few of the contributors delved far into the mind of Franz Boas or the degree to which he intended the book as a paradigmatic statement of his position. The cumulative stereotypes of our inherited Boas are long overdue for revision. This chapter revisits Boas's ongoing influence on anthropology, linguistics, and Native American history, identifying and debunking stereotypes where necessary and concluding that *The Mind of Primitive Man* in 1911 set out the theoretical position that would preoccupy Boas for the remainder of his career. I argue that he was fully cognizant of the integration of his core ideas and that MPM, in both its 1911 and 1938 editions, therefore legitimately constitutes a scientific paradigm statement. In this work, Boas formulates both explanatory and descriptive theory and provides a systematic program for the Americanist tradition in anthropology (see Darnell 1998, 2001).

The elements of this paradigm are explicitly articulated. Boas set a high standard for theory, insisting that it be based on scientifically rigorous methodology even when dealing with qualitative ethnographic or psychological phenomena. Human biological variability, more amenable to such methodology, was his starting point for the study of the mind as well as the body. Culture, in his view, was dynamic and grounded in a specific environment, operating in history. Traditional classifications of race, language, and culture were noncomparable phenomena and had to be kept separate analytically. Biological determinism, whether phrased as eugenics or everyday racism, was dangerous to the very existence of civilization. Only science and scientific method could counter its toxicity and reveal the positive potentials inherent in human diversity. Boas foresaw inevitable mixture of races over time and lamented the counterproductive blinders imposed by European American ethnic prejudice. Freedom of thought, the sine qua non of science, could be protected only by valuing racial and cultural diversity. Although Boas's analytic lens shifted systematically from the biological to the cultural and back again, he refused steadfastly to consider them independently of their intersections and mutual entailments. The axioms of this paradigm worked together across subject matters and inductive or deductive methods to explore human nature, history, and "civilization" (a term that appears more frequently in this text than "culture").

One of the most persistent of our inherited stereotypes is that Boas was not a theorist. His legendary six-foot shelf of Kwakiutl ethnography, replete with blueberry recipes, has been ridiculed by some as the height of descriptive ethnography, a meaningless empiricism (Maud 2003), glossing over the significance of blueberries to the cultural practices and livelihood of the Kwakwaka'kwak (the people he called Kwakiutl). If Boas had any theoretical ideas, they have long since outlived their utility, or so goes the metanarrative (see also Bauman and Briggs 2003; Freed 2012; Williams 1996). It seems clear today, however, that his critique of evolution has been relegated to the past primarily because that battle has been won, at least on the fronts that Boas envisioned it. He argued persuasively that the approach of the evolutionists to their own embodiment as the culmination of human civilization was based on premature generalization about both human nature and human history. Such a position might be construed merely as a theory of absence based in negation—except that Boas did not stop there. Rather, he offered a methodology, a mentalist standpoint epistemology, that entailed fundamental rethinking of the verities of science and the purported objectivity of scientific method (Darnell 2001). It does not follow, of course, that a mentalist theory is atheoretical, though it may be deemed nonrigorous by some when judged by the criteria of their own nonmentalist theory. Boas carefully avoided such reductionism.

Another facile stereotype suggests that Boas was a theorist for one shining moment in 1911 when he published both his introduction to the *Handbook of American Indian Languages* and his monumental *The Mind of Primitive Man*. Never again, we are to assume, did he attempt to synthesize his theoretical position. The 1911 cut-off date for George W. Stocking Jr.'s (1974) compilation of Boas's writings, for example, assumes that Boas's "theory" already was set in stone by that time. Boas's most comprehensive biographer, Douglas Cole, ends even earlier, with Boas's resignation from the American Museum of Natural History in 1906. Thereafter Boas concentrated on consolidating his institutional leadership of American anthropology within the academy. On the subject of theory, Cole (1999) recapitulates Stocking (1968, 1974) and the positivists without further analysis, despite the presence of substantial revisionist scholarship in the interim (see Baker 2010; Bunzl 2004; Darnell 1998, 2001; Hyatt 1990; Jonaitis 1995; Kendall and Krupnik 2003; Stocking 1996; Vermeulen 2015).

Most commentators recognize two critical ideas that emerged in the 1911 statements: The essential position of the *Handbook* introduction, that race, language, and culture are analytically independent variables, was incorporated into the methodological exegesis of MPM. In the latter, more extensive work, Boas further argued for the universality of the human mind across geographic regions, "forms of life" (i.e., subsistence patterns), and cultures, regardless of the biological make-up of the societies or their individual members. These insights, of course, are now so taken for granted that they appear to be common sense rather than the theoretical breakthrough away from ethnocentrism that they were when Boas first formulated them. Contemporary scholars and intellectual heirs too often cite these 1911 propositions as though heroically isolated from Boas's otherwise atheoretical narrative. That is, it is simply assumed that Boas was not by temperament or creative genius a theorist, even though some theoretical commitments may have been implicit in his oeuvre.

This tenor of the Boasian legacy requires historicist contextualization. Postwar anthropologists in North America and Britain alike engendered a turn to positivism and placed their faith in technology as the harbinger of modern progress. Mentalism was out of fashion, and that side of Boas's thought seemed increasingly old-fashioned, though he continued to be revered by generations of students and students of these students. Anthropologists, like high-energy physicists, wanted to be scientific (ironically, since physics itself increasingly has challenged the parameters of linear logic and stable dimensions). Many of Boas's successors preferred to explore revitalized, presumably more nuanced, and sophisticated (neo)evolutionary paradigms. Among the most vociferous critics of Boas as hindering the theoretical development of anthropology, Leslie White (1963) and Marvin Harris (1968) continue to be taken at face value by many commentators without returning to the originals.

In the interim, the theoretical pendulum of the social sciences has shifted again, back toward mentalist alternatives to formal modeling and rational actor approaches. Despite tensions between seemingly incommensurable methodologies, the former carries renewed legitimacy. In the present anthropological climate, therefore, Boas stands out as far ahead of his own time for his effort to develop a single paradigm for mind and body. He called for an anthropology that was prescient in his day but is even more robustly resonant in our own. I argue that Boas used the opportunity of his "course of lectures" delivered at Boston's Lowell Institute and at the National University of Mexico in 1910–11 to consolidate under a single umbrella the position he had been developing in a series of published papers beginning in the 1880s and lightly reworked for his synthesis. Each paper had worked through one or more planks of his emerging theory of mind, and in 1911 he finally was prepared to bring them together.

Boas's preface listed the previously published works that were incorporated into his lectures. Despite the repetition of content already in the public domain and the close correspondence of chapters in MPM to these prior publications, Boas baldly asserted that the constituent pieces were "revised," "enlarged," and "embedded" in a new framework (1911b:n.p.). This embedding involved a juxtaposition adding up to more than the sum of its parts: it was intended as a paradigm statement.

"Human Faculty as Determined by Race," presented to the American Association for the Advancement of Science at the Chicago World's Fair in 1893 and published in the *Proceedings* the following year, argued that "race" was a misleading, emotionally laden, and scientifically inaccurate term for attested human variability. Two years later, in *Science*, "The Limitations of the Comparative Method of Anthropology" articulated the critique of unilinear evolution. In 1901 Boas tried out what would become the label for his developing paradigm, providing the title for his 1911 book, "The Mind of Primitive Man." This paper was presented to the American Folklore Society, where Boas might have deemed mentalist topics particularly welcome, folklore being concerned with the products of mind and the histories of the communities producing them. To the same audience in 1904, "Some Traits of Primitive Culture" debunked stereotypes about the primitive; the folklore audience included literary scholars for whom ethnographic folklore was unfamiliar, and a champion was needed to attest to its comparable value. In 1909 Boas's anthropometric studies were rising to prominence, and he outlined his emerging synthesis of biology and culture in "The Race Problem in America," published in *Science*, the preeminent national arbiter of professional debates on science. His intervention in the public issues of race would reach a wide audience through this venue. "Psychological Problems in Anthropology" appeared in the *American Journal of Psychology* only a year before MPM. Psychology, as the science of the mental, was a critical discipline for the legitimization of mentalist anthropology. Boas (1912) also noted his use of parts of the introduction to the *Handbook of American Indian Languages* and data from his report entitled "Changes in the Bodily Form of Descendants of Immigrants" to the United States Census Commission. The latter two works appeared virtually concurrently with MPM and were integral to the consolidation of his paradigm at this juncture of his career.

In 1911 Boas had already laid out the four-field approach that continues to hold sway in North American anthropology, albeit more as nostalgic norm than as uniformly reflected in departmental practices or professional identities. What Boas did in MPM that was so remarkable is in the first instance methodological. Because he believed that method and theory were inseparable in science, Boas's innovations of method, many of which were effectively thought experiments in the absence of conclusive data, allowed him to articulate his theory. This transformed everything. He began to talk about the "mind" of his title, "primitive" or otherwise, by talking about body, about human biological variability. He adopted this strategy because the methods of biological science were far more advanced than those for studying culture, and he was prepared to reason analogically from one to the other.

Yet another inaccurate inherited stereotype about Boas is that he was a culturalist and that his theory of culture was static. In MPM, however, the term "culture" rarely appears independently. Boas's binary to biology is not culture but environment (see Darnell 2015). He wants to know why one group of people is different from another and turns to biology as explanation only as a last resort and when forms of life, including ways of gaining a living, can be held constant. Boas deploys a method of defamiliarization that toggles back and forth between one set of variables and another. From the standpoint of biology, plasticity is the core of variability, and culture is held constant, with environment as its explanatory mechanism. The inductive method in the face of limited data is parallel to that of Darwin's theory of natural selection. From the standpoint of environment/culture, however, variability is rampant, and the possibility of equal "value" to "civilizations" other than our own holds constant an equal species-level capacity for mental development:

> It is somewhat difficult for us to recognize that the value which we attribute to our own civilization is due to the fact that we participate in this civilization, and that it has been controlling all our actions from the time of our birth; but it is certainly conceivable that there may be other civilizations, based perhaps on different traditions and on a different equilibrium of emotion and reason, which are of no less value than ours, although it may be impossible for us to appreciate their values without having grown up under their influence. (1911b:207)

"Value," like the plasticity of bodily form, is a matrix that operates in the eye of the beholder. The predictability of biological form, cultural form, the histories of particular groups, and environmental context all potentially dissolve into a sea of multivariate complexity that broadens the desiderata of adequate theory: biology, culture, archaeology, language. Any classification is arbitrary, because variability necessarily exceeds its bounds when one switches the beholder's classificatory lens again: hence the analytic discreteness of race, language, and culture. Interestingly, the classificatory value of language is not central to MPM, although Boas developed this side of his argument in the *Handbook* introduction and in much of his later work.

A final distorting stereotype comes from the reputation of the Boasian paradigm as represented by Boas's classic first generation of students. They all acknowledged, though sometimes chaffed against, his institutional leadership, which created a consensus for anthropology, a normal science in Kuhnian parlance. None of the students matched the breadth of Boas's own work; rather, each specialized in some part of the package (see Darnell 1998, 2001): Alfred Kroeber attributed to Boas his own culturalist predilections for the "superorganic"; Edward Sapir pushed for history or "time perspective" based on inferences from historical linguistics as extended to encompass unwritten languages; Robert Lowie created typologies of social structure not dependent on set evolutionary sequences; Paul Radin developed life history methods to capture what Boas called "the native point of view" through dialogue with the anthropologist; Ruth Benedict and Margaret Mead explored the relationship of individual personality to cultural pattern and socialization. The students concentrated on developing theory within their own chosen specializations and rarely articulated the common assumptions of what became recognizable in the years following MPM as the Americanist Tradition, that is, the Boasian paradigm.

Toward the end of his life, after his forced retirement in 1936, Boas turned to ensuring the legacy of his paradigm (though of course the term "paradigm" is anachronistic, its present use stemming from Thomas Kuhn [1970] two decades after Boas's death). What the discipline remembers is Boas's late-career activism against Nazi racism and his 1928 *Anthropology and Modern Life*. Crucially, however, he also revised

MPM in 1938 and compiled a selection of his published essays titled *Race, Language and Culture* in 1940. These were the works he hoped to enshrine as the culmination of his life's work.

As in MPM, Boas begins *Race, Language and Culture* with the relative methodological rigor of race/biology and ends with culture/ethnology. The final section is explicitly labeled methodology. Most tellingly, in this compendium, language has a more explicit mediating role in the analytic triad of 1911. Both historical and synchronic linguistics (extended to unwritten languages by Boas and his students) promise methodological rigor closer to that of biology than of culture. Language is an attractive starting point because it is more akin to culture than is biology. Indeed, language is part of culture and thereby holds the potential to bring culture into greater analytic clarity on analogy with the structures of language. The logic of inference (i.e., theory) is directly parallel to that of MPM. Boas saw himself as a scientist, first and foremost. The problem was to deal with mental phenomena in scientifically rigorous ways by applying insights from more fully studied or easily measured arenas of study to others until the whole succumbed to scientific method, thereby mitigating the relative fuzziness of culture considered in isolation.

In the preface to the 1938 edition, Boas emphasized that "much work has been done since 1911 in all the branches of science" engaged in his topic, that is, heredity, "the influence of environment upon bodily form and behavior," and the "mental attitudes of 'primitive' man." Interestingly, "primitive" was problematized here by quotation marks, as it is not in the 1911 edition. The language of anthropological theory was changing, in good part because of the work of Boas and his students. Boas acknowledged the need to rewrite and rearrange parts of his text but nonetheless insisted that he had come to "an ever-increasing certainty of his conclusions" that "no fundamental difference in the ways of thinking of primitive and civilized men" can be identified by science (1938:v). The updated scientific results from overlapping disciplines were described as "new points of view," a position that maintained the standpoint of the scientist at the center of his epistemology. He contrasts the "logical as well as . . . biological" revisionism in which biology, psychology, and anthropology "concur" in challenging "popular prejudice based on earlier scientific and popular tradition." He further laments that science gives way to prejudice when dictators attempt to control the flow of "trustworthy science" (vi). In 1938 gathering clouds over Hitler's Europe underscored the urgency of effectively disseminating his views. He observed darkly: "The suppression of intellectual freedom rings the death knell of science" (vi).

THE ARGUMENT FOR MIND AND BODY

Let us turn now in more detail to the consistencies versus the modifications in the text. The critical mass of material in both editions deals with the logic underlying the mentalist paradigm. I have elsewhere highlighted two issues: first, the reasoning by analogy from biology as rigorous and culture as less amenable to measurement and manipulation; and second, the emphasis on environment rather than culture as the methodologically preferable option (Darnell 2015). The foremost goal of Boas's mentalist theory is to counter biological determinism, that is, racism. The bookends in both editions are an introduction about race prejudice and a conclusion about the scientific incoherence of popular misconceptions of race. The work of Boas as theorist is framed alongside the convictions of Boas as activist that science can resolve many of the dilemmas of modern society.

Boas's biological argument relies on his review of the laws of heredity as understood in 1911 to show that variability within "races and types" far exceeds the "range of variation in each type" (1911b:94). In 1938 he notes that "heredity" in his initial treatment now is termed "genetics" (1938:54). In both editions he calls for the study of family lines (e.g., 1938:63) and emphasizes that small isolated populations develop relatively uniform physical characteristics because of the limited number of individual ancestors. The human type is more variable in "instable" populations with larger numbers and greater mobility. The fundamental question for Boas is demographic: "how far . . . human types are stable" and "how far variable under the influence of environment." Because we can never assume "a permanent stability of bodily form," causes of variation (e.g., environment) become crucial to explaining observed variations (1911b:40, 41). The short time span of ethnological inquiry, moreover, has precluded study of longer-range trends.

Despite the absence of conclusive evidence from the science of the day, Boas concludes that "mental development follows laws quite analogous to those of physical development" (1911b:49). His demonstration of the plasticity of human biological types "necessarily" leads to "a great plasticity of the mental make-up of human types" (64–65). This chain of inference places the burden of proof on those who would argue for the stability (i.e., determinism) of mental forms. Boas cites his own census research with southern Italians, central Europeans, northern Europeans, and "an extended series of East European Hebrews" (54). Differences in head form and other bodily traits develop in childhood and persist throughout life. He concludes that the "advance of civilization" creates conditions for rapid response to environment with consequent instability of type, by inference mental as well as physical (75).

In 1938 Boas set up his argument about the "composition of the human race" by demonstrating the impossibility of clearly distinguishing race and culture, with culture standing alone, as it did not in 1911 (1938:35). The difficulties of maintaining a definition of race by objective biological criteria for variation based on common descent remain difficult to overcome. Unfortunately, the very "concept of type develops in our minds from general impressions" (47). However, even a purely statistical treatment cannot resolve the problem, because the types themselves are not discrete.

In the 1938 edition Boas devotes a chapter to "the morphological position of races," concerning himself particularly with the possibility of parallel development of similar traits without descent from a particular set of ancestors. Such "convergence" (1938:100) is plausible because the traits that most distinguish humans from animals are distributed across otherwise divergent groups.

In 1911 Boas reviewed "the evolutionary viewpoint" in terms of social rather than biological evolution. Similar forms (e.g., of religion, social organization, art, etc.) occur around the world, which demonstrates "the fundamental unity of the mind of all the races of man, but also of the truth of the theory of evolution of civilization" in which "our present civilization" appears as the culmination (1911b:280–281). Evidence is potentially available from early written history, survivals in modern civilization, and archaeology—with only the latter germane to "people that have no history" (182). Boas sees no evidence that "every people in an advanced stage of civilization" must have passed through the same stages (184). Nor is it necessarily the case that the same forms result from the same causes. Further methodological problems arise because comparability of data cannot be assured. The theory of evolution assumes development from simple to complex "under more or less rationalistic impulses" (193). Many human activities, unlike technology, do not depend on reason for their development. In sum, "there is no close relation between race and culture" (196).

In 1911 the comparison of primitive and civilized mental traits begins with the comparison of animal and human mind under "varying conditions of race and environment" and quickly establishes that reason is the critical human faculty. Nonetheless, the differences are more apparent than real (1911b:95, 114). In 1938 "physiological and psychological functions of races" are grouped together (1938:116). In both cases, more complex elements are more variable. Family lines and individual variability both confound the possibility of accurately describing formal contrasts. Boas uses his own immigration data and Otto Klineberg's data on Indian and white girls' ability to reproduce beadwork patterns, concluding that social experience trumps innate ability. Posture and gesture attest that the "motor habits of groups of people are culturally determined and not due to heredity." Boas declines to speculate about personality on methodological grounds: "Unfortunately, the methods of studying personality are highly unsatisfactory because the features to be investigated lack clarity" (126, 127 128). Boas's former students, in particular, Ruth Benedict, Margaret Mead, and Edward Sapir, were developing culture and personality as a field, but none of them shared Boas's insistence on objective and scientific measurement. The tenor of culture and personality remained configurational, more ethnographic than comparative. Note that Boas did not use the term "cultural relativism," though it is regularly attributed to him as evidence of his purported culturalism and unwillingness to judge cultural phenomena on objective, potentially universal grounds. In any case, he concludes that "the effect of civilization upon the mind has been much overestimated. . . . We should then be clear in our minds regarding the differences between the phenomena of culture themselves and the abstract concepts of qualities of the human mind that are deduced from cultural data but have no cultural meaning if conceived as absolute, as existing outside of a culture" (140–141).

"The interpretations of culture" have too often yielded to premature generalization, with Darwinian evolution as an exemplar of inadequate methodological rigor (1938:175). Boas's former student Alexander Goldenweiser's theory of totemism, foreshadowing Claude Lévi-Strauss, illustrates the psychological distinctiveness of ethnological patterns such that comparison of forms alone is meaningless. Indeed, culture is better interpreted by geographical environment than by evolution. Boas cautions that geography can modify culture but is not in itself creative. "Anthropo-geography" has overstated the case for determinism of cultural development. Mind is the intervening variable and draws the influence of environment into the realm of "social life" (192).

In the 1938 edition Boas glosses the question as one of "mind and progress." He begins with assumptions about the "advance of culture" and its relationship to "primitiveness." Because every group of people experiences foreign influences, "cultural values" cannot be taken as discrete (1938:198). Boas suggests that both technological innovation and "intellectual work" require leisure. An objective measure is accumulation of experience and rational increase in knowledge (202). Boas also points out that cultural achievements are not shared by all members, whether in primitive or civilized cultures. Moreover, progress itself is difficult to define in such realms as social organization. Boas uses language as an example of the need for some sort of classification of experience, although very diverse forms of classification may serve this function. Languages most differ, he argues, in their obligatory forms, in the distinctions that must be expressed.

Boas believes, however, that rationality has increased as whatever classifications are provided by a given language rise to consciousness, allowing systematization of "the whole field of knowledge." In science, exemplified by the survival of the fittest, "the dominating idea determines the development of theories." Science cannot progress by exploring the uniqueness of phenomena but depends on generalization. Rather, progress depends on folklore, "the character of the traditional material," rather than on the individual. Despite the enormous variability of linguistic structures, thought is not restricted in capacity in any human language (1911b:220–223).

In 1938 the chapter title expands to include culture as the third typological variable, the one that would provide Boas with the title for his collection of his own essays. Recapitulating his arguments for the instability or nonpermanence of (bodily) type, language, and culture and for their independent variability, he notes that "the Aryan problem" disintegrates when the lack of covariation is acknowledged. "Culture" is more in focus here than in the first edition. But Boas emphasizes that it is a "vague" term, representing developments at different times in different aspects of the life of a people. "Culture areas" are simply "conveniences for the treatment of generalized traits of culture" and are normally based on geography, economics, or material culture. There is no progressive series, as claimed by the evolutionary theorists (1938:151, 155, 156).

In 1911 Boas frames the question of "the universality of cultural traits" as one of debunking the existence of "a lower cultural stage." Observed "analogues" of cultural traits occur in contexts that clearly have no shared historical roots. Environment provides inadequate explanation, because different groups in the same environment "show often marked differences." Environment, at best, places a limit on "the special forms of customs and beliefs," which themselves arise from historically determined cultural conditions (1911b:155, 158, 161, 163).

In 1938 Boas begins a chapter on "early cultural traits" by presenting a concise definition of culture as "the mental and physical reactions and activities that characterize the behavior of the individuals comprising a social group collectively and individually in relation to their natural environment, to other groups, to members of the group itself and of each individual to himself. It also includes the products of these activities and their role in the life of the groups. The mere enumeration of these various aspects of life, however, does not constitute culture. It is more, for its elements are not independent, they have a structure" (1938:159). Using these customary criteria, parallel animal behavior could be cited for most forms. "If we were to define culture by observing behavior alone there is little in the fundamental elements of human behavior that has not some kind of parallel in the animal world" (163). But the variability of human behavior, learned through tradition, makes them different. In the case of a particular culture, folklore provides the best entrée to considering "its inner growth as well as the effect of its relations to the cultures of its near and distant neighbors" (169).

REFORMULATING THE PARADIGM
FOR A CHANGING WORLD

On the surface, Boas's most salient rationale for a revised edition would seem to have been updating the biological, psychological, and ethnological database available to support his argument. Indeed, the 1938 edition provides far more references to the work of others and adds a new "Historical Review," largely using history of anthropology to debunk the views of earlier scholars. Boas states his problem not as biology and mind but as race and culture, the relationship of which he deems "influenced too often by racial, national, and class prejudice." He reviews various theorists (e.g., Gobineau, Klemm, Carus, Nott and Glidden, Chamberlain) whose purported generalizations about racial type are in fact based on cultural rather than the biological grounds they claim. American polygenist Samuel G. Morton is singled out for relegating Australians, Eskimos, and others to a permanent inferior "degree of civilization" (1938:20, 22). His arguments conveniently justify slavery in the United States. Madison Grant's "dogmatic assumption" that positive cultural characteristics must reflect otherwise unattested Nordic ancestry further illustrates the failure of such pseudoscience to ground itself in evidence. Boas takes on American eugenics here, the enemies close to home in America (see Baker 2010). He declines to trace a similar historical development for "modern theories" that "racial descent determines the mental and cultural qualities of the individual" (28). Having demonstrated the inadequacy of the biologically based theory of race, Boas remains willing to assume that the cultural will follow in even greater degree.

Ethnologists, not immune from disciplinary blinders, have been remiss in ignoring race and environment altogether. They gloss over actual bodily differences in an effort to "justify the assumption of a fundamental sameness of the human mind regardless of race." The ethnological paradigm assumes that "social and psychological conditions" are common to all mankind, with differences manifested through "the effects of historical happenings and of natural and cultural environment." The psychology of Wilhelm Wundt and the evolutionary sociology of William Graham Sumner err equally in paralleling social to organic evolution and in equating all peoples "on similar levels of culture." Boas concludes that ethnologists recognize a major divide between "culturally primitive man" and "civilized man" (1938:33–34). Interestingly, this distinction perpetuates the attribution of "culture" to the primitive and reserves "civilization" for the modern. Boas's own ethnology, however, more often speaks of the "civilization" of the so-called primitive. Stocking (1968), for example, emphasized the importance of Boas's pluralization of the concept of culture and its discreteness from the elite culture of the European literati. But the extension of "civilization" to all those of human stock, as of equal mental capacity, at least in 1911, is the alternative to the rigid dichotomy between "us" and "them."

In 1911 Boas begins with "Racial Prejudices," somewhat ironically depicting the equation of a self-satisfied white race with "civilization." The "naïve" and "unproved" assumption of "superior aptitude" judges everything by its own standards (1911b:3). "Civilization," like "mental faculty," cannot be the exclusive possession of a single group. Rather, the history of Europe's antecedents documents intermingling of cultures, each according to its own "genius." If the white race is distinguished, it is only by its capacity for assimilation from myriad sources. From "genius" Boas moves directly to the potential for "equal value," citing New World civilizations as evidence. He explores reasons for the favorable "conditions for assimilation" of the white race (7, 13). These include demographic (small population size over wide territory; degree of colonial control/settlement), geographic (isolation), historical (length of contact), medical (disease and epidemic), technological, and cultural (degree of difference in customs and physical appearance among peoples in contact). On the one hand, Mohammedans, Chinese, and Arabs have developed their own civilizations quite independently. On the other hand, obstacles to progress of the "negro race" in America can hardly be attributed to aptitude alone. In 1938 he puts it: "Several races have developed a civilization of a type similar to the one from which our own has sprung, and a number of favorable conditions have facilitated its rapid spread in Europe. Among these, similar physical appearance, contiguity of habitat and moderate difference in modes of manufacture were the most potent. When, later on, Europeans began to spread over other continents, the races with which they came into contact were not equally favorably situated" (1938:15). We could "hardly . . . predict" Negro achievements "if he were able to live with the Whites on absolutely equal terms" (15).

Boas makes short shrift of presumed biological evidence. All human groups are vastly divided from animals, making bestial analogies ridiculous. Differences in the central nervous system, which in 1911 could be measured only by such indices as brain weight and cranial capacity, are dismissed equally rapidly. Indeed, the "process of evolution" still continues, and human characteristics across the species cannot be assumed to be "stable." "Modern biological concepts" document the "intensity" and "varying directions" of human traits, making separate human types impossible to identify and clearly differentiate, particularly over time (1911b:20, 22).

In 1938 Boas elaborates on the multivalence of the term "primitive" as applied to both "bodily form and culture" (1938:3). Popular stereotypes persist due to the "racial isolation of Europe and the social segregation of races in America." Reasoning by equating "higher civilization" with innate racial aptitude is based in emotion, not science. This "idea" of superiority is deeply rooted. Both "race" and "civilization" are terms of judgment whose relationship must be clarified before "the form and growth of culture" can be adequately studied. More than in 1911, Boas emphasizes the terminology in which the problems of race are delineated. Here he talks about the "germs of civilization" of the white race (6, 10). The primitiveness of biological differences and how they may or may not lead to permanent inferiority must be distinguished from correspondence of racial groups with "the traits of the mental and social life of those people whom we call primitive from a cultural point of view" (18).

The 1938 introduction ends with an enlargement of the scope of the question from America to "our globe," within which diverse races and cultural forms exist (1938:17). This makes it ever more urgent that questions of race and culture be resolved by science. As nationality replaces race in categorizing human groups, the emotional urge to rigidify artificial categories enforces an unscientific determinism on complex and as yet answerable questions. Answers from science still fail to offer closure after a quarter century of further study.

THE SCOPE OF THE RACE PROBLEM

Race was the single most pressing question Boas addressed over his career. His stature as a public intellectual reflects his refusal to take up the cause of a single race subject to oppression and discrimination in a single time and place. Although he was in the first instance a specialist in the aboriginal peoples of the Americas, Boas also addressed everyday racism in the lives of Negroes and Jews in America. Science overruled personal standpoint—his theories of the relation of mind, body, environment, and culture operated the same way regardless of the group in question. Boas did not consider his own Jewish background germane to his analysis of prejudice against "the Hebrews." He presented himself as an American and a scientist, considering his unmentioned Jewishness a question of culture that no longer applied to his personal identity (Glick 1982:84, 545–565). Throughout his lifetime, Boas tenaciously and publicly opposed what we now call "scientific racism," including eugenics, restricted immigration policy, forced assimilation, and all other indignities to human freedom arbitrarily imposed on grounds of group membership.

In both the 1911 and 1938 editions, a chapter on race forms the culmination of the argument. It is the underlying motivation for the coalescence of anthropology's potential contribution to the often virulent and irrational public debate about race. The immediate targets of Boas's own vitriol, however, responded to then-contemporary events. In 1911 he attacked the American eugenicists who opposed miscegenation, supported strict segregationist laws, and blocked Negro civil and legal rights. The everyday racism of white America was deeply embedded in the "trammels of tradition" and required vigilant attention to science rather than emotion and fear of difference. By 1938 "Race Problems in the United States" had become "The Race Problem in Modern Society," a critique both of modernity's arrogant claim to represent the pinnacle of civilization and of the dehumanization of Jews in Hitler's Europe. The structure of the argument and most of the prose are unchanged from the first edition to the second, but they are reframed in more explicitly paradigmatic terms. Anthropology could provide both moral guidance and scientific evidence.

"Our modern civilization," particularly in America, was the starting point of the 1911 argument. Boas set out the urgency of the race question given the increasing heterogeneity of an immigrant nation. He asserted the relevance of anthropological knowledge while simultaneously acknowledging that key questions for political policy could not be answered "at the present time with scientific accuracy" (1911b:251). The problem was defined as a mentalist one—Boas presented "to our minds" a narrative of American history tailored by British victors. He dismissed the biological effect of Native Americans or Asians on the national gene pool (in contemporary terminology). The demographic valence of the Negro, however, had far more potential impact.

The "pure racial types" of the European history in which most Americans took great pride proved to be a comfortable fiction from a scientific point of view. Processes of historical change recurrently redistributed peoples and mingled them both biologically and culturally. The "causes" of presently observed group diversity were multiple: survival from past "stock" (a more neutral term than "race"), incursion of new physical types, or environmental change. Convergent evidence from difference sources might or might not enable reconstruction of the history or dominant factors in particular cases. A "peculiar selective process" in each case, involving complex intersections of race, language, and culture, precluded prediction of the direction or intensity of change across cases (1911b:257). Only the existence of change itself could be assumed. The sole thing unique about such multivariate processes in America was population density (which was growing rapidly in all modern societies, so the difference was a matter of degree). The discreteness of intermingling communities could be maintained more effectively when larger numbers permitted interaction of like groups. A small group, in contrast, would become virtually homogeneous by the fourth generation. Therefore, according to Boas's math, European communities in America could not maintain "the continuance of racial purity of our nation" even if such a state had existed in a prior golden age (260).

Boas then turns to the potential for "degradation of type" through racial mixture, moving from historical antecedents to "a biological standpoint." His own data for the 1910 Census Commission demonstrate that environment is far more significant than heredity in disrupting the stability of European types. "The most fundamental traits of the body" are subject to rapid environmental modification, even more so for bodily traits developed through maturation rather than fully present at birth (1911b:261, 262). Therefore, Boas asserts "with a high degree of confidence that mental traits as well as physical traits will be modified by the effect of the environment." The reasoning by analogy depends on the implicitly entailed plasticity of the mental relative to the physical, reinforcing the more adequately measurable phenomena. It then follows that environmental factors will preclude degeneration based on original type. Boas cautions that "speculation is as easy as accurate studies are difficult" but that the fears of biological degradation are already demonstrably imaginary. American racial mixtures differ "only in a sociological" sense built up by "the public mind" and "by a credulous public" into a fearsome shibboleth. He sticks to the biological side of the race question, because "mental life is so plastic, that no heredity inability [to cope with modern life] can be assumed to exist in any of the peoples of Europe." Therefore, judgments of inferiority are unjustified for the "bulk" of the white or Negro populations. Indeed, any traits that might bear on "vitality and mental ability are much less than the individual variations in each race" (264, 268, 269).

These questions are too important to be left to emotional speculation. Boas asserts that good census data focused on family lines and the relative fertility of different groups could answer many of these questions. Longitudinal studies over at least 20 more years would be required to provide the evidence for more explicit population modeling. He cautions, however, that statistics are not directly comparable from one group to another, because circumstances of migration vary considerably (e.g., single men vs. families, mobility in the new country, extended family structures, etc.). The barriers to intermixture producing rapid blending are social, not biological. But "racial cohesion" cannot be assessed based on existing data. Forthcoming 1910 census results will clarify many of these trends for particular groups. Boas asserts that his statistical analysis of the biology of racial mixture "is quite in accord with the result of ethnological observation." The achievements of Africans in Africa stand in point. Although differences in physical and mental characteristics doubtless exist, on the basis of "an unbiased estimate of the anthropological evidence so far," they are not sufficient to "stigmatize" full participation in "our social organization" (in "modern life") (1911b:268, 269, 272).

Boas also turns an anthropological lens to the emotional "instinct and fear" embedded in European tradition and the urge to maintain "a distinct social status" to prevent mixture. These strong emotions lead us to "call such feelings instinctive," but they are not determined by biology. In sum, "the data of anthropology teach us a greater tolerance of forms of civilization different from our own" and indicate the wisdom of "a fair opportunity" for all to contribute to "cultural progress." He laments the failure of governments or scientific institutions to attack the question of the American Negro but does not make explicit the sharing of popular prejudices by science and statesmen as a cause of the myopia (1911b:274, 273).

The 1938 edition of MPM features a new introduction, broadening the issue of race beyond the internal schisms of American society. The virulent racism "of the present day" is a recent thing in Europe, becoming "a foundation of public policy" only at the turn of the twentieth century as nationality became increasingly identified with racial unity and national characteristics were attributed to biological descent. In Germany in 1880, for example, Jews who assimilated were acceptable. Soon after, their racial character was redefined as "definite, unalterable" (1938:253). The same deterioration of racial relations occurred with the Negro in America. These increasingly impermeable social barriers run counter to the progress of science: "Serious scientists, whenever free to express themselves, . . . have been drifting away from the opinion that race defines mental status." Boas sideswipes here at political control of science in interwar Germany and pointedly excludes those scientists hung up on hereditary morphological determinism from his ameliorative definition of science. Sadly, too many politicians share the race prejudice of "the uninformed public." Boas's own position is unequivocal. He refers to "the errors which underlie the theory that racial descent determines mental and social behavior. The term race, applied to human types, is vague. It can have a biological significance only when a race represents a uniform, closely inbred group, in which all family lines are alike.... These conditions are never realized in human types and impossible in larger populations" (254).

Boas acknowledges the difficulties of measuring "the range of variation of biologically determined personalities within a race" in part because personality itself cannot be defined independently of its cultural context. However, he confidently concludes that "a very general primitive attitude of mind" is reflected in "the identification of the characteristics of an individual with the supposed typical characteristics of the group" (1938:255). The sharpness of this 1938 critique is far from Boas's 1911 optimism that Americans might rise to the challenge of accepting scientific evidence of equal capacity of races. The political policies of Nazi racism are "primitive" because they pander to the worst of public stereotypes and reflect what must surely be willful blindness to the data of science.

Boas assumes the existence of "laws" that would explain the development of particular types but acknowledges that we do not yet know these laws. We do know that Europe has no pure stocks and that moral judgment is impossible based on scientific probability to date. His review of European evidence for group intermixture over time recapitulates the 1911 argument and denies any evidence of "causes for the behavior of a people other than historical and social conditions." We do not know enough about the actual movements of people to establish detailed "historical facts." Recent movements of peoples resulting from "political terrorism directed against political opponents" are trivial in population terms, however significant they may be for individuals, compared to the effects of mass migration from Europe to America (1938:259, 260).

As in the American case in 1911, Boas regrets the still unanswerable questions about race, because "the political question of dealing with these groups of people is of great and immediate importance." Science, he repeats in 1938, rather than emotion must prevail. He emphasizes that the "modern transatlantic migration" is far from unique; social rather than biological barriers divide so-called races. Rapid migration facilitates the break-down and intermixture of types through environmental influence. What Boas cannot predict may be answered by "energetic" studies "on a sufficiently large scale." The recent population studies of Frank Lorimer and Frederick Osborn are especially promising.

Race, language, and culture, rather than biology alone, should influence the distribution of "hereditary constitutional types into social classes." The aim of eugenics to "improve constitutional health" is "highly commendable" but unattainable in practice on both moral and pragmatic grounds (1938:261, 266, 267).

The Negro in America reflects the same problem as the Jew in Germany: "Ethnological observation does not countenance the view that the traits observed among our poorest Negro population are in any sense racially determined." He reiterates the litany of African achievements in Africa and the insignificance of biological and mental differences that doubtless exist. He also reiterates the indifference of American science to resolving these issues, citing the recent work of his former student Melville Herskovits as an exception.

To evaluate individuals on the basis of the class to which we have already assigned them is "a survival of primitive forms of thought." Whatever characteristics exist in populations are never realized in "a single individual." "Freedom of judgment," then, turns to the attested merits of individuals. We must, Boas exhorts, "treasure and cultivate the variety of forms that human thought and activity has taken, and abhor, as leading to complete stagnation, all attempts to impose one pattern of thought upon whole nations or even upon the whole world" (1938:272). In the language of science, then, Boas pleads for the application of evidence to real-world decisions, for science to be valued above the wiles of nation-states, and for the obligation of the citizen to resist emotional restriction of human potential for scientifically invalid reasons. His theory and his practice merge.

The theoretical work revisited in this chapter demonstrates Boas's concern for his own legacy. His intentions, manifested in efforts at and after his formal retirement to provide a popular textbook on anthropology and modern life, a second edition of MPM, and a volume of his selected essays highlight pieces of his paradigm that were important to him and remarkably consistent over his long career but that have not always been in focus for his intellectual descendants. The thread that tied these projects together was the emancipatory potential of anthropology as he understood it. That Boasian commitment motivates revisionist scholarship and persists into the contemporary era of anthropology despite considerable changes in the discipline and the social, cultural, and political context in which it has moved beyond modernism.

NOTES

1. Conferences on the subject were organized at the University of Western Ontario by Regna Darnell, at the Wenner-Gren Foundation for Anthropological Research by Nene Panagourgiá, and at Yale by Isaiah Wilner. I am grateful to participants in these various events, which have reinvigorated scholarly reassessment of Boas's oeuvre. My own formulation of the Boasian paradigm relies especially on the insights of Lee D. Baker, Frederic W. Gleach, Robert L. A. Hancock, Stephen O. Murray, Joshua Smith, and the late George W. Stocking Jr.

REFERENCES

Baker, Lee D. 2010. Anthropology and the Racial Politics of Culture. Durham NC: Duke University Press.
Bauman, Richard, and Charles Briggs. 2003. Voices of Modernity: Language Ideologies and the Politics of Inequality. Cambridge: Cambridge University Press.
Boas, Franz. 1911a. Introduction to the Handbook of American Indian Languages. Bureau of American Ethnology Bulletin 40.
———. 1911b. The Mind of Primitive Man. New York: Macmillan.
———. 1912. Changes in Bodily Form of Descendants of Immigrants. New York: Columbia University Press.
———. 1928. Anthropology and Modern Life. New York: W. W. Norton.
———. 1938. The Mind of Primitive Man. 2nd ed. New York: Macmillan.
———. 1940. Race, Language and Culture. New York: Free Press.
Bunzl, Matti, ed. 2004. Special issue, American Anthropologist 106(3).
Cole, Douglas. 1999. Franz Boas: The Early Years: 1858–1906. Vancouver: Douglas and McIntyre.
Darnell, Regna. 1998. And Along Came Boas: Continuity and Revolution in Americanist Anthropology. Amsterdam: John Benjamins.

———. 2001. Invisible Genealogies: A History of Americanist Anthropology. Lincoln: University of Nebraska Press.

———. 2015. Mind, Body and the Native Point of View: Boasian Theory at the Centennial of the Mind of Primitive Man. *In* Franz Boas as Public Intellectual: Theory, Ethnography, Activism. Regna Darnell, Michelle Hamilton, Robert L. A. Hamilton, and Joshua Smith, eds. Pp. 3–17. Lincoln: University of Nebraska Press.

Freed, Stanley. 2012. Anthropology Unmasked: Museums, Science and Politics in New York City. Wilmington OH: Orange Frazer Press.

Glick, Leonard B. 1982. Types Distinct from Our Own: Franz Boas on Jewish Identity and Assimilation. American Anthropologist 84:545–565.

Harris, Marvin. 1968. The Rise of Anthropological Theory. New York: Thomas Crowell.

Hyatt, Marshall. 1990. Franz Boas, Social Activist: The Dynamics of Ethnicity. New York: Greenwood.

Jonaitis, Aldona, ed. 1995. A Wealth of Thought: Franz Boas on Northwest Coast Art. Seattle: University of Washington Press.

Kendall, Laurel, and Igor Krupnik. 2003. Constructing Cultures Now and Then: Celebrating Franz Boas and the Jesup North Pacific Expedition. Washington DC: Arctic Studies Center, National Museum of Natural History, Smithsonian Institution.

Kuhn, Thomas S. 1970. The Structure of Scientific Revolutions. Chicago: University of Chicago Press.

Lewis, Herbert. 2014. In Defense of Anthropology: An Investigation of the Critique of Anthropology. New Brunswick NJ: Transaction.

Maud, Ralph. 2003. Transmission Difficulties: Franz Boas and Tsimshian Mythology. Vancouver: Talonbooks.

Stocking, George W., Jr. 1968. Race, Culture and Evolution: Essays in the History of Anthropology. New York: Free Press.

———. 1974. The Shaping of American Anthropology, 1883–1911: A Franz Boas Reader. New York: Basic Books.

———, ed. 1996. Volksgeist as Method and Ethic. Madison: University of Wisconsin Press.

Vermeulen, Han. 2015. Before Boas: The Genesis of Ethnography and Ethnology in the German Enlightenment. Lincoln: University of Nebraska Press.

White, Leslie. 1963. The Ethnology and Ethnography of Franz Boas. Bulletin of the Texas Memorial Museum 6.

———. 1966. The Social Organization of Ethnological Theory. Rice University Studies 52:1–66.

Williams, Vernon J. 1996. Rethinking Race: Franz Boas and His Contemporaries. Lexington: University of Kentucky Press.

MICHAEL E. HARKIN

2

"We Are Also One in Our Concept of Freedom"

The Dewey-Boas Correspondence and the
Invention of Postmodern Bourgeois Liberalism

Franz Boas is known for his political activism, which both shaped his anthropology and was informed by it. In "Anthropology as Kultur-kampf," George Stocking (1992:92–113) argues for understanding Boasian anthropology within the framework of progressive and reformist politics, which shifted during various phases of Boas's life. As I have argued elsewhere, I believe that this trajectory continued beyond Boas's lifetime and that American anthropology of the late twentieth and twenty-first centuries has become identified with a particular political worldview: what Richard Rorty (1983) called "postmodernist bourgeois liberalism." It is important to note that while Rorty claims Dewey as a direct ancestor and inspiration, it has been argued that Rorty's is a more conservative political position (Shusterman 1994:391). In part this is owing to Rorty's prioritization of preserving such liberties as exist over securing new ones (Shusterman 1994:395). This conflict resonates as well in contemporary anthropology. One could argue that in recent years, anthropology has taken on a more radical complexion, with prominent scholars such as David Graeber espousing anarchistic political positions, but it is difficult to say from the perspective of the present whether this will amount to an important long-term trend. Moreover, I am not arguing that the great diversity of American anthropology in the twentieth and twenty-first centuries, which includes both scientific racism and a range of Marxist and feminist perspectives, can be defined by this Boasian arc. However, American anthropology has been, and will apparently remain, among the most politically engaged of the social sciences; I believe that the underlying perspective is one that combines cosmopolitanism, antiracism, and a concern for social justice.

What certainly *is* a structure of the longue durée is the parallel trajectories of American cultural anthropology and philosophical pragmatism and neopragmatism. Certainly the closest connection between anthropology and pragmatism was the personal relationship between Boas and John Dewey near the beginning of the development of both disciplines. Their correspondence, albeit modest in quantity, reveals allied political and theoretical perspectives. It is also notable that many of the early-generation Boas students, such as Ruth Benedict, Gene Weltfish, and Alexander Lesser, took courses with Dewey and considered themselves "Deweyans" as much as or more than "Boasians" (Colón Torres and Hobbs 2015:142). Boas and Dewey in fact taught a seminar together in 1914–15 and obviously shared students.

Colón Torres and Hobbs (2015) and Loren Goldman (2012) argue for the significance of Boasian anthropology in the development of pragmatism. Specifically, Goldman argues that Dewey's "cultural turn" away from the notion of "experience" was grounded in Boas's ethnographic conception of culture. (This is similar but not identical to Rorty's [1983:72–98] argument in favor of the cultural turn.) Similarly, Colón Torres and Hobbs argue that Dewey's use of both "culture" and "nature" draws heavily on Boas's adaptationist notion of anthropology.

On the other side of this equation, Herbert Lewis (2000) has argued that Boas was influenced by Deweyan pragmatism. Other figures such as William James and George Herbert Mead were also influential (Colón Torres and Hobbs 2015:141). As I have argued, both Boas and Dewey drew inspiration from the Keatsian notion of "negative capability," which can be seen as a posture of skepticism used to undermine positivism, evolutionism, and a priori reasoning. Although a major biographer of Dewey downplays the connection, I argue with Lewis and other scholars for the importance of the intellectual connection between pragmatism and anthropology more broadly and the personal one between Boas and Dewey (Ryan 1997:167).

The personal and small-scale can shed light on larger-scale and seemingly more important themes, as microhistory and certain versions of ethnography, biography, and literature can teach us. I propose to

examine the relation between Dewey and Boas through their correspondence. First, a note about sources: the body of correspondence
between them is fairly sparse. There exists a box in the Boas collection
of the American Philosophical Society in Philadelphia. Surprisingly,
there exists no counterpart in the Dewey archive at Southern Illinois
University. Boas did seem to be fairly fastidious about collecting both
outgoing and incoming correspondence, so perhaps the archive we
have is all that ever existed. I suspect, however, that additional papers
that would have been in Dewey's possession at the time of his death
were lost. Drawing on extant documents, I will examine some of the
more important topics they discussed.

COMPARATIVE ETHICS

Boas suggests that an empirical study of ethics cross-culturally would
bear fruit for developing a philosophical anthropology. In particular, he
argues for a universalist understanding of ethics, suggesting an antire-
lativistic position, which Stocking (1992:111) suggests and I have long
argued for in understanding Boas:

> One of the most important problems that I think should be solved
> in order to gain a satisfactory basis for ethical studies is the question
> in how far, in cultural types that have grown up independently of our
> own, distinctive ethical concepts occur. The matter has never been
> investigated in detail. . . . So far as I have been able to look into prob-
> lems of this kind, the indications are that the fundamental, I might
> say instinctive, ethical tendencies are the same everywhere where
> social factors do not exert a disturbing influence. In other words, if
> we investigate the ethics of the poor in various tribes, we find that
> the same altruistic tendencies that are the foundation of modern eth-
> ical concepts occur with equal vigor. As soon, however, as the ethics
> of the property-owning class or of people of higher social standing
> are investigated, we find that the conflict between the obligations
> towards property or towards their social class are apt to outweigh
> the more general ethical reactions. (Boas to Dewey, March 29, 1916)

One small point: coming as this does less than a year after their joint
seminar, it is likely that this was indeed the topic. This in fact coincides

with Robert Lowie's (1956) recollection, although it is contradicted by others (see Colón Torres and Hobbs 2015:143). Additionally, it is consistent with his letter to Dewey the year prior to the seminar of his intent to use Edvard Westermarck's *Origin and Development of Moral Ideas* (Boas to Dewey, October 20, 1913). Boas goes on to suggest a large-scale comparative study of ethics from West Africa, the Northwest Coast, the northern Plains, and elsewhere. This no doubt reflects the geography of Boas's students—his particular emphasis on Crow and his statement that he knew a good young anthropologist working there no doubt refer to Lowie. This vision of a sort of proto–Human Relations Area Files project focused on ethics is compelling, and its lack of execution is disappointing. One can only imagine what such a project may have meant for the development of American anthropology and how it may have provided a more solid foundation for anthropology's political interventions throughout the subsequent century.

A more important point here is Boas's assumption of a natural or "instinctive" morality based on altruism as a human baseline. Thus one would expect to encounter similar ethical regimes in far-flung places, for instance, around rules of hospitality. The key point is the way that particular cultural arrangements deform this default altruism, what he defines as "the obligations toward property or towards their social class." Thus, it is in classless societies or in the lower reaches of complex societies that one finds the uncorrupted human ethical order. This would seem to reflect the influence of Lewis Henry Morgan and even Rousseau but was probably equally the result of Boas's German cultural background and his familiarity with Herder's valorization of the *Volk*, as well as with Ferdinand Tönnies's (Boas's contemporary) concept of *Gemeinschaft*. It is, however, rather surprising that the usually skeptical Boas could espouse such an uncritical, inherently Romantic theory, one that, moreover, he was well equipped to critique. His experience with diverse cultures in North America should have given him pause. The Eskimo with whom he initially worked surely possessed a sense of ethics different from that of the Northwest Coast groups. Notions of hospitality, for instance, were central in both cultures; only in the latter did it develop into agonistic giving and ostentatious displays of wealth.

It seems that here Boas is feeling the pull of philosophy and of Dewey in particular. Obviously, part of this is the latter's desire to resituate ethics away from Kantian foundations and to base it instead on human nature as modified by culture. It is surprising that Boas was willing to move so far in the direction of universalism and even implicitly biological foundationalism, although, as I have argued elsewhere, his critiques of biologism and even racial theories were surprisingly modest. Although the sentiments expressed here would disappear from Boasian anthropology and perhaps even from Boas's mind (although not from the second edition of *The Mind of Primitive Man*), this formulation clearly informed a political agenda, one that Boas and Dewey would pursue jointly in the decades ahead.

WORLD WAR I AND THE ANTIWAR MOVEMENT

The first major issue on which Boas and Dewey were united was opposition to American entry into World War I. The sole extant exchange between them on this topic is curious but reveals an important aspect of their relationship. Boas had been contemplating writing one of his many letters to the editor on the topic of opposition to the war. Dewey states that he agrees with Boas but counsels him thus: "Everybody who reads it who doesn't already know you scientifically and judge you from that standpoint will see the German name. . . . [I]t would tend to reduce your future influence" (Dewey to Boas, March 9, 1917). In addition to illustrating the colloquial meaning of "pragmatism" (a term Dewey mostly eschewed), this is a surprisingly blunt statement. Boas is advised against speaking out because he will be taken for just another German by those unaware of his reputation in the academy. Dewey is also concerned for Boas's "future influence" and, perhaps, even his safety, as examples of anti-German violence in many American cities were frequent. Boas's reply reveals a deepening rift between the two on the matter of the war:

My Dear Professor Dewey,
I thank you very much for your opinion. I have not yet quite made up my mind what to do, but I do not believe that the question of my future influence will determine my action. What I feel at the present time is that everybody who is for peace needs stiffening of

the back, and while I am quite clear in my mind that nobody wants to be convinced, I do believe that the other point of view is worth considering.

Besides this I cannot get over the feeling, and I acknowledge this as a feeling, that it is our business to show that we cannot be intimidated. (Boas to Dewey, March 12, 1917)

Underlying this exchange is a major point of difference and disagreement between them. Boas was opposed to the war for the reason that most German Americans were: a lingering sense of loyalty and patriotism toward Germany and an affinity for German language and culture. (This was, obviously, true of a number of Boas's early students as well [Dinwoodie 2014].) Dewey's initial opposition was based on the ethical stance of pacifism, which was connected to the seminar theme of a baseline panhuman morality. However, by the following summer, Dewey's opposition to the war had waned, and he declared himself to be among "those who still thought of themselves as fundamentally pacifists in spite of the fact that they believed our entrance into the war a needed thing" (quoted in Cywar 1969:581).

While this action placed Dewey and Boas on different sides of the war issue (Boas continued to oppose it after the U.S. entry), on a deeper level it demonstrated a commonality. In the mode of what Rorty would later call "ironic ethnocentrism," both Dewey and Boas had fundamental allegiances to a particular cultural heritage despite their espousal of liberal, cosmopolitan perspectives. Indeed, the latter provides a significant part of Dewey's justification of the war. He felt that the war would usher in a world order that would realize many of the goals of progressives. Writing in the magazine the *Independent* in the final months of the war, he argued that the Spencerian law of unintended consequences would help to create a radically new postwar order:

In executing our immediate purpose we have to use forces which are outside our intent. Once released, however, they continue to operate, and they bring with them consequences which are unexpected and which in the end may quite submerge the objects consciously struggled for. Such an immense undertaking as the present war is no exception. The will to conquer describes the immediate aim. But in order to realize that end all sorts of activities are set going; arrangement made, organizations instituted, as incidental means. After they have been called into being they cannot be whisked out of existence merely because the war has come to an end. (Dewey 1918)

He foresees, with considerable accuracy, the rise of multinational institutions such as the League of Nations and increasing economic and political interdependency. At the same time he sees the fulfillment of the promise of nineteenth-century liberalism, the liberation of smaller nations such as Poland, and decolonialization in India and elsewhere. He also sees, again with some accuracy, the widespread reaction to war profiteering and the nationalization of many industries, as would indeed happen in Europe but not the United States. He sees the attainment of socialism and "true democracy":

But if we are to have a world safe *for* democracy *and* a world *in* which democracy is safely anchored, the solution will be in the direction of a federated world government and a variety of freely experimenting and freely cooperating self-governing local, cultural and industrial groups. It is because, in the end, autocracy means uniformity as surely as democracy means diversification that the great hope lies with the latter. The former strains human nature to the breaking point; the latter releases and relieves it—such, I take it, is the ultimate sanction of democracy, for which we are fighting. (Dewey 1918)

What he did not foresee was, of course, the rise of Nazism out of the ashes of the Great War, a topic that would reunite him with his colleague Boas. (In fairness, he was among the first to warn of Hitler as early as 1933.)

ACADEMIC POLITICS

As important as the war and Germany were to Boas, he never ceased to be actively involved in academic politics in the United States, which would eventually lead him back to Germany. The political landscape of science in the early decades of the century was dominated by, as George Stocking said, "the waspish hard-science leaders of the National

Research Council," whose only use for anthropology was "physical anthropology strongly tinged with racialism" (1992:105). Boas had to fight a lifelong battle to ensure that anthropology retained its status as a science, a cause to which Boas was profoundly committed. He relied on Dewey, whose fame and acceptability to the WASP establishment was much greater than his own, to further his agenda. Thus, in 1912 Boas asked for Dewey's help in securing a position in the National Academy of Sciences for Jesse Fewkes, the Harvard-trained zoologist turned archaeologist who was an important ally of Boas and who was instrumental in bringing a contingent of early Boas students to the Southwest (Boas to Dewey, December 27, 1912; Stocking 1992:292). Six years later he asked for Dewey's help in having Alfred Kroeber appointed to the same body (Boas to Dewey, October 3, 1918).

Dewey also enlisted Boas in his battles, which were mainly focused on academic freedom and the professionalization of the professoriate. Thus, he requested Boas's assistance at a panel discussing the formation of an "association of university professors" at the 1913 meeting of the National Academy of Science (Dewey to Boas, October 31, 1913). This entity was to become the American Association of University Professors, founded two years later.

The correspondence drops precipitously after the war. One can only speculate what this signifies about the state of their relationship. It is likely that Boas, like other antiwar progressives, felt betrayed by Dewey's possibly opportunistic support for U.S. entry into the war (Cywar 1969:579). For Boas, there was of course the additional grievance of Dewey's anti-German views. Nevertheless, Dewey's name remained valuable currency. In 1923 Boas, who was active in the efforts to restore German educational and cultural institutions (he made many personal contributions to the cause, including giving a large number of books to the University of Kiel), asked Dewey to lend his name to a letter supporting the Emergency Society for German and Austrian Science and Art (Boas to Dewey, January 8, 1923).

THE 1930S

The 1930s were the decade in which both men would retire. Facing typical late-in-life issues such as retirement in the midst of the ongoing crisis, they experienced a rapprochement, one filled with more personal statements of support and affection. At one point Dewey confided in Boas regarding financial woes he was experiencing in his retirement at Key West due to the Depression-era reduction of his pension allowance by one-third (Dewey to Boas, January 6, 1939). Personal birthday greetings were exchanged and sentimental feelings expressed (e.g., Dewey to Boas, October 28, 1939). These statements are often intermixed with expressions of regret that circumstances had forced them apart. The hyperpolite tone of these late letters also suggests the sense that both men felt the relationship had been damaged and remained fragile.

In addition to the personal reconciliation, political forces aligned themselves so as to bring the two men back into active alliance. With the rise of Nazism in Germany and anti-Semitism much more broadly, both men were compelled to be active in these issues, mostly from within the academy. Many of the issues in which they were involved were in a sense parochial but reflecting these larger trends. Thus, for instance, there was the case of Lienhard Bergel, a comparative literature professor at Rutgers who was fired for alleged incompetence when in fact his dismissal was due to the Nazi sympathies of the department chair (Boas to Dewey, January 7, 1936; see Oshinsky 1989). This was a cause that Dewey gladly signed on to, as it related to his core interest in academic freedom.

Far from parochial was the campaign to award Carl von Ossietzki the Nobel Peace Prize. Ossietzki was imprisoned in Germany for writing about Nazi Germany's clandestine rearmament. Boas approached Dewey, who had been involved with the Nobel's centennial celebrations, about nominating Ossietzki, which Dewey in fact did (Boas to Dewey, January 15, 1936; Dewey to Boas, January [?], 1936). Ossietzki received the award, dying two years later in a hospital under military guard, becoming a cause célèbre for the anti-Nazi movement.

Similarly, Boas was able to identify numerous academics who were victims of the Nazis. One of them was Helmut Kuhn, a philosopher who lost his job in Germany (Boas to Dewey, February 8, 1935). It was natural that Boas would turn to Dewey, who, in addition to having considerable clout in the American academy, was one of the founders of the New School, which became a refuge for European refugees, including scholars such as Claude Lévi-Strauss, whom Boas would personally mentor. In the same period, Boas warned against visiting German scholars supported by the Nazi government: "I feel a good deal concerned about the various professors who are sent to this country by the German government in order to make propaganda and perhaps even more so by the present conditions of the exchange students. These are selected by the government in Berlin and have to report, according to a published statement of the government, to one of the most objectionable persons abroad, a Mr. von Leers, the author of the book, 'Juden Se en dich an' ('Jews are Looking at You')" (Boas to Dewey, May 31, 1934). Although there is no extant reply from Dewey, it is likely that Dewey relied on Boas as a well-situated observer of the German scene. His assessment of who was worthy of support versus those suspected of being Nazi mouthpieces would certainly have affected Dewey's strategy to support foreign scholars.

As the war in Europe ramped up, Boas was furiously engaged in a campaign of letter and petition writing. At times it was literally impossible to keep track of who was supporting which group and petition, as is evident from this exchange: "I have just learned that you have prepared a letter, addressed to the American Jewish Committee, in which you say that while I signed the petition of the Committee in which you are interested regarding the Dies Committee I didn't sign that of the Committee in which Mr. Trager is interested. Your first statement is of course true; the second is incorrect[.] I did sign the petition of the Committee for Cultural Freedom" (Dewey to Boas, February 8, 1940). The significance of the distinction between the two petitions is unclear but no doubt represents the narcissism of small differences in the very active arena of Jewish and anti-Fascist activism in New York during that period. Clearly, Dewey's signature remained very valuable, coming from a famous scholar who was also a WASP. It is unclear whether Boas deliberately misstated the situation for some now obscure tactical reason or was simply mistaken. The latter seems most likely, as Dewey was traveling at the time. In any case, he replied to Dewey with extreme promptness: "I am more sorry than I can say that these affairs should in any way affect our personal relationship. I am quite sure that fundamentally we take the same positions. I wish you would let me know when you come back so we can have a personal talk and I am sure that every apparent conflict will be cleared up" (Boas to Dewey, February 10, 1940).

This is a leitmotif cropping up again and again in their correspondence: the danger that the vicissitudes of political life and the ill will of those who would, for their own purposes, try to separate Dewey and Boas would lead to damage to their personal relationship. In point of fact, this certainly did happen, as was clear in the post–World War I era. Two years before his death, Boas sent what amounts to a valediction, summarizing the relationship between the two on intellectual and political grounds:

Dear Dewey:
I am exasperated by the constant attempts that are being made and that come to me from the most diverse sides to make it appear as though you and I in our public activities had fundamentally different objectives.

I believe that this is absolutely untrue.

There are two matters to which I am devoted: absolute intellectual and spiritual freedom, and the subordination of the state to the interests of the individual; expressed in other forms, the furthering of conditions in which the individual can develop to the best of his own ability—as far as this is possible with a full understanding of the fetters imposed upon us by tradition; and the fight against all forms of power policy of states or private organizations. This means devotion to the principle of a true democracy. I object to the teaching of slogans intended to befog the mind, of whatever kind they may be.

It has always seemed to me that under present political conditions we are impotent to influence the governments of foreign states and that, in order to attain our ends, we must confine ourselves to act for the ideals of intellectual freedom and of service of the state for the benefit of the individual in our own country.

I believe we are also one in our concept of freedom. In our complex economic system absolute freedom of the individual to reach his own ends must be restricted by a consideration of the effects of his actions upon his fellow citizens, even upon the rest of mankind. Whenever his activities threaten the welfare of others the general interests of society demand that his freedom of action be controlled, the more so as economic exploitation is made possible only by the existence of our society. The developments of the last century prove that the necessity of such restrictions and of the protection of the individual against the effects of our modern methods of production is being recognized.

I agree to the necessity of economic control, but this has no relation to intellectual and spiritual freedom. (Boas to Dewey, November 6, 1939)

Dewey responded tersely but in agreement: "I share fully your resentment against efforts put forth to make it appear that our aims are different or that there is any significant opposition between our respective social or economic beliefs" (Dewey to Boas, November 12, 1939). Boas is here arguing for a version of democratic socialism that above all respects individual freedom, but he is willing to control the economy to minimize the excesses of unbridled capitalism. It is worth pointing out that in the context of the 1930s this was a very common position in the United States, especially among writers and academics. Nevertheless, this formulation does reflect a common trajectory that both men had, making detours through various versions of socialism, antiracism, and individual liberation.

CONCLUSION

During the course of a shared career at Columbia spanning four decades, Franz Boas and John Dewey developed strong intellectual ties and a political alliance that was broken only by their differing opinions on entering World War I. Their cotaught seminar on comparative ethics forged a paradigm that would influence, at its earliest stages, not only the history of American anthropology via the first generation of Boasians but also, as Colón Torres and Hobbs (2015) have argued, the development of pragmatic philosophy. This common filiation has been occasionally remarked upon (e.g., by Herbert Lewis [2000]) but for the most part ignored in both disciplines. When we look at the work of neopragmatists such as Richard Rorty (1983), we can still hear the strong echoes of the Boas-Dewey collaboration.

Among the most important points, at least from the standpoint of contemporary American anthropologists, to emerge are these:

Boas rejected naive cultural relativism. In fact, what he believed was almost the opposite. It is culture alone (specifically class relations, but I imagine Boas would have a place for religious ideology there now, if not then) that can deform the natural tendency of humans toward altruism.

Boas did envision a superior society, one that contained elements of liberal Germany mixed with those of cosmopolitan New York. The ultimate goal of a just and equal society in which the freedom of all could be ensured was achievable through a combination of scientific knowledge, education, and political activism, which would combat racism, prejudice, and religious intolerance.

The excesses of capitalism were to be reined in. Class relations, as we saw, are one of the main causes of corruption of the natural morality practiced by most people.

The opposition to capitalism should never become so powerful that it becomes a coercive force. Rather, it should be a force of liberation. In particular, it should never threaten science, as in the Soviet Union, where "anthropology must be Marxian and Lewis Morgan, otherwise it is not allowed" (quoted in Stocking 1992:109).

More broadly, individual freedom of expression and conscience must be respected above all else, which included broad room for political activism, something Boas and Dewey were deeply engaged in.

Rorty had a term for this: "postmodernist bourgeois liberalism."

REFERENCES

Boas Papers, box 21. American Philosophical Society, Philadelphia.
Colón Torres, Gabriel Alejandro, and Charles A. Hobbs. 2015. The Intertwining of Culture and Nature: Franz Boas, John Dewey, and Dew-

eyan Strands of American Anthropology. Journal of the History of Ideas 76(1):139–161.

Cywar, Alan. 1969. John Dewey in World War I: Patriotism and International Progressivism. American Quarterly 21(3):578–594.

Dewey, John. 1918. What Are We Fighting For? Independent, June 22, 1918.

Dinwoodie, David. 2014. Boas on Nationalism: Positions Taken in the Circumstances Surrounding WWI. Paper presented at World War I, Sociopolitical Escalation/Destabilization, and the Production of Anthropology panel, AAA Annual Meeting, Washington DC.

Goldman, Loren. 2012. Dewey's Pragmatism from an Anthropological Point of View. Transactions of the Charles S. Peirce Society 48(1):1–30.

Lewis, Herbert. 2000. Boas, Darwin, Science, and Anthropology. Current Anthropology 42(3):381–406.

Lowie, Robert. 1956. Reminiscences of Anthropological Currents in America Half a Century Ago. American Anthropologist 58(4):995–1016.

Oshinsky, David. 1989. The Case of the Nazi Professor. New Brunswick NJ: Rutgers University Press.

Rorty, Richard. 1983. Postmodernist Bourgeois Liberalism. Journal of Philosophy 80(10):583–589.

Ryan, Alan. 1997. John Dewey and the High Tide of American Liberalism. New York: W. W. Norton.

Shusterman, Richard. 1994. Pragmatism and Liberalism between Dewey and Rorty. Political Theory 22(3):391–413.

Stocking, George. 1992. The Ethnographer's Magic and Other Essays in the History of Anthropology. Madison: University of Wisconsin Press.

3

What Would Franz Boas Have Thought about 9/11?

To ask what Franz Boas would have thought of 9/11 is obviously to engage in an act of historical and biographical imagination, but also one of self-examination. I would argue that we anthropologists, especially those of us trained in the great Americanist tradition of cultural anthropology and historical ethnography, feel that we know Boas. Indeed, we have internalized him in some way, like a beloved dead relative, and so, in some sense, his reaction is our reaction. As in any time of crisis, the crisis of the past decade that was ushered in on that bright September morning and that shows little sign of abating is a test of our worldview, of our epistemology and ethics, of our way of making sense of and acting in the world in our historical moment.

I argue that Boas is to be understood primarily as an advocate for a progressive view of a multicultural, open, egalitarian society, which he believed could be achieved in the United States. In this he was allied with his Columbia colleague John Dewey, with whom he had a long-term friendship and political alliance on matters both within the academy and, more importantly, beyond it. Boas of course was also an ethnographer with a desire to present non-Western cultures in a generally positive light. However, Boas was in the end no cultural relativist. Rather, he was a partisan of a liberal, cosmopolitan, pluralistic, democratic society, and he was capable of embracing any number of ethnic and cultural minorities. In his lifetime, the great enemies of this vision of society were the advocates of Jim Crow and restricted immigration and, of course, the anti-Semites and Nazis. A similar challenge to this model of society today comes from religious extremists, primarily Islamists and Christianists. This is not a debate on which Boas would have been silent. It is time for anthropology, especially in its American version, so directly the product of Boas and Boas's students and protégés, to acknowledge this reality. Not only can anthropology never stand as a culturally neutral observer and mediator (the very claim to which is logically absurd), but it must be admitted that this particular discipline is in many ways the distilled ideological essence of what Richard Rorty (1983) calls "postmodernist bourgeois liberalism."

My goal here is to link Boas's thought to that of the pragmatists, especially Dewey, and to trace that genealogy into the present via neopragmatists such as Rorty and Cornel West. By reconnecting with the pragmatic tradition, I believe anthropology can not only achieve a greater understanding of its own origins and philosophical underpinnings but also become more relevant in contemporary debates. Not only is this Boasian-Deweyan-Rortyan vision of liberal society threatened from without (and here I would include domestic Christianist terrorists), but in the face of these threats we see the prospect of a total surveillance state and permanent warfare. If anthropology is to be relevant to these debates, it must understand how it is historically, philosophically, and ethically situated.

Had Franz Boas been alive in 2001, we can imagine him taking his usual ferry from the Jersey side (the evocatively named suburb of Grantwood) across the Hudson River. Had he been crossing at around 9:00 a.m. or a little earlier, he would have seen the first tower burning, perhaps the plane striking the second tower. Perhaps he would have seen in the bright sunlight the "pink mist" of vaporized humanity created by the crash, or the burning people jumping from top floors of the building. I think we know from many points of view the depth of Boas's humanity, and so we know he would have been horrified and indeed "terrorized" by this awful spectacle, as were almost all New Yorkers and Americans and indeed many people around the world who saw the scenes on television. The fact that this attack was carried out by a group motivated in part by virulent anti-Semitism and a hatred for the sort of open society that is necessary for the existence of critical social science and whose improvement is its ultimate object would have had its effect as well. No doubt Boas would have expressed indignation. I do not see him being among the leftist intellectuals who seemed to blame American society itself for these attacks (the validity of some of these remarks having been completely overwhelmed by their awful timing and the howling public reaction). Nor do I think that Boas would have been taken in by throwaway pronouncements claiming that 9/11 represented the "end of irony" or of feminism. Indeed, like many of us, one suspects Boas would have found irony an increasingly central and necessary trope as the Bush-Cheney administration engaged in misdirection to undertake a war unrelated to 9/11 and to transform American society away from the very openness that made it the prime target of the terrorist attacks in the first place.[1] Indeed, it would be in keeping with Boas's pacifism to have agreed with many Bush critics on the left that terrorism was a direct response to American military action in the Middle East and elsewhere.

What *is* in question regarding Boas's reaction to 9/11 is what effect it would have had in the middle term, several years after the attacks, as the United States began wars in Afghanistan and Iraq, as new terror attacks occurred in Madrid and London, as the depravity of the Baathist regime in Iraq and the primitive brutality of the Taliban became matters of public record. Would a way of life based on a delusional reading of religious texts and violent repression of people, especially women, have come under the umbrella of cultural relativism? Could the stoning to death of a pair of teenagers who made the mistake of having romantic feelings for each other or a woman who had been raped ever become mere ethnographic data to be dispassionately interpreted?

It is true, of course, that Boasian anthropology has been operationalized in the context of American military intervention, most famously by Ruth Benedict's analysis of Japanese culture during World War II and more recently with the Human Terrain program. In fact, ethnography can be employed in such situations as a means of understanding the motivation of enemies. That is, relativism is in this instance purely methodological. However, Boas, in both his anthropological and his political efforts, sought a space in which people of different races and cultural traditions could coexist.

It is obviously not merely a question here of the West versus Islam or a certain version of each, although this is undeniably part of it. Just as in the Cold War, when the United States and the USSR were in many ways mirroring each other, so in the United States and the West the rise of a theocratic, intolerant, misogynistic, and extremely violent segment identifying with fundamentalist Christianity (although not necessarily practicing it, as I discuss below) mirrored Al Qaeda. The terrorist acts in Oklahoma City and Norway and the attendant rise of virulent right-wing political organizations such as the Tea Party in the United States and the National Front in France have moved these societies in a direction closer to our putative adversaries, even as the specter of Islamic terrorism is used as justification. "Sharia law" may be the bugaboo of the American Right, but something very similar to it, and indeed based on the same foundational text, would be quite acceptable to them.[2] Thus the dilemma for the anthropologist is both intellectual and existential. As the radical Right is already committed to "rounding up" certain classes of people (borderlands Hispanics primarily at the moment), it is reasonable to wonder where it will end and whether, say, Jewish urban liberal social scientists would suffer under an administration run by such people. If that sounds too far-fetched, it takes little imagination to envision the implementation of a national security state in which the rights to privacy, free speech, and criticism of the government would be radically curtailed, leaving little room for public intellectuals such as Boas. Indeed, a third Bush term would likely have resulted in just that, and the willingness of the Obama administration to continue these policies is certainly a cause for alarm.

The intellectual challenge is equally great. A social philosophy based upon a high degree of tolerance for cultural difference and a pragmatic cultural relativism finds that it has become the epitome of the Western way of life, at least in the eyes of its conservative enemies. Can the worldviews of these enemies, either Taliban or Tea Party, be given equal standing under the principle of tolerance, or is it necessary in this singular case for liberalism to stand up for itself, rather than cede the point, as does Robert Frost's liberal: "I mean so altruistically moral / I never take my own side in a quarrel"? If so, upon what ground does an antifoundational science stand?

The Franz Boas of *The Mind of Primitive Man* (1938[1911]) stakes out a position for anthropology as a science in largely negative terms. That is, he sees the highest value of science being its self-critical function, what Karl Popper called the "falsifiability" of scientific propositions. Boas is, throughout the book, calling into question the broader claims of racialist, evolutionary, and eugenicist models while nonetheless refusing to deny altogether the legitimacy of such approaches. It is surprising to the modern reader that he concedes a great deal to these deterministic models, as when he states that it is "highly probable" that cranial capacity, which was believed to be higher in whites and in males, was positively correlated with intelligence, as Francis Galton stated, and that, moreover, within the white race it closely tracked intelligence (Boas 1938[1911]:26). There were likely environmental and historical factors as well, according to Boas, and so one could not assume that such effects were purely the product of "Mendelian genetics." This was a question for study, not a matter to be settled in a priorist fashion. Indeed, Boas respected and to a certain degree mimicked Darwinian evolutionism. As Herbert Lewis (2000) has argued, Boas shared with Darwin an interest in the contingency of events and outcomes and a preference for probabilistic and statistical analysis as opposed to system building. We cannot take this line of argument too far, for certainly the Darwin of *The Descent of Man* is somewhat drawn to systematic thought. However, this remains an accurate description of Boas.

Indeed, Boas epitomizes the Keatsian principle of "negative capability," described as being "capable of being in uncertainties, Mysteries, doubts without any irritable reaching after fact & reason" (Wu 2005:1351). This concept is demonstrated in "Ode to a Nightingale," in which the poet rejects the aspirations of Romanticism, in particular to attain a state of ecstatic union with nature. His realization of transience, death, and perspectivalism forces him to circumscribe any such ecstatic moments with an awareness of their insufficiency. Similarly, in the realm of science, the moments of presumed insight into the workings of nature and of course culture are circumscribed. Boas was content with "half-knowledge," unlike Keats's colleague Coleridge, at whom this passage was directed. One can well imagine Boas averring that half-knowledge of which one was certain was preferable to a complete account, such as Galtonian eugenics, based on unproved assumptions.[3]

Another side of this is Boas's willingness to entertain multiple modes of causality. In this way he is, as Lewis argues, very much a creature of our own age (although few would follow Lewis in calling Boas a post-modernist). In particular, Boas characteristically argues against purely biological or hereditarian models. His argument with Galton is not really over the feasibility or even desirability of eugenics but rather over the role of environment, racial history, and other extrasomatic factors in producing individuals with particular capacities. We cannot help but notice that this moves the entire discussion in a much more liberal and to us congenial direction: such a take on eugenics could lead to campaigns for childhood nutrition programs, improved education, workers' rights, and the like. However, the Galtonian model is not so much rejected as qualified, with a "yes, but" style of argument, the characteristic mode of Boasian skepticism.

On the question of race itself, with which we associate the progressive legacy of Boas most particularly, we find this sort of qualified acceptance, as in the passage early on in *The Mind of Primitive Man* discussing the unique accomplishments of the "white race": "The fact deserves attention, however, that at present practically all members of the white race participate to a greater or lesser degree in the advance of civilization, while in none of the other races has the civilization that has been attained at one time or another been able to reach all the tribes or peoples of the same race" (Boas 1938[1911]:10). Boas scrupulously produces numerous caveats having to do with the historical situation of Western Europeans as opposed to Arabs, Africans, and others, but this is hardly a clarion call for multiculturalism. Rather, it seeks to bring in other determinisms, such as disease, technology, and geography, much in the way that Jared Diamond does in *Guns, Germs, and Steel*.

My argument here is not that Boas was complicit with the more sinister sorts of social theories produced in the early twentieth century (Lewis 2001). However, negative capability is an epistemological position incapable of producing an autonomous and coherent theoretical perspective. It is always piggybacking on those positions that it critiques. Boas was utterly dependent on evolutionary, racialist, and eugenic theory in his formulation of a general anthropological model in *The Mind of Primitive Man*. Given that, it is also true that by dint of the sheer weight of the partial objections raised throughout the text,

Boas reaches a point, at least rhetorically, late in the book where he effectively dismisses deterministic and racialist thought. In the famous final paragraph, he offers a beatific expression of hope for the future course of anthropological research: "The data of anthropology teach us a greater tolerance of forms of civilization different from our own, and . . . we should learn to look upon foreign races with greater sympathy, and with the conviction, that, as all races have contributed in the past to cultural progress in one way or another, so they will be capable of advancing the interests of mankind, if we are only willing to give them a fair opportunity" (Boas 1938[1911]:278). Here we have the expression of Boasian cultural relativism familiar to any student of an introductory anthropology course in the United States. To point out that it is less a conclusion to the book that preceded it than a giant non sequitur is merely to note that there were two distinct sides to Boasian thought. On the one hand is the negative capability: the lawyer raising questions of reasonable doubt in the teeth of simplistic theories, not with the intent of introducing alternative theories or even dismissing those that are critiqued, but rather introducing uncertainty and complexity to the picture. This is essentially a centrifugal force. On the other hand is the integrative, aesthetic appreciation of a culture's "genius," which is centripetal in nature and leads us to a holistic, integrative appreciation of that culture, much as Boas achieved with respect to the Kwakiutl.

This holistic approach allows the anthropologist to take a view of a cultural complex as integrated and seamless. While it would appear to the outside observer to be composed of "heterogenous" elements, this is not the perspective of the cultural insider, and indeed the anthropologist can replicate this perspective through consideration of the various dimensions of culture—language, psychology, symbols, race, geography, and so on—in the context of what Ruth Benedict called "configurations." Thus we can see that Boas had in mind two distinct functions for anthropology: on the one hand to critique deterministic models in general anthropology, and on the other to construct or reconstruct models of individual cultures through an aesthetic, interpretive sensibility.

These two functions are distinct, with the latter taking precedence in the vast majority of the Boasian corpus. Indeed, it is mainly in *The*

Mind of Primitive Man that Boas systematically sets out the former. Although these functions are distinct, it is possible to view both of them within the context of a broad pragmatism that defines Boas's intellectual paradigm. On the one hand, we have the epistemological side: skepticism, historicism, inductivism, and a tolerance for messy facts and incomplete descriptions characteristic of negative capability. On the other hand, we have the interpretive, ethical, and aesthetic dimension that leads us to a Deweyan notion of progress in society brought about by the abandonment of metaphysical presumptions.

Franz Boas and John Dewey were not merely colleagues at Columbia University. They were political allies and friends as well. At one point Boas stated bluntly in a letter written to Dewey on November 6, 1939, that he feels that he and Dewey "are one" with respect to their political and philosophical perspectives. He goes on in a second letter to stress their many points in common, for instance, their shared view of freedom:

> I believe we are also one in our concept of freedom. In our complex economic system absolute freedom of the individual to reach his own ends must be restricted by a consideration of the effects of his actions upon his fellow citizens, even upon the rest of mankind. Whenever his activities threaten the welfare of others the general interests of society demand that his freedom of action be controlled, the more so as economic exploitation is made possible only by the existence of our society. The developments of the last century prove that the necessity of such restrictions and of the protection of the individual against the effects of our modern methods of production is being recognized. (November 6, 1939)[4]

Thus Boas asserts a model of the modern state in which liberty, while valued, must be measured against the effects of any action on others. This is a clear consequence of a pragmatic philosophical position. For Boas, this pertains particularly to the economic sphere, where unfettered liberty clearly leads to exploitation: "I agree to the necessity of economic control, but this has no relation to intellectual and spiritual freedom" (Boas to Dewey, November 6, 1939). Thus, in a society in which "intellectual and spiritual freedom" was absolute (although for Boas this would not have included many of the ideologies current in the 1930s, such as racism), when it came to material action in the economic sphere, the worker must be protected from the excesses of capitalism (of course, this was a common position in the 1930s and by no means restricted to Boas, Dewey, and their circle).

In the same letter Boas expands on his notion of the desired form of society, a statement reminiscent of several he makes in *The Mind of Primitive Man*:

> There are two matters to which I am devoted: absolute intellectual and spiritual freedom, and the subordination of the state to the interests of the individual; expressed in other forms, the furthering of conditions in which the individual can develop to the best of his own ability—as far as this is possible with a full understanding of the fetters imposed upon us by tradition; and the fight against all forms of power . . . of states or private organizations. This means devotion to the principle of a true democracy. I object to the teaching of slogans intended to befog the mind, of whatever kind they may be.

"True democracy" thus rests on the principle of freedom of thought and belief. Moreover, this requires not just a negative freedom but "the furthering of conditions in which the individual can develop to the best of his own ability," that is, public education, a central theme of Dewey's advocacy to which Boas himself contributed in his curation of the ethnological exhibits at the American Museum of Natural History. What threatens this condition of pure democracy is the incursion of the political power of the state or private interests (we can imagine Boas's horror at the post–*Citizens United* entry of private wealth into electoral politics), demagogic "slogans that befog the mind" (which he would hear soon enough as the war got under way and which certainly persisted through the postwar Red Scare), and, interestingly, the "fetters imposed upon us by tradition." Elsewhere he refers to "the shackles of tradition" not only as the phenomenon of political conservatism but as the constraints that culture places upon worldview. This, again, is consistent with a pragmatic understanding of the human subject as always situated within a particular epistemological framework. Transcendental truth was an illusion: the best that could be hoped for was an awareness of the biases and constraints inherent in any such perspective.

Superficially it is then supremely ironic that Boas wished to fight these shackles (to the degree possible) within his own society but made a career of studying and preserving the traditions of others. Even more than his contemporaries, Boas was committed to describing "pure" traditions detached from the forces of culture change and assimilation. Thus, in studying Kwakiutl (Kwakwaka'wakw) culture around the turn of the century at a time of rapid change, he diligently scrubbed out these incursions, even as the main object of his analysis, the potlatch, was itself the product of transcultural flows (Bracken 1997).

This is indeed a common argument made about many anthropologists: they are radicals at home and Burkeans "in the field"; that is, they support an idealized version of traditional culture as purveyed by elites. However, in the case of Boas (and I imagine others) a rather different logic is operating. For Boas, the starting point was an awareness of the power of tradition and its constraint on the development of "true democracy." While liberals within the Kantian tradition might argue against tradition based on an imagined transcendental perspective, for Boas and other pragmatists the only (and arguably the more effective, in any case) possibility was to *relativize* these traditions by pointing out analogues within other traditions. Thus Boas's desire to bring to the general public the esoterica of the Kwakiutl and other indigenous cultures had the intent of forcing people to consider their *own* cultural tradition from a relativistic perspective. This was certainly not a farfetched notion, especially in the New York of the early twentieth century. Visitors to the Great Hall of the American Museum of Natural History in New York represented traditions from well beyond northwestern Europe, reaching into the Middle East, Asia, and elsewhere. This, then, was a second desired result of the relativizing of tradition: the acceptance of something like a multicultural society. If no one tradition could be absolute, then the end result of the evolution of American society would be a metatradition in which there would be room for many specific traditions, provided they gave up their claims to absolutism. This state could only be achieved in the United States once the hegemony of the WASP traditions could be overcome. This was indeed a major goal of American anthropology during the twentieth century.

Clearly, then, Boas, like his friend and ally Dewey, imagined American society as many other progressives have: if not perfectible, then meliorative. It would be possible to achieve at least some of the conditions of "true democracy" through public education (including that taking place in museums), the progressive enfranchisement of new groups such as immigrants and African Americans, and the beating back of vested interests and the forces of reaction. For Boas, the ultimate desideratum of such an open, free, and pluralistic society was more important than the anthropological arguments that got him to that point. One could say that the structure of *The Mind of Primitive Man* reflects the structure of his professional life: the careful work of his critical anthropology provided the building blocks of the sort of society that he wished to live in. When he died in the Columbia University faculty club on that winter's day in 1942, Claude Lévi-Strauss said that his last words were "I have a new idea on race." I would suggest that this was not a scientific theory of race, a concept that he effectively demonstrated to be of limited value, but rather the race problem, which remained the greatest stumbling block to the realization of "true democracy" in the United States.

In this context it is fair to ask whether the interpretive mode of Boasian thought would be of any value in attempting to understand cultural formations that embrace racism itself, as in fact many do. Here the territory becomes hopelessly muddy. Obviously, it would be absurd to try to understand, say, Hindu culture without reference to the concept of *varna*. Yet while *varna* is a foundational concept of that culture, it could in no way be presented as exemplary; at the same time, it could not be condemned outright, lest Boas violate his own principle of showing "greater sympathy" to other cultures, especially those exploited by colonial powers. This is, I think, what Boas means by "heterogenous" cultural traits.

To return to the theme of 9/11, what does a Boasian anthropologist make of a cultural formation based on nihilism, misogyny, anti-Semitism, and a profound fear of modernity that characterizes some of the extreme forms of Islamism. Should we treat that cultural formation as an aberration, a type of mental illness on the collective plane, despite its deep roots in Arab civilization? In this case, Boas's term "heterogenous" may be read as "irrational," although we would have to stipulate, along with Rorty, that we do not mean this in an absolute sense. Indeed, there is no transcendental ground upon which we can base notions of rationality or justice; we must recognize that such concepts are always freighted with culturally specific value and that we all are, as Rorty says, inescapably ethnocentric (Voparil and Bernstein 2010:47). Anthropology has historically sought to create a space of cultural neutrality, but clearly this is an illusion. We have been fooling ourselves if we have believed that anthropology is anything other than a mode of understanding specific to the West, intrinsically and pragmatically linked with bourgeois capitalist society. It is the very notion of multiculturalism, a product of the anthropological worldview, that has particularly incited Islamist terrorists, especially in the United Kingdom. That is, far from operating in an interstitial space between cultures, Boasian anthropology becomes in fact the epitome of "postmodernist bourgeois liberalism," in Rorty's memorable phrase. A discourse that rejects injustice based on race, sex, and religion and favors pluralism is radically incompatible with religious fundamentalism of any stripe. As the latter comes increasingly to define the major alternative to capitalist democracy, it is no longer possible for anthropology to proclaim its neutrality, much less its objectivity.

The issue here is not fundamentally one of relativism versus antirelativism, which has played the role of red herring in similar discussions for most of anthropology's history. Boas's operational relativism is not to be confused with philosophical relativism, which is, as Rorty points out, "self-refuting" but also represents a metaphysical position to the extent that we can pretend to make judgments about the moral value of other cultures: "The view that every tradition is as rational or as moral as every other could be held only by a god, someone who had no need to use (but only to mention) the terms 'rational' or 'moral,' because she had no need to inquire or deliberate. Such a being would have escaped from history and conversation into contemplation and metanarrative" (Rorty 1983:589). Rather, we are capable of making judgments about other cultures only from within our own historical tradition. There is no Quinean "God's-eye view" available to anthropologists or anyone else (see Quine 1951). While the anthropologist generally will do well to strive to understand disturbing cultural practices from the context of his or her own culturally embedded understandings, much as Boas did with respect to Northwest Coast cannibalism, it is not a foregone conclusion that any particular bit of "heterogenous" material will be easily digested, nor does the judgment of the anthropologist ultimately matter that much—certainly not in the sense of absolute truth. We live in a deeply imperfect world, but one in which evil, like everything else, is distributed according to a cultural logic. What is relatively familiar to us—handgun violence, military drone attacks that kill children in Afghanistan—is less noticeable and disturbing than that which exists outside our ken, such as genital mutilation or suicide bombing. In acknowledging the moral failings of our own historical tradition we at least can attain the level of interpretive sophistication represented by Terence's dictum "Homo sum, humani nihil a me alienum puto" (I am human, and nothing of that which is human is alien to me).

Thus anthropology does not have a particular role to play in adjudicating points of cultural difference, in determining which bad practices are tolerable and which are not. We are always coming at it from deep within our own historical tradition, and as American anthropologists, we have tended to inherit a great deal from Boas's own tradition of secular liberal German Judaism. We can never be neutral in such a situation, because ultimately our liberal worldview depends on the existence of a liberal society. If we do not realize this, we risk irrelevance and extinction.

Rorty suggests a role for philosophy that consists in "redescription" (2010:432), or working and reworking our narratives to include broader notions of humanity and perhaps eventually reaching a sort of consensus that would achieve through globalized discourse what Kantian universals claimed by fiat. This is a congenial perspective for the anthropologist, employing imagination and an aesthetic understanding to come to terms with historical traditions well outside our own: a sort of talk therapy for the schizophrenia of the modern world. In this way it is much like Boas's interpretive modality. Can we achieve this, expanding the discursive community beyond our own tradition, eventually to include the Islamists and Christianists themselves? Can we render their "heterogenous" elements in such a way that we can see them with the eyes of a cultural insider?

Several caveats suggest themselves. First, and most obviously, this is little more than a genial, dressed-up form of colonialism. This discursive regime is, as we have noted, associated with liberal bourgeois capitalism and relies on its central tropes such as free speech and the weightlessness of both capital and information as they cross the globe. Indeed, such a project would end by imposing a hegemonic discourse of Western liberalism. And yet, given the events of the Arab Spring, it is not clear that such an outcome would be unwelcome in much of the world. Here again we face a fundamental contradiction between our substantive beliefs and our intellectual habits.

A second problem is its impracticality. Despite the pronouncements of cheerleaders of globalism such as Thomas Friedman (2005), the world is much more an Einsteinian universe than Flatland. The barriers to the flow of capital and digital information may have been greatly reduced due to technological and political changes in the past quarter century, but the vast majority of meaningful human interactions (and even economic transactions) exist on the local level. How does one find an interlocutor for a conversation that would inevitably take place in English, in the rarefied terms of anthropology or philosophy, who is truly a representative of another historical tradition? Would not such a conversation necessarily take place only among elites who share a common commitment to universal standards in a field such as science or commerce? Moreover, Rorty's impoverished sociology makes a person's identity a matter of an atomistic subject being affected by seemingly random factors in her social environment: "For purposes of moral and political deliberation and conversation, a person just is that network, as for purposes of ballistics she is a point-mass, or for purposes of chemistry a linkage of molecules. She is a network that is constantly reweaving itself in the usual Quinean manner—that is to say, not by reference to general criteria (e.g., 'rules of meaning' or 'moral principles') but in the hit-or-miss way in which cells readjust themselves to meet the pressures of the environment" (Rorty 1983:586). Most social scientists would instead argue that while individuals are indeed affected by their networks (and their position within those networks), there exist as well perduring, overlapping identities that may appear to the actor as fundamental and even primordial. He or she may choose to enact certain ones (e.g., religion, ethnicity) at the expense of others (sexuality, political beliefs), but each has the possibility of connection with a larger community and historical tradition. Thus, to truly capture such identities within our globalizing anthropological narrative, we would need to take into account literally millions of stories. Less a Diderotian philosophical meeting of the minds on great issues such as sexual morality and private property, a global anthropology would consist in the small, everyday markers of lived experience. This is a project for which not even anthropologists have demonstrated a particular zeal, at least when it comes to reading colleagues' ethnographies.

Indeed, this raises a third objection to the project of "redescription," one that rests on the very sort of ironic sensibility that Rorty championed. As the world becomes increasingly "flattened" (relative to, say, the days before the internet, cheap long-distance flights, and satellite television), globalizing forces have challenged local traditions and identities, which has created a crisis for those both in the West and outside it. One of Boas's most eminent protégés, Claude Lévi-Strauss, identified what we might call "cultural entropy" as the defining condition of the modern era: "It is differences between cultures that make their meetings fruitful. Now, this exchange leads to progressive uniformity: the benefits cultures reap from these contacts are largely the result of their qualitative differences, but during these exchanges these differences diminish to the point of disappearing. Isn't that what we are seeing today?" (Lévi-Strauss and Eribon 1991:149). This, too, is profoundly ironic. The chief benefit of cultural difference (indeed, in the context of Lévi-Straussian theory, its *purpose*) is the reciprocal exchange that brings about greater symbolic and material wealth and the possibilities for marriage and alliance. However, in the modern context, aided by advances in communication and transportation technology, this reciprocity threatens to overwhelm the cultural boundaries themselves. As an idea or product becomes ubiquitous (e.g., Buicks in China), it ceases to have the function of representing the Other in absentia and serves to remind us of the increasingly porous cultural boundaries and the difficulty in constructing an identity out of such a hybridized mélange. More recently, Lévi-Strauss has suggested that there exists an "optimum diversity" both among and within cultures (2011:55–57). The key factor is the possibility of distinctive identities constructed in terms of opposition and reciprocity. As societies become larger, the internal divisions become more important. As Lévi-Strauss recognized during Boas's lifetime, the fundamental human need for identity is always connected to the possibility of difference.

This of course resonates with Boas's own concerns, as he felt the traditional way of life of the Kwakiutl and other Native American groups slipping away in the reservation period. As Barber described on the macrolevel, the spread of a globalized version of Western capitalism, with its characteristic brands (McDonald's, Coca-Cola) and language (English), has led to a reaction in many parts of the world, especially the Middle East, which has been characteristically violent (Barber 1995). The problem of "debranding" and "rebranding" the person at the margins of the global system is arguably the central problem of our era.[5] The problem is not, as Lévi-Strauss seemed to believe, that a global monoculture would truly take over the world (although this particular belief was probably shared widely among members of the Académie française) but rather that the choices of meaningful identity, which, as Lévi-Strauss reminds us, is always seen within an oppositional context, are reduced, thus impoverishing our lives. New "brands"—jihadist, Christian soldier—present themselves as novel if unsustainable possibilities. As Timothy McVeigh was created out of the rubble of a devastated industrial working class in the "rust belt" of the 1980s and 1990s (as deftly portrayed in the Michael Moore film *Roger and Me*), so Mohamed Atta was deracinated, stripped of his identity while attending university in Germany to study engineering. While both took on the mantle of their religious/racial traditions, neither was a religiously devout person, nor is Anders Behring Breivik. Rather, for them, it is the role of religion as diacritic that matters. Atta was clearly an Islamist rather than a follower of Islam, while McVeigh and Breivik may be accurately called "Christianist." As Olivier Roy (2009) argues in *Holy Ignorance*, the rise of fundamentalism is preceded by a thorough secularization of society. The Islamist and Christianist actors are removed from their own religious traditions to the degree that they embrace customs that are tangential to it (e.g., the celebration of Christmas, belief in "the Rapture") or indeed antithetical to it (the "gospel of wealth") but that nevertheless function as markers of identity and solidarity.

Religion, even forms of it that are demonstrably inauthentic to their tradition, fulfills this function better than other, more transient identities, such as those related to capitalist production and consumption (e.g., occupation, identification with consumer brands). Although religious identity can be assumed with relatively little effort, it has the aura of primordialism, so that even those who may be recent converts or connected to a tradition in a shallow way may claim it as a central, motivating feature of their identity. Unlike Rorty's view of human individuals as atoms in Brownian motion buffeted by an array of impersonal forces, an anthropological perspective would view people such as Atta as actors imbued with limited but real agency. This agency is deployed most effectively in constructing an identity based on separation from the secularizing, globalizing world.

To answer the question with which I began this essay, I think that Boas, like most of us, would be on the horns of that particular sort of dilemma that comes from being faced, in an immediate and unignorable way, with the fact that "it is turtles all the way down." Much as we may have been aware of this fact intellectually and may, like Clifford Geertz (1984), have celebrated our discipline's antifoundationalism and "anti-anti-relativism," we find that we must now defend our discipline and the type of society on which it depends and that it has shaped without resorting to metaphysical arguments against foes with a surplus of them. Nor will pragmatic skepticism suffice. In a passage of great insight, Boas speaks of how the concept of race had in his time replaced "nationality," which in turn had "replaced that of group allegiance to the feudal lord, and the religious bond holding together all Christianity—a tie still potent in Islam" (1938[1911]:39). To speak of our own era, it must be acknowledged that we are, to some degree, postracial and that we have returned to some of these earlier categories as principles of identity and difference. This is not to say that we have defeated racism in all contexts but rather that racism as an official discourse has been marginalized and largely (although not yet completely) exiled from the academy. While Boas could chip away at the foundations of racialist thought with his method of negative capability, such a strategy would be useless in countering claims based not on scientific (or pseudoscientific) argument but on absolutist, metaphysical positions.

If the first part of the Boasian method is of little use to us in our historical moment, the second—the ethnographic imagination—most certainly is, and is perhaps more critical than ever before. Although, as I argued above, serious problems are connected with Rorty's project of redescription, it is perhaps the best alternative we have. If we give up the idea that we can ever achieve something more than partial, provisional understandings of other historical traditions or that we can eventually reach a utopian end of global democracy—that is, if we can deploy our own negative capability—the goal of creating dialogic space is a worthwhile one. To extend our understanding (with the "our" being unapologetically a postmodern, bourgeois, liberal Western perspective) in new directions, to engage with new interlocutors in an expanding, democratic dialogue is perhaps, to paraphrase Churchill, a terrible idea, but far better than all the others.

NOTES

1. Bush was seemingly correct if crude in saying that terrorists envied or hated our "freedoms"; his solution was to curtail them.
2. In *Kingdom Coming* the journalist Michelle Goldberg describes the rise of an extreme right-wing theocratic movement called Dominionism whose aim is to establish religious rule in the United States. Two of the three front-runners in the 2012 Republican presidential race subscribe to this ideology. The differences between this and Wahhabism or Shi'ite fundamentalism are ones of degree.
3. John Dewey was aware of Keats's concept, although it is unclear if his Columbia colleague Boas was or not. Nevertheless, as a principle consistent with early pragmatic philosophy, it was certainly consistent with a major strain of Boasian thought.
4. Dewey was in agreement with Boas's assessment of the situation. Although they were occasionally on different sides of specific issues,

Dewey emphasizes their commonality of purpose and perspective: "I share fully your resentment against efforts put forth to make it appear that our aims are different or that there is any significant opposition between our respective social or economic beliefs" (John Dewey to Franz Boas, November 12, 1939, Boas Papers).

5. See Robert Foster (2007, 2008, 2013). I am indebted to Foster for his development of the concept of branding in the anthropological sense. I am using it in a somewhat different context that is detached from market mechanisms, but I believe in a similar sense.

REFERENCES

Barber, Benjamin. 1995. Jihad vs. McWorld: Terrorism's Challenge to Democracy. New York: Ballantine Books.

Boas, Franz. 1938[1911]. The Mind of Primitive Man. Revised edition. New York: Macmillan.

Boas Papers, box 21. American Philosophical Society, Philadelphia.

Bracken, Christopher. 1997. The Potlatch Papers: A Colonial Case History. Chicago: University of Chicago Press.

Foster, Robert. 2007. The Work of the "New Economy": Consumers, Brands and Value. Cultural Anthropology 22:707–731.

——— . 2008. Commodities, Brands, Love and Kula: Comparative Notes on Value Creation. Anthropological Theory 8:9–25.

——— . 2013. Things to Do with Brands: Creating and Calculating Value. HAU: Journal of Ethnographic Theory 3:44–63.

Friedman, Thomas. 2005. The World Is Flat: A Brief History of the Twenty-First Century. New York: Farrar, Straus and Giroux.

Geertz, Clifford. 1984. Anti-anti-relativism: 1983 Distinguished Lecture. American Anthropologist 82:263–278.

Goldberg, Michelle. 2006. Kingdom Coming. New York: W. W. Norton and Co.

Lévi-Strauss, Claude. 2011. L'anthropologie face aux problèmes du monde moderne. Paris: Seuil.

Lévi-Strauss, Claude, and Didier Eribon. 1991. Conversations with Claude Lévi-Strauss. Trans. Paula Wissing. Chicago: University of Chicago Press.

Lewis, Herbert. 2000. Boas, Darwin, Science, and Anthropology. Current Anthropology 42:382–406.

——— . 2001. The Passion of Franz Boas. American Anthropologist 103:447–468.

Quine, W. V. O. 1951. Two Dogmas of Empiricism. Philosophical Review 60:20–43.

Rorty, Richard. 1983. Postmodernist Bourgeois Liberalism. Journal of Philosophy 80:583–589.

————. 2010. Ethics without Principles. *In* The Rorty Reader. Christopher J. Voparil and Richard J. Bernstein, eds. Hoboken NJ: Wiley-Blackwell.

Roy, Olivier. 2009. Holy Ignorance: When Religion and Culture Part Ways. New York: Columbia University Press.

Voparil, Christopher J., and Richard J. Bernstein, eds. 2010. The Rorty Reader. Hoboken NJ: Wiley-Blackwell.

Wu, Duncan. 2005. Romanticism: An Anthology. Hoboken NJ: Blackwell Publishing.

DAVID W. DINWOODIE

4

Boas and the Young Intellectuals

Exploring the American Context of
Anthropology and Modern Life

Alongside the study of innovation in so-called primitive societies, Franz
Boas began operationalizing the anthropological study of (rather than
reiterating the theoretical possibility of) the construction of the social
position of newly minted social elites in *Anthropology and Modern Life*.
In this chapter I will explore the American circumstances through which
Boas articulated what we might call, following George W. Stocking Jr.
(1965), *enlightened anthropological presentism*.

The history of anthropology has rightly emphasized the rich European roots of Franz Boas's scholarship and political commitments
(Bunzl 1996; Cole 1999; Liss 1996; Stocking 1968, 1996). In this chapter I will explore the possibility that Boas saw the achievements of the
"Young Intellectuals" of the twentieth-century United States as an inspiration for reshaping American anthropology and for reconfiguring its
intellectual commitments and institutional foundations. I explore the
possibility that Boas expanded upon Randolph Bourne's critiques of
the hegemony of Anglo-Saxons and Anglo-centric intellectuals when
broadening the scope of anthropology in *Anthropology and Modern
Life*. What the Young Intellectuals offered, in addition to a fresh critique of basing civil institutions on social precedence, was a model of
success—even if transitory—in developing new institutions for new
material circumstances. Given Boas's preexisting concern about the
continuing dependence of turn-of-the-century anthropology on the
American establishment, the possibility of fashioning a new institutional foundation likely held more than a little appeal.

At the outset I must admit, however, that evidence for Boas's active
uptake of the Young Intellectuals' ideas is not definitive. Nowhere to

my knowledge does Boas detail his intellectual debt to Bourne. Despite shared political interests, shared place of residence, shared involvement in the life of Columbia University, and shared public visibility, no significant body of correspondence between Boas and Randolph Bourne survives, none at least that I have located. And, somewhat to my surprise, I have located no commentary of any substance on the Boas-Bourne relationship in the correspondence of Elsie Clews Parsons, a close acquaintance and longtime interlocutor to each. Why? Boas and Bourne both lived in New York. Perhaps correspondence was not the primary mode of communication. Is it relevant that from the time of the onset of World War I both were under close scrutiny for expressing radical political views during a time of national paranoia? Perhaps. The possession of the correspondence of either could have proven to be a political liability for many in their circle. If there was correspondence, I have not been able to locate it. In any case, I have not found direct documentation of Boas's active uptake of Bourne's ideas.

There is evidence, nonetheless. A key piece of evidence and the point of departure for my exploration is the fact that Boas published a radical paper for a social scientist in Bourne's radical publication, the *Dial*. The publication occurred at a key juncture in Bourne's effort to challenge the political influence of the academy; that circumstance corresponded to a key juncture in Boas's thinking about the scope of anthropology. The paper in question was titled "The Mental Attitudes of the Educated Classes." It appeared in 1918. By publishing the paper in the *Dial* at that particular moment, Boas—at the time a noteworthy Columbia professor and a visible public intellectual—legitimated Bourne's suggestion that we look critically at the ideas of the establishment. But the paper also represented an innovation in the practice of anthropology. Boas was in the process of shifting the field away from its received focus on so-called primitive man. In his previous major works Boas (1911a, 1911b) had challenged the idea that so-called primitives were categorically other, arguing instead that differences were culturally mediated and essentially historical. In "The Mental Attitudes of the Educated Classes" Boas initiates the concrete exploration of the construction of the formal education-based and typically experience-free authority of modern experts and, by implication, of modern social

62 DAVID W. DINWOODIE

positionality in general, themes that he more fully elaborates in his book *Anthropology and Modern Life*.

In her innovative recent book *On Creating a Usable Culture: Margaret Mead and the Emergence of American Cosmopolitanism*, Maureen A. Molloy argues that the primary goal of Margaret Mead's anthropology was not that of empirical social science but rather the questioning of what it meant to be American, of what that "nation/self might be or what it might become."[1] Mead, according to Molloy, was fully involved in a project initiated by intellectuals and artists converging on New York City in the 1920s. Mead was not the only anthropologist involved in the American avant-garde who was rethinking self and nation. According to Molloy, there is much more to learn about the relationship between American modernism and American anthropology: "Studies of anthropology have tended to focus on that discipline's formation in and complicity with earlier phases of Euro-American imperialism and colonialism. Yet anthropology and anthropologists, especially in the eastern United States, were centrally engaged in debates about the nature and meaning of modern life. Elsie Clews Parsons, Franz Boas, Ruth Benedict, and Edward Sapir, each a mentor of Mead, participated in vigorous, not to say ferocious, debates in nonacademic venues about the meanings of domesticity, sexuality, race, and culture" (2008:3). Mead's formative cultural milieu, argues Molloy, was the circles of the new intelligentsia, the American modernists, without which her anthropological work is incomprehensible. Molloy acknowledges the critiques of the scientific aspects of Mead's work while offering a new appreciation of it.

Following Molloy, I explore Franz Boas's involvement in American debates about the nature and meaning of modern life and how that involvement shaped his anthropological vision. I will first examine the relationship between the writings of Bourne and Boas on modern life. I will sketch Bourne's critique of modern dependence on an archaic establishment and Boas's new vision for anthropology as articulated in *Anthropology and Modern Life*, and I will highlight the fact that there was a link between the two, namely, Boas's paper "The Mental Attitudes of the Educated Classes." Second, I will provide historical background on the Young Intellectual movement. Third, I will examine Bourne's relationship with Elsie Clews Parsons. Finally, I will briefly reflect upon the legacy of the Boas-Bourne relationship. I will argue that the relationship opened social scientific inquiry into the anthropology of expertise (Carr 2010); the philosophy, political science, and anthropology of civil religion (Beiner 2011; Deneen 2005; Gray 1998; Silverstein 2003); and the problem of Western social science's dependence on the institutions of the Western establishment (Graeber 2004, 2012; Sahlins 1976). These phenomena illuminate Western modernity's eternal imbrication in the human condition and the urgency of social scientific reflexivity.

ANTHROPOLOGY AND MODERN LIFE: BUILDING UPON BOURNE'S CRITIQUE

Provoked by a letter published in the *Atlantic Monthly* in 1911, a "Letter to the Rising Generation," Randolph Bourne challenged our reliance on elders, elders' ideas, and relatively old (though obviously not very old) institutions. Bourne proposed that whereas the previous generation had concerned themselves with personal salvation, the religion that would mean something to the rising generation would be based on social ideals, ideals that would supply a real working platform for addressing social injustice. Bourne proposed that the rising generation was motivated by "the scientific attitude toward the world" (1967[1913]:48–49) instead of Victorian Christianity. In his sequel, Bourne initiated an analytic explanation of the character of the ideas of the older generation:

> Old men cherish a fond delusion that there is something mystically valuable in mere quantity of experience. Now the fact is, of course, that it is the young people who have all the really valuable experience. It is they who have constantly to face new situations, to react constantly to new aspects of life, who are getting the whole beauty and terror and cruelty of the world in its fresh and undiluted purity. It is only the interpretation of this first collision with life that is worth anything. For the weakness of experience is that it so soon gets stereotyped; without new situations and crises it becomes so conventional as to be practically unconscious. (Bourne 1967[1913]:12–13)

In order to act decisively, effective leaders should be "coincident with the conditions of the world as [they] find them" (Bourne 1967[1913]:15). And yet, according to Bourne, experience can become "so conventional as to be practically unconscious" (12). Bourne questioned the character of the experience of elders, who could be unconscious regarding the conditions of the world and yet strategic in pursuit of their own interests.

In an essay published in 1917 Bourne also questioned academics' claims to universal knowledge:

> A war made deliberately by the intellectuals! A calm moral verdict, arrived at after a penetrating study of inexorable facts! Sluggish masses, too remote from the world-conflict to be stirred, too lacking in intellect to perceive their danger! An alert intellectual class, saving the people in spite of themselves, biding their time with Fabian strategy until the nation could be moved into war without serious resistance! An intellectual class, gently guiding a nation through sheer force of ideas into what the other nations entered only through predatory craft or popular hysteria or militaristic madness! A war free from any taint of self-seeking, a war that will secure the triumph of democracy and internationalize the world! (Resek 1999[1964]:3)

Bourne urged us to cultivate a critical stance toward the idea that self-styled experts are disinterested and toward ostensibly scholarly rationales for political interventions.

Though his essays exhibit a distinct voice, Bourne was not alone in challenging the elite of the day. He was one among a group that sometimes called themselves the Young Intellectuals. The group included Van Wyck Brooks, Randolph Bourne, Waldo Frank, James Oppenheim, Paul Rosenfeld, and Herbert Croly. In order to envision a new, more vital, more cosmopolitan American culture, they challenged Anglo-Saxon primacy, the politics of the Gilded Age, the genteel tradition of criticism, and the obsolete institutional structure of politics and media (May 1959:281; Wertheim 1976:xii).

As is well known, shortly after his arrival in the United States, Boas had became suspicious that the so-called anthropology practiced in the United States was less than fully scientific, less than fully conversant with the fundamentals of Enlightenment debate. Boas suspected that the American version of the extension of the idea of evolution from biology to social development by such figures as Daniel Garrison Brinton, for example, represented not science but a facsimile thereof. Already by 1887 he had publicly questioned the theoretical coherence of Otis Mason's presumed typological evolutionary approach to displaying ethnographical specimens in the U.S. National Museum (Bunzl 1996:56). Boas also developed an account in his introduction to *The Handbook of American Indian Languages* of how socially foundational behaviors, whether grammatical or cultural, can become so routinized as to not seem conscious. Both of these ideas—the importance of a critical examination of the claims of received experts and the idea that many forms of behavior that are apparently grounded in real conditions are predicated on unexamined categories—originated with Boas, not Bourne. Nevertheless, Bourne's innovation was to suggest that the attitudes of modern intellectuals and elites must be analyzed. And Bourne extended the idea that key forms of behavior are practiced without conscious control when he suggested that elites in particular often act on social prerogative without any clear apprehension of contemporary conditions.

Boas built upon these Bournean innovations (which were based on Boas's ideas), in my view, in his interwar re-visioning of anthropology. Of all his works that reveal the relationship between his scholarship and his politics, *Anthropology and Modern Life* (2008[1928]) has received less critical attention than *The Mind of Primitive Man* (1911b), the introduction to *The Handbook of American Indian Languages* (1911a), and his Kwakiutl ethnology (Briggs and Bauman 1999; Stocking 1968, 1992b).[2]

Anthropology and Modern Life can be divided into three sections. As in his previous major works, the introduction to *The Handbook of American Indian Languages* and *The Mind of Primitive Man*, *Anthropology and Modern Life* opens with a discussion of the race concept and a critique of so-called scientific racism. This discussion is followed by an unprecedented examination of the counterintuitive dynamics surrounding stability and adaptability in large versus small societies. Whereas so-called primitive societies appear to be static, history shows that some have changed extensively in the face of new circumstances. Whereas modern societies appear to be dynamic, closed institutions and closed minds are often constructed within them. Nationalism is a modern institutional-ideological complex that can either expand the scope of human relations or constrain it. Education is a modern institutional-ideological complex that can either open minds to empirical realities or inculcate obedience to authority. In practice, the two impulses are not clear in the minds of contemporary actors. Rather, argues Boas, they are often in conflict. Finally, Boas addresses the question of how anthropology might play an active role in engaging the dilemmas of modern life. He argues that anthropology can draw on the full range of human history and human experience to critically evaluate the interventions proposed by contemporary experts, whether they are rationalized in terms of empirical science or of "tradition." Mentioning some of the most revered ideas of the time—"progress," "the greatest good for the greatest number," geographical determinism, and economic determinism—Boas suggests that all are amenable to anthropological contextualization. Overall, Boas initiates the study of what will later be called "acculturation"; he suggests that anthropology has a special responsibility to question the claims of Western experts. And in the way he lays out his arguments, he also points toward the study of the construction of social position and authority in modern societies no less than so-called primitive societies.

What is the link between Bourne and Boas? "The Mental Attitudes of the Educated Classes," a manuscript now in Boas's professional papers at the American Philosophical Society, was republished verbatim as the second half of chapter 8, "Education," of *Anthropology and Modern Life*. In this epitomizing section of the book, Boas argues that the nation is neither a natural nor an ideal political arrangement but rather "a segregated class, a closed society," the characteristic feature of which is that its members accord its ideals priority over those that are general and human (2008[1928]:194). He continues in observing that, due to long periods of isolation in apprenticeship, academics in America too represent a closed society in which class interests prevail over general human interest. As a result of the length of training and of increasing specialization, Boas argues that the application of the critical attitude was becoming limited to one narrow area of study and not extended to other aspects of culture (193, 195). Boas sums up:

> Combined with the thoroughness with which the intellectuals have imbibed the traditions of the past, [the absence of strength of char-

acter] makes the majority of them in all nations conventional. It has the effect that their thoughts are based on tradition, and that the range of their vision is liable to be limited. . . .

I should always be more inclined to accept, in regard to fundamental human problems, the judgment of the masses rather than the judgment of the intellectuals, which is much more certain to be warped by unconscious control of traditional ideas. (Boas 2008[1928]:196–197, 199)

"The Mental Attitudes of the Educated Classes" was originally published in the radical periodical the *Dial* in 1918. It was very likely solicited by the editor, Randolph Bourne, in the context of Bourne's efforts to challenge John Dewey's position on American entry into the war.

Boas's relation with Dewey is not entirely straightforward. They were colleagues at Columbia. They were both reformers and shared many causes. Later, Boas quarreled with Dewey. Dewey formed the Committee for Cultural Freedom in May 1939 apparently to counter or subsume a similar committee Boas formed not long before, the Lincoln's Birthday Committee for Democracy and Intellectual Freedom. Boas questioned Dewey's actions in correspondence (on this issue, see Boydston 1988:488–489). It is possible that their relationship was already ambivalent by 1918.

Elsie Clews Parsons was a supportive interlocutor of Bourne as he developed a critical attitude toward Dewey and other academic elites. Based on her strong ties to Boas (she was a patron and former student) and her intuitions regarding the shared interests of the two, I think it is likely that she mediated the inclusion of Boas's paper in the *Dial* (see Lamphere 1989 for more on Parsons's anthropological legacy).

The emergence of a felt need for anthropologists to think critically not only in relation to Catholicism in feudal regimes or Protestantism among the Victorian bourgeoisie but also in reference to secular elites and intellectuals marks an important moment in anthropology. Boas theorized the point, and there is no doubt that it is to him that the credit should go for its anthropological formulation (Stocking 1992c). Nevertheless, it appears that Bourne was influential. Perhaps Boas came to see that Bourne had opened a space for positioning the field of anthropology beyond the new "civil religious" current of the twentieth-century mainstream.

THE YOUNG INTELLECTUALS AND RANDOLPH BOURNE

As observed above, the Young Intellectuals formed in the 1910s in New York City. As Henry F. May explains, exactly "for the same reason Henry James shuddered and conventional middle-class progressives shook their heads, the Young Intellectuals exulted: New York, whatever else it was, was not Anglo-Saxon. This meant more than cheap and good French and Italian restaurants; it meant a serious invitation to attack the dominant concept of culture exactly where it was weakest, in its narrow exclusiveness" (1959:282). In the big picture, the Young Intellectuals were the avant-garde of the age of reform, though, curiously, they are not mentioned in Richard Hofstadter's classic *The Age of Reform* (1955), perhaps due to his focus on politics over culture. For May the Young Intellectuals deconstructed American innocence and ushered in our contemporary world of polarization, media, abrupt discontinuities, innovation, destruction, and general trepidation: "On one side of some historical boundary lies the America of Theodore Roosevelt and William Jennings Bryan, of Chautauqua and Billy Sunday and municipal crusades, a world so foreign, so seemingly simple, that we sometimes tend, foolishly enough, to find it comical. On the other side of the barrier lies our own time, a time of fearful issues and drastic divisions, a time surely including the Jazz Age, the great depression, the New Deal, and the atom bomb" (1959:ix).

The Young Intellectuals were a part of a movement that Arthur Frank Wertheim designates the New York Little Renaissance. Wertheim sees four groups shaping the Renaissance: (1) "the radical writers and artists affiliated with *The Masses* magazine and The Eight group of painters," including Max Eastman, John Reed, and Floyd Dell; (2) "the apolitical iconoclasts on *The Smart Set* staff, especially H. L. Mencken and Willard Huntington"; (3) "the avid cultural nationalists associated with *The Seven Arts* and *The New Republic* magazines," literary and social critics including Van Wyck Brooks and Randolph Bourne; and (4) the modernists, including "the poets published in *Others* magazine, the Stieglitz circle of artists, and the members of the various little theatre movements" (1976:xi–xii). The Young Intellectuals were primarily critics who first came together at the *New Republic*. In their publications Herbert Croly (a student of Josiah Royce), George Santayana, and Charles Eliot Norton at Harvard began to develop a concept of critical cultural nationalism and sought to build institutions that might bring about change. In 1914 Croly, Walter Lippmann, and Walter Weyl founded the *New Republic*; Lippmann became the editor. Croly and Lippmann emphasized politics, and Francis Hackett and Randolph Bourne were hired as critics of arts and of books. As the *New Republic* was drawn more into the politics surrounding possible entry into World War I its commitment to cultural criticism receded.

With funding from the socialite Mrs. A. K. Rankine, James Oppenheim founded the *Seven Arts* to better address the role of the arts in creating a new society. Oppenheim hired Waldo Frank as associate editor. Frank recruited Van Wyck Brooks, Paul Rosenfeld, and, eventually, Randolph Bourne. Bourne was not on the editorial staff but played an influential role, according to Wertheim, particularly during 1917, when Bourne was publishing his antiwar articles, including what became his signature piece, "War and the Intellectuals" (Resek 1999[1964]:3–14; Wertheim 1976:167–176). The *Seven Arts* became the most influential periodical of socially significant art. With the publication of his book *America's Coming-of-Age* in 1915 Van Wyck Brooks came to be the most refined and broadly influential member of the Young Intellectuals. Randolph Bourne, conversely, became the group's punk-rock icon for youth and, not incidentally, the point of contact for Boas (May 1959:323). Unlike the many Harvard-educated Young Intellectuals, Bourne had been a Columbia student, a student of John Dewey, and even a student of Boas himself (Resek 1999[1964]:x).

In the writings of William James, Friedrich Nietzsche, and Henri Bergson, Bourne found "an absolution from ancestral dogma" (Resek 1999[1964]:x). In his early publications, particularly "The Two Generations" (1911) and "Youth" (1912), Bourne became spokesman for the twentieth-century youth movement (Bourne 1967[1913]; Deacon 1997:168; Resek 1999[1964]:vii). As Eric J. Sandeen observes, Bourne attained remarkable stature, and it was reflected in the judgment of his distinguished friends. The music critic Paul Rosenfield observed that

Bourne had the rare "power to organize the contrary forces of his times, to categorize influences, to act as the cutting edge in the search for truth," and this enabled him to surmount "the disorienting chaos of the cultural material with which he was working." Through the "forceful application of the power of his mind, he was able to exert influence on social conditions" (Sandeen 1981:3). For Van Wyck Brooks, Bourne's ability to internalize the complexities of society, his sense of social responsibility, and his ability to draw together the sociological and artistic perspectives on society into one all-encompassing, comprehensive vision were key elements of his leading role among the young intelligentsia (3).

Recent critics, according to Sandeen, have "returned to and amplified the view of Bourne's contemporaries" (1981:5). Christopher Lasch, for example, saw that Bourne was committed to progressive education and to the possibility that contact with society led to valuable experiences that would shape students and enable them as a collective to contribute to the reformation of society. Ideally, the developing youth was "placed in an organic functional relationship with a society in which there was a clear relationship between thought and action. . . . The problem for Bourne, as Lasch sees it, was how to take the spirit of youth with him into middle age, how to maintain the stance of the reformer, separated from the social structure by both age and perspective, while at the same time assuming social responsibility" (6).

Bourne was born in Bloomfield, New Jersey, in 1886. His mother's side of the family was, according to Carl Resek, "relentlessly aristocratic. Proud of ancestors among the first generation of settlers in New England, they owned Bloomfield's finest real estate, married in their own social class and sent their sons to college and law school. They voted Republican and regularly attended the town's First Presbyterian Church. Randolph was raised on one Bible verse a day and, as he later recalled, on frequent entreaties to be a gentleman" (1999[1964]:vii). His background notwithstanding, Bourne developed into a critic of the aristocratic Puritan class. In a letter to Elsie Clews Parsons, Bourne states, "You are the only other renegade Anglo-Saxon I know besides myself" (July 4, 1916, Parsons Papers). Factors shaping his apostasy included his mother's family's rejection of his father (at his uncles' bidding his father left the household); the restraining influences of small-town life and small-town schools; and six years working in factories and then in minstrel and vaudeville shows, which caused him to develop a "sensitivity to human exploitation" (Resek 1999[1964]:ix).

Bourne entered Columbia in 1909, excited by the great revolt against rationalism, and he attended classes taught by John Dewey, James Harvey Robinson, and Franz Boas. After publishing "Two Generations" and several other radical, energetic, and stylish pieces in such venues as the *Atlantic Monthly*, in the early 1910s he developed a respectable following (Resek 1999[1964]:x).

Five of Bourne's essays are relevant for thinking about his influence on Boas: "Two Generations" (*Atlantic Monthly*, May 1911), "Youth" (*Atlantic Monthly*, April 1912), "Transnational America" (*Atlantic Monthly*, July 1916), "War and the Intellectuals" (*Seven Arts*, June 1917), and "Twilight of Idols" (*Seven Arts*, October 1917). The first two, "Two Generations" and "Youth," while perhaps echoing aspects of Boas's earlier thought, including his skepticism of received authority and his argument that people are generally not conscious of the linguistic and cultural foundations of perception and practice, develop key features of the arguments Boas develops in "The Mental Attitudes of the Educated Classes" and *Anthropology and Modern Life*, namely, that elites are relatively disconnected from their times and, what is worse, blissfully unaware of this fact. In contradiction to the modern ideology of progress, structural features of modern society favor insularity and stasis, especially in the face of changing circumstances. Contrasting Boas's work with Ralph Linton's *The Study of Man* (1936) illustrates the originality of Boas's argument within the field of anthropology. *The Study of Man* was organized around the premise that World War I had demonstrated that the greatest threat to humanity came not from "primitives" living in, as Hobbes put it, a "state of Warre" but rather from civilized men, who, with contemporary technology, now had the capacity to destroy humanity itself. Linton proposed that anthropology might examine small-scale societies for what they reveal about integration and stability. In "The Mental Attitudes of the Educated Classes," Boas suggested that while we assume the educated classes are attuned to the world, their quasi-feudal institutional practices inhibit empirical inquiry along novel lines. Boas's *Anthropology and Modern Life* includes a chapter, "Stability of

Culture," whose title suggests a concern parallel to Linton's. However, in it Boas subtly reverses widespread assumptions regarding the difference between so-called moderns and so-called primitives, suggesting that whereas we expect so-called primitive societies to be closed and stable, in fact they are sometimes open, dynamic, and even plural. And while we expect so-called modern societies to be open and dynamic, they can cloister themselves from unpleasant realities.

Bourne's essay "Transnational America" identified the parochial character of chauvinistic nationalism and sketched out a political ideological alternative, transnationality. As he phrased it, "The contribution of America will be an intellectual internationalism which goes far beyond the mere exchange of scientific ideas and discoveries and the cold recording of facts. It will be an intellectual sympathy which is not satisfied until it has got at the heart of the different cultural expressions, and felt as they feel. It may have immense preferences, but it will make understanding and not indignation its end. Such sympathy will unite and not divide" (Resek 1999[1964]:119).

In "The War and the Intellectuals" Bourne exposed John Dewey's and others' literal rationalization of America's entry into the war and their defensive attribution of rational motives as a way of avoiding a material analysis of motives:

> To those of us who still retain an irreconcilable animus against war, it has been a bitter experience to see the unanimity with which the American intellectuals have thrown their support to the use of war-technique in the crisis in which America found herself. Socialists, college professors, publicists, new-republicans, practitioners of literature, have vied with each other in confirming with their intellectual faith the collapse of neutrality and the riveting of the war-mind on the hundred million more of the world's people. And the intellectuals are not content with confirming our belligerent gesture. They are now complacently asserting that it was they who effectively willed it, against the hesitation and dim perceptions of the American democratic masses. (Resek 1999[1964]:3)

In "Twilight of Idols" Bourne develops a different take on John Dewey. "What concerns us here," Bourne observes bluntly, "is the relative ease with which the pragmatist intellectuals, with Professor Dewey at the head, have moved out their philosophy, bag and baggage, from education to war," from areas in which they have genuine expertise, to areas in which an aura of expertise might be all that is necessary to resolve political indecision (Resek 1999[1964]:56). Here Bourne profanes Dewey by association, and he highlights the supplicatory character of the attitudes upon which Dewey's following is based:

> It may seem unfair to group Professor Dewey with Mr. Spargo and Mr. Gompers, Mr. A. M. Simons, and the Vigilantes. I do so only because in their acceptance of the war, they are all living out that popular American "instrumental" philosophy which Professor Dewey has formulated in such convincing and fascinating terms. On an infinitely more intelligent plane, he is yet one with them in his confidence that the war is motivated by democratic ends and is being made to serve them. A high mood of confidence and self-righteousness moves them all, a keen sense of control over events that makes them eligible to discipleship under Professor Dewey's philosophy. (Resek 1999[1964]:58–59)

In *Anthropology and Modern Life* it is the ideas of the very figures identified by Bourne, the hegemonic sages of the modern ages, that Boas argues demand anthropological scrutiny.

MEDIATING BETWEEN BOURNE AND BOAS: ELSIE CLEWS PARSONS

Elsie Clews Parsons was born in 1874 to Henry and Lucy Madison Worthington Clews. Henry Clews was born in England. He immigrated to the United States in 1850 and, enriched by the Civil War, was by 1870 the model of a "new man," running a successful banking and investment firm. While Elsie's mother met Henry Clews at a White House ball, and while Lucy grew up in the border states among northern sympathizers, she remade herself during her marriage as a southern belle. Lucy "never made a new role for herself as the wife of a 'new man,'" according to Desley Deacon. "Instead, she clung with even greater tenacity to the role of hostess and beauty" (Deacon 1997:5).[3]

Elsie Clews graduated from Barnard College in 1896 and continued on at Columbia, receiving her MA and PhD in sociology in 1897 and 1899. Her dissertation was published as her first book, *The Educational Legislation and Administration of the Colonies* (Hare 1985:19). While she married Republican politician Herbert Parsons in 1900, she considered it an "experimental relationship," and throughout her life she continued her effort to critically examine the conventions of Victorian society.

Deacon argues that Elsie's parents' marriage was a source of Elsie's "critical bent." Deacon brilliantly analyzes the structural circumstances behind the problems with Elsie's parents' marriage, structural circumstances that illuminate some of the dramatic changes under way in the turn-of-the-century United States. In the mid-nineteenth century, politics and business were overseen by a small number of well-positioned families. The end of this era was punctuated by the Belknap scandal. Gen. William Belknap, Elsie's mother's brother-in-law, was disgraced for selling traderships in the Oklahoma Territory. Elsie's mother's sister, Belknap's wife, tried to save the family fortunes by "deflecting the blame onto herself." Puss, as she was known, was made a scapegoat in the press and was subject to "a tirade of misogyny." Whereas in antebellum family-based politics, women played an integral role as "behind the scenes partners of men," they were removed in the new system, which centered on the politics of parties. Puss and her family were put forward as models of old-fashioned morality.

By marrying Henry Clews, Elsie's mother, Lucy, joined herself to the new order that was displacing the old family-based system. However, as time went on she emphasized her identification with the past, including maintaining "the role of hostess and beauty" (Deacon 1997:5).

With the decline of the family-based political system, the women's movement sought to develop itself effectively as a new separate constituency with institutions of its own (Deacon 1997:4). In this transitional environment, Elsie Clews's parents diverged, and the marriage became formal and dissonant. The result for Elsie was an unhappy family experience: "Although her parents had abandoned, for their different reasons, the authority of the past, they clung to the forms of a traditional marriage and a social life which seemed to their daughter to be without substance. This sense of the past's weakness and inutility gave the young Elsie the motivation to question her parents' sexual and social world, and the confidence to set about building her own moral universe" (7).

According to Peter H. Hare, Parsons's career had two stages. In the early stage she identified as a feminist, and her writing was devoted to deconstructing the conventions associated with women's roles. In that stage she wrote *The Old Fashioned Woman* (1913) and *Fear and Conventionality* (1914), and she contributed to the *New Republic* (Hare 1985:19). On the basis of her early writing, she became "a central figure" in the New York avant-garde (Deacon 1997:152). In the second stage of her writing, she pursued ethnographic study in anthropology. Due to her energy, intelligence, style, and, not least, her established position in the avant-garde, anthropologists welcomed her interest and ratified her participation (Deacon 1997:152; Hare 1985:19).

As World War I escalated and as the United States debated whether to participate, Parsons attempted to encourage clear thinking by questioning whether Americans were being drawn into the war on the basis of either pressing interests or cultural patterns. When she wrote "A Warning to the Middle Aged" in the *New Review* in 1915, she attracted the attention of another young intellectual, Randolph Bourne. They met in 1915, "probably at one of the elegant New Republic lunches" (Deacon 1997:167, 8). They developed a relationship at social clubs and in correspondence. Eric J. Sandeen characterizes the relationship:

> The letters benefit from the difference in the circumstances of the correspondents. Parsons was a decade older than Bourne; she was 40 when he began corresponding with her in 1915 at the age of 29. To him she represented maturity and he solicited her advice; occasionally, her letters to him appropriated the stance of an older sister or aunt. Parsons was also a person of wealth and position. . . .
>
> She was used to being the benefactor—in future years she would sponsor with her own checkbook research programs for budding anthropologists—and, despite his radical views, he sought a patron. (1989:493–494)

Bourne found Parsons to be a meaningful interlocutor regarding the antiwar movement. "Both viewed the war," as Deacon explains, "as part of a larger struggle between youth and age that encompassed sexuality and education as much as militarism" (1997:169).

During the period of their correspondence, Parsons was shifting away from her critiques of modern America and toward ethnographic study of so-called primitives. Bourne was in the midst of writing the antipaternalism, antiwar works that made his reputation. He was at the peak of his literary influence. As Sandeen puts it, "Most fame has [come to] Bourne . . . through his principled opposition to the war" (1981:1).

Though the relationship between Parsons and Bourne has attracted the interest of both Bourne scholars and Parsons scholars (Deacon 1997; Sandeen 1989; Zumwalt 1992), their correspondence has not attracted the attention of historians of anthropology to my knowledge. Nevertheless, the issues they address bear on the field in a variety of interesting ways. Questioning the character of the jingoistic patriotism of the time, for example, Parsons wrote in a letter to Bourne:

> "Americanism" is becoming such a burlesque that I really think people will wake up to it some morning with a laugh.
>
> I must tell you a private joke. Somebody at Hunter's College telegraphed me would I make the commencement address there. Fired by those articles of Kallen's I wrote him I would if I could talk on democracy v. melting pot. Something to that effect, but as I knew that brand of Americanism was not popular in school circles he must not hesitate to withdraw his invitation if he so wished. He withdrew it. So they'll lose a few Zuni anecdotes and a few references to Anglo-Saxon arrogance. (June 14, 1916, Bourne Papers)

In the same letter, Parsons expressed her view that the assumed linkage between unity and nationality was aggressive and unnecessary: "I am for practical & definite pacifism in nursery & school and for democratic tolerance of all nationalities as against the melting pot propaganda."

In a letter to Parsons, Bourne objected to the use of pragmatism, a self-styled departure from traditionalism, to rationalize vulgar conservative political endeavors: "Did you see Dewey's article in a recent NR on the Conscientious Objector? This seems to me to show Dewey's own philosophy up in the weakest spot. I wrote a reply trying to show that the pragmatist, from his own philosophy, could never accept war, or consent to its use as a technique" (July 16, 1916, Parsons Papers).

In another letter to Parsons, Bourne showed his sensitivity to the need to freshen his criticisms of the elites, lest his views be pigeonholed as unpatriotic or even treasonous:

> The NR is getting—or FH is—a little weary of my anti-Americanisms and my peevishness and my stock is running very low. I shall make another try to hold my own, but see my income slipping away from me.
> When does your book come out? (October 3, 1916, Parsons Papers)

What of evidence for the Bourne-Boas relationship? While there is no direct evidence, there is circumstantial evidence. In a letter to Parsons that likely elucidates the circumstances in which Franz Boas submitted "The Mental Attitudes of the Educated Classes" to the *Dial* during Bourne's editorship in 1918, Bourne reveals his radical and brilliant conclusion that the new progressivism had become a dogma: "Your article is delightful. I foresee a next book on the subject of 'Social Progress.' The intellectuals must be exposed" (May 9, 1917, Parsons Papers). Parsons could not have missed the appeal that this insight would hold for Franz Boas, particularly for his long-standing effort to question whether American anthropology was not part and parcel of a national tradition (Lomnitz 2005:167–169).[4]

CONCLUSION: THE LEGACY OF BOAS'S RELATIONSHIP
WITH THE YOUNG INTELLECTUALS

As has been well documented, Boas's thought has roots in the German Enlightenment, in the intellectual resistance to French imperialism, in the critical perspectives that figures like Johann Gottfried Herder and Immanuel Kant brought to the great debates among Jeremy Bentham, David Hume, John Locke, the marquis de Condorcet, Baron de Montesquieu, Jean-Jacques Rousseau, Voltaire, and so many others. But in America, even in an America that was not as cosmopolitan as he had hoped, Boas found new insight and new motivation, and he reconfigured his representation of his anthropological vision accordingly. In 1928 in *Anthropology and Modern Life* Boas expanded the scope of anthropology to include study of the historical dynamics of so-called primitive societies and the means through which social hierarchy, ideological closure, and the appearance of stasis are effected in so-called modern societies. In 1918 Bourne had published Boas's preliminary analysis of the construction of expertise and structural authority in educational practice. "The Mental Attitudes of the Educated Classes" was then republished as a key part of the transitional section of *Anthropology and Modern Life*. Bourne's critique of intellectuals thus appeared as a key element of Boas's vision of a new anthropology for a new century, a new world order.

For the history of anthropology, attending to Boas's links to Bourne and other Young Intellectuals and the part played by the Young Intellectuals in shaping a historical moment provides a richer sense of the critical energy of the field in its modern formative moment. Though short-lived as social presences, the Young Intellectuals' ideas and critical energy live on in another sense in the modern vision of anthropology.

As mentioned above, several lines of anthropological inquiry that have come into their own only recently have their origins in the Bourne-Boas relationship dialogue. One important contemporary research focus pioneered in the Bourne-Boas relationship is the anthropology of expertise. E. Sumerson Carr (2010) reframes a Foucauldian theme within an empirically productive social semiotic approach. On the one hand, Carr's work is cutting edge, but on the other, it is a line of inquiry that runs at least as far back as Bourne and Boas. During the early twentieth century, the Victorian mass mobilization of Protestantism was losing ground to socialism and pragmatism. Along with William James and John Dewey, Bourne did what he could to expedite the shift, enhancing the appeal of pragmatism and socialism by imparting to them salvational overtones (for Bourne, see "Two Generations" in Resek 1999[1964]:48–49; for Dewey, see Deneen 2005:166–188). With Dewey's shift in favor of American entry into the war, however, Bourne and Boas took exception to the uncritical acceptance of expertise.

Related to questions surrounding the bases of expertise is a second theme that has recently emerged as a full-blown subject of inquiry, namely, civil religion. Ronald Beiner characterizes civil religion as "the appropriation of religion by politics for its own purposes" (2011:1). Jean-Jacques Rousseau coined the phrase for a phenomenon he saw as necessary to the modern world but one that was dangerous nonetheless. It was necessary because people are not moved by mere ideas. Governance could not rely on ideas alone. Rousseau saw civil religion as bad, if necessary, "in that it is founded on errors and lies, it deceives men, making them credulous and superstitious" (1994[1762]:163).

From the vantage point of the present, I think it is possible to identify civil religion as having been a pressing concern in the interwar years. Certainly it is a pressing issue now. It is another contemporary issue the anthropological study of which was pioneered in the Bourne-Boas relationship. While the concept of civil religion has been much discussed since Jean-Jacques Rousseau introduced it in *The Social Contract* (1994[1762]) and since sociologist Robert Bellah (1967) revisited it during the social unrest of the 1960s, it has only recently become a central analytic focus of inquiry in political science and anthropology. In the context of the intensification of Western ideology production in the post-Soviet environment, a loosely linked body of scholarship turned to the critical examination of civil religion as a key element of modern political regimentation (Beiner 2011; Deneen 2005; Gray 1998; Silverstein 2003).

A third area of contemporary anthropological interest pioneered in the Bourne-Boas relationship, and the last I will discuss, is the need for a principled examination of the implications of the dependence of social science, including anthropology, on the institutions of the establishment of Western society, or to put it into the starkest relief, what we might characterize as the dependence on the example of one single society among all the societies of the world. I would argue that the broad appeal of contemporary anthropologist David Graeber's writing centers on the fact that he is highlighting the distortions imposed on the public imagination by our overwhelming dependence on capitalist institutions; Graeber (2004, 2012) cultivates a version of anthropology that illuminates our dependence and then sets about challenging it. Slightly earlier in time, Marshall Sahlins challenged widespread assumptions regarding the basis of "practical reason" in his brilliant *Culture and Practical Reason* (1976). But anthropological inquiry originates not in the near present. It goes back to Bourne and Boas. Paul Rosenfeld saw Bourne at his best not as the proponent of a position but as a "dialectical machine" (Sandeen 1981:2). For Bourne, the point became not to be a member of any single political party or of a generic transcendent transnationality but rather to consciously strive against passively accepting an exclusionary nationalism, to maintain a vibrant critical self-awareness through dialectic inquiry. For Bourne, the point was to sustain a transnational, transgenerational, and transfaith dialectic.

In *Anthropology and Modern Life* Boas reframed Bourne's dialectic of nationality in social scientific terms. The critical stance taken toward the devotional attitudes surrounding the ostensibly "progressive" ideas of the educated classes is what makes *Anthropology and Modern Life* so fresh today. I believe the evidence shows that in articulating his critical stance toward intellectuals, Boas appropriated language and ideas *authored*, in Erving Goffman's sense of the term, by Randolph Bourne and Elsie Clews Parsons as key members of the group that came to be known as the Young Intellectuals. For Boas, the goal was to distance anthropology from the Victorian establishment by positioning it in—or by *voicing* it in relation to—the critical space established by the Young Intellectuals (Goffman 1983; Dinwoodie 2013; Keane 1999).

American anthropology's German roots are rich indeed, and no doubt there is much more to learn about them. The relations between Franz Boas, his students, and the avant-garde in New York also warrant considered attention. Randolph Bourne died unexpectedly of influenza shortly after Woodrow Wilson entered the war. Whether it was because of the loss of Bourne or the tidal wave of patriotism triggered by the formal declaration of hostility, the Young Intellectuals' meager institutional footing quickly eroded. Still, the passing moment when Bourne and Boas may have interanimated a critical anthropology has the potential to enkindle anthropological purpose and disciplinary reflexivity today, tomorrow . . .

NOTES

This chapter was originally presented as a paper at the session "The Contextualization of Contemporary Engagements: George W. Stocking Symposium in the History of Anthropology," organized by David W. Dinwoodie and Sergei Kan, at the annual meetings of the American Anthropological Association, November 20–24, 2013. Ira Bashkow, Robert Brightman, Raymond Fogelson, Maria Lepowsky, Johanna Radin, Michael Scott, Michael Silverstein, and two anonymous reviewers have provided meaningful comments. The chapter's shortcomings cannot be blamed on anyone but me.

I hereby register my gratitude to the American Philosophical Society and the Randolph Bourne Archives at Columbia University for having organized and maintained the papers of Franz Boas, Elsie Clews Parsons, and Randolph Bourne and for making them accessible. The Rare Book and Manuscript Library owns only the physical objects in the Randolph Bourne Papers and Elsie Clews Parsons Papers, not the copyright to these items, and will neither grant nor deny copyright permission regarding such materials, according to Tara C. Craig, MLS, reference services advisor (October 2, 2014). The APS holds the rights to the Parsons Papers and the Boas Papers but not to the Bourne Papers, even the material that is in the Elsie Clews Parsons Papers, so the APS cannot give permission to quote these materials, according to Charles B. Greifenstein, associate librarian and curator of manuscripts (October 2, 2014).

1. Michael Silverstein directed me to Maureen Molloy's work. He reviewed *On Creating a Usable Culture* (Silverstein 2009).
2. Works that discuss the contributions of *Anthropology and Modern Life* within the Boasian corpus include Herb Lewis's afterword to the reissue of *Anthropology and Modern Life* (Lewis 2008) and George W. Stocking Jr.'s classic "Anthropology and *Kulturkampf*" (1992a).
3. Deacon's *Elsie Clews Parsons: Inventing Modern Life* (1997) represents a remarkable synthesis of historical particularity within a theoretically informed approach to history, an inspiration for anthropological inquiry into sociopolitical history.
4. In his important paper on the relationship between his intellectual ideas and his politics, George W. Stocking Jr. (1992a) observes that Boas was generally committed to universal values, including the ideas that reason would gradually triumph over tradition and that people would come to live peacefully within ever-larger social units. Boas's commitment to what Stocking terms universal values waivered, however, during World War I. In the face of the xenophobic nationalism that arose in the United States upon the onset of the war in Europe, Boas participated extensively in German American organizations and expressed open criticism of the universal values used to justify American entry into the

war. In this context, Stocking (1992c:102) judges, Boas began to place a greater emphasis on the localized solidarity of sentiment as opposed to the universal solidarity of reason. While one cannot but pause and admire Stocking's nuanced understanding of the vicissitudes of Boas's personal orientation, I think it is helpful to see that Boas's (along with Bourne's) skepticism was directed toward the use of professedly universal values to justify the pursuit of national self-interest; he was not openly doubting the need to transcend local values.

REFERENCES

Bauman, Richard, and Charles L. Briggs. 2003. Voices of Modernity: Language Ideologies and the Politics of Inequality. Cambridge: Cambridge University Press.

Beiner, Ronald. 2011. Civil Religion: A Dialogue in the History of Political Philosophy. Cambridge: Cambridge University Press.

Bellah, Robert. 1967. Civil Religion in America. Daedalus 96(1):1–21.

Boas, Franz. 1911a. Introduction. *In* Handbook of American Indian Languages, Part 1. Franz Boas, ed. Pp. 5–83. Bureau of American Ethnology Bulletin 40. Washington DC.

———. 1911b. The Mind of Primitive Man. New York: Macmillan.

———. 1918. The Mental Attitudes of the Educated Classes. Dial.

———. 2008[1928]. Anthropology and Modern Life, with a New Introduction and Afterword by Herbert S. Lewis. New Brunswick NJ: Transaction Publishers.

———. N.d. The Mental Attitudes of the Educated Classes. Manuscript in Boas Papers and Manuscripts.

Boas Papers and Manuscripts. American Philosophical Society, Philadelphia.

Bourne, Randolph Silliman. 1967[1913]. Youth and Life. Freeport NY: Books for Libraries Press.

Bourne, R. S. Papers. Rare Book and Manuscript Library, Columbia University, New York.

Boydston, Jo Ann, ed. 1988. John Dewey: The Later Works, 1925–1953. Vol. 14: 1939–1941. With an introduction by R. W. Sleeper. Carbondale: Southern Illinois University Press.

Briggs, Charles L., and Richard Bauman. 1999. "The Foundation of All Future Researches": Franz Boas, George Hunt, and the Textual Construction of Modernity. American Quarterly 51(3):479–528.

Bunzl, Matti. 1996. Franz Boas and the Humboldtian Tradition: From

Volksgeist and *Nationalcharakter* to an Anthropological Concept of Culture. *In Volksgeist* as Method and Ethic: Essays on Boasian Ethnography and the German Anthropological Tradition. George W. Stocking Jr., ed. Pp. 17–78. Madison: University of Wisconsin Press.

Carr, E. Sumerson. 2010. Enactments of Expertise. Annual Review of Anthropology 39:17–32.

Cole, Douglas. 1999. Franz Boas: The Early Years. Vancouver: Douglas and McIntyre; Seattle: University of Washington Press.

Darnell, Regna. 1969. The Development of American Anthropology 1879–1920: From the Bureau of Ethnology to Franz Boas. PhD dissertation, University of Pennsylvania.

Deacon, Desley. 1997. Elsie Clews Parsons: Inventing Modern Life. Chicago: University of Chicago Press.

Deneen, Patrick J. 2005. Democratic Faith. Princeton NJ: Princeton University Press.

Dinwoodie, David W. 2013. "He Said He Would Show [the Tobacco] to M. Ogden": Voice and Historical Role in the Tsilhqut'in Fur Trade. *In* Transforming Ethnohistories: Narrative, Meaning, Community. Sebastian F. Braun, ed. Pp. 97–112. Norman: University of Oklahoma Press.

Goffman, Erving. 1983. Footing. *In* Forms of Talk. Pp. 124–157. Philadelphia: University of Pennsylvania Press.

Graeber, David. 2004. Fragments of an Anarchist Anthropology. Chicago: Prickly Paradigm Press.

———. 2012. Debt: The First 5,000 Years. Brooklyn: Melville House.

Gray, John. 1998. False Dawn: The Delusions of Global Capitalism. New York: New Press.

Hare, Peter H. 1985. A Woman's Quest for Science. Buffalo NY: Prometheus Books.

Hofstadter, Richard. 1955. The Age of Reform: From Bryan to F.D.R. New York: Vintage Books.

Keane, Webb. 1999. Voice. Theme issue, "Language Matters in Anthropology: A Lexicon for the Millennium," Journal of Linguistic Anthropology 9(1–2):271–273.

Lamphere, Louise. 1989. Feminist Anthropology: The Legacy of Elsie Clews Parsons. American Ethnologist 16(3):518–533.

Lewis, Herbert S. 2008. The Passion of Franz Boas. Afterword to Franz Boas's Anthropology and Modern Life. Pp. 247–324. New Brunswick NJ: Transaction Publishers.

Linton, Ralph. 1936. The Study of Man. New York: D. Appleton-Century Co.

Liss, Julie. 1996. German Culture and German Science in the *Bildung* of Franz Boas. *In Volksgeist* as Method and Ethic: Essays on Boasian Ethnography and the German Anthropological Tradition. George W. Stocking Jr., ed. Pp. 155–184. Madison: University of Wisconsin Press.

Lomnitz, Claudio. 2005. Bordering on Anthropology: Dialectics of a National Tradition in Mexico. *In* Empires, Nations, and Natives: Anthropology and State-Making. Benoit de L'Estoile, Federico Neiburg, and Lydia Sigaud, eds. Pp. 167–196. Durham NC: Duke University Press.

May, Henry F. 1959. The End of American Innocence: A Study of the First Years of Our Own Time 1912–1917. New York: Alfred A. Knopf.

Molloy, Maureen A. 2008. On Creating a Usable Culture: Margaret Mead and the Emergence of American Cosmopolitanism. Honolulu: University of Hawaii Press.

Parsons, Elsie Clews. Papers. American Philosophical Society, Philadelphia.

Resek, Carl, ed. 1999[1964]. Randolph S. Bourne, War and the Intellectuals: Collected Essays, 1915–1919. Indianapolis: Hackett Publishing Company, Inc.

Rousseau, Jean-Jacques. 1994[1762]. The Social Contract. A new translation by Christopher Betts. Oxford: Oxford University Press.

Sahlins, Marshall. 1976. Culture and Practical Reason. Chicago: University of Chicago Press.

Sandeen, Eric J., ed. 1981. The Letters of Randolph Bourne: A Comprehensive Edition. Troy NY: The Whitston Publishing Company.

———. 1989. Bourne Again: The Correspondence between Randolph Bourne and Elsie Clews Parsons. American Literary History 1(3):489–509.

Silverstein, Michael. 2003. Talking Politics: The Substance of Style from Abe to "W." Chicago: Prickly Paradigm Press.

———. 2009. *Review of* On Creating a Usable Culture: Margaret Mead and the Emergence of American Cosmopolitanism, by Margaret A. Molley. Journal of the Royal Anthropological Institute 15(1):181–182.

Stocking, George W., Jr. 1965. On the Limits of "Presentism" and "Historicism" in the Historiography of the Behavioral Sciences. Journal of the History of the Behavioral Sciences 1(3):211–218.

———. 1968. Race, Culture, and Evolution. Madison: University of Wisconsin Press.

———. 1992a. Anthropology and *Kulturkampf. In* The Ethnographer's Magic and Other Essays in the History of Anthropology. Pp. 92–113. Madison: University of Wisconsin Press.

———. 1992b. The Boas Plan for the Study of American Indian Languages. *In* The Ethnographer's Magic and Other Essays in the History of Anthropology. Pp. 60–91. Madison: University of Wisconsin Press.

———. 1992c. Ideas and Institutions in American Anthropology: Toward a History of the Interwar Years. *In* The Ethnographer's Magic and Other Essays in the History of Anthropology. Pp. 114–177. Madison: University of Wisconsin Press.

———, ed. 1996. *Volksgeist* as Method and Ethic: Essays on Boasian Ethnography and the German Anthropological Tradition. Madison: University of Wisconsin Press.

Wertheim, Arthur Frank. 1976. The New York Little Renaissance: Iconoclasms, Modernism, and Nationalism in American Culture, 1908–1917. New York: New York University Press.

Zumwalt, Rosemary. 1992. Wealth and Rebellion: Elsie Clews Parsons, Anthropologist and Folklorist. Urbana: University of Illinois Press.

5

Ruth Benedict

Synergy, Maslow, and Hitler

The onset of World War II left Boasians in a quandary. There was a belief that anthropology had significant lessons to teach about being human and the plasticity of so-called human nature. There was also a strong stricture against generalizations, or at least generalizations at that time. However, although opposed to overgeneralization, Boasians did feel that there was a need to go beyond mere statements of specifics that bordered on exoticism. Alfred Kroeber, for example, wrote a textbook, *Anthropology*, outlining the general ideas of the field. In private, moreover, Kroeber poked fun at Boas's opposition to general laws.

Alternatively, culture and personality studies were in conformity with many of Boas's ideas. Margaret Mead's *Coming of Age in Samoa* and Ruth Benedict's *The Chrysanthemum and the Sword* highlighted this trend. Benedict's friendship with Boas and his growing reliance on her over the years allowed her to extend his ideas, especially with the coming of the challenges of the Second World War, when demands on anthropology and anthropologists exceeded anything else in their history.

BACKGROUND TO THE CONCEPT OF SOCIAL SYNERGY

Ruth Benedict (1887–1948) studied with Boas at Columbia and received her PhD in 1923. She joined the faculty that same year. Two of her outstanding students were Marvin Opler and Margaret Mead. Benedict held that each culture chooses from vast possibilities but a small number of traits. These traits form a gestalt that shapes personalities within the culture. Her *Patterns of Culture* remains influential, though it has been criticized as too general, and it is still remarkably readable and interesting. Benedict was among the few who applied anthropology to complex cultures in its early days. Like Boas, she was strongly drawn to social causes, and she also opposed racism and the bigotry of some so-called religious people, using anthropological data to combat these biases.

Consequently, Ruth Benedict, an anthropologist who had helped pioneer the concept of cultural relativism, found herself with a major dilemma when faced with the inhumanity, intolerance, and brutality of Nazi Germany. She could not blithely state that Hitler's system was equal with others and needed to be judged simply on its own terms. Cleverly, she adapted the concept of synergy from the physical sciences and applied it to human cultural systems under the term "social synergy." Through diligent cross-cultural controlled comparison of a number of societies, she noted that societies that promote nonaggression foster a cultural climate in which the individual acts to serve both the group's well-being and his or her own. This fact does not mean that Zuni, for example, are somehow more unselfish than, say, Ojibwa or Kwakiutl or that Zuni are nicer people in themselves. It means that their cultural patterns promote what she termed "synergy." She noted that societies have low synergy or high synergy. Moreover, those societies with high social synergy are not either more or less "evolved" in technological terms. The same is true of societies with low social synergy. Examples of high and low synergy are found at every level of technological development, from hunters and gatherers to industrial society. What is true, nevertheless, is that low synergy is correlated with aggression, and high synergy is correlated with more peaceful conflict resolution and personal fulfillment (cf. Maslow and Honigman 1970; McElroy 1985).

Abraham Maslow, a good friend of Benedict, was working along the same lines. His concept of self-actualization paralleled Benedict's social synergy. He borrowed part of her manuscript on synergy and with John Honigman, a cultural anthropologist, published the notes and expanded on them. With the concept of social synergy Benedict drew attention to life-affirming versus life-denying cultures. The concept has echoes of Edward Sapir's idea of genuine as opposed to spurious cultures. Genuine cultures are those that promote the needs and personal fulfillments of individuals. B. T. Grindal (1976) draws out the clear connection between genuine culture and synergy. Grindal begins with Sapir's genuine culture and then asserts that it came to its full fruition in Benedict's concept of synergy. Benedict framed her idea in this manner: "Any society that is compatible with human advancements is a good one, but a society that works against basic human goals is anti-human and evil, and can be judged as such" (Stonewall Society, Ruth Benedict, 1887–1948, http://www.stonewallsociety.com/famouspeople /ruth.htm). Clearly, Benedict saw Nazi Germany as the embodiment of evil. This idea patently fits into Maslow's idea that self-actualization should emerge through the person's dialogue with community but does not solve the problem of who gets to judge what is life affirming or denying and when.

THE ANNA HOWARD SHAW LECTURES

For many years anthropologists accepted as general truth that Benedict's Shaw Lectures were lost, destroyed by Benedict herself. Maslow and Honigman (1975) stated this as fact. Margaret Mead, Benedict's executor, had noted that the lectures were lost. However, Virginia Heyer Young (2005:334 n. 6) notes that in 1995 Nancy McKechnie found four of the six lectures Benedict delivered. One other lecture was found in the Research Institute for the Study of Man. Indeed, Benedict published the first lecture in the *American Scholar*, giving the lie to another accepted truth that she was not happy with any of the lectures.

An invitation to give the Anna Howard Shaw Lectures was a great honor. The terms of the lecture series are as follows: "The Anna Howard Shaw Lectureship was founded at Bryn Mawr College in 1928 as a memorial to Dr. Shaw and takes the form of a course of lectures given every three years by persons, preferably women, eminent in politics, social science or other fields" (Young 2005:90). Certainly, Benedict was eminent in social science, and her work over the next few years extended her political influence as well. The scope of her lectures gives some idea of what she sought to do in that winter of 1941.

Human Nature and Social Institutions

1. Monday, February 10, "The Problem of Anthropology"
2. Monday, February 17, "Human Nature and Man-Made Cultures"
3. Monday, February 24, "Individual Behavior and the Social Order"
4. Monday, March 3, "Socializing the Child"

5. Monday, March 10, "Anthropology and Some Modern Alarmists"
6. Monday, March 17, "Anthropology and the Social Bases of Morale"

It is obvious what Benedict was seeking to do and how her later work was prefigured in these lectures. Simply, she was seeking to discover the cultural and social roots for aggression, including warfare, and the manner in which a culture and social structure can shape individual constitutions in differing ways. The consistency of her argument is brought home through subtle arguments in each topic. In moving to the general level, she does not lose the enormous value of understanding the specific cultures she discusses. In my opinion, she unites cultural relativity and sound generalization in the same work, demonstrating the need for both perspectives in a full anthropological view.

It is also important to note the importance in Benedict's thinking of the writing of her book *Race: Science and Politics* in 1940. She drew heavily on the work of Franz Boas and asked him to check the manuscript and write a blurb for the book. The book showed Benedict that she could reach a large audience and translate anthropological concepts into lay terms, a point driven home more strongly when she and Gene Weltfish adapted the book as a pamphlet in 1944 as *The Races of Mankind*. Unfortunately, the book also demonstrated the intensity of race hatred in the United States, including the U.S. Congress, a story for another time. However, the success of her book on race led Ruth Benedict into popular presentations and causes of which the Shaw Lectures were a major example.

Benedict provides strong evidence of where the ideas expressed in these lectures arose. They were a development of some of Boas's most strongly held values and concepts. For example, in the manuscript "Contributions to Ethnology" (1943), Benedict states, "He himself often said that this problem was the relations between the objective world and man's subjective world as it had taken form in different cultures. He wanted to study man's cultural constructs with the same inductive methods that had proved indispensable in the study of the natural world." She continued the argument, stating that "it has never been sufficiently realized how consistently throughout his life Boas defined the task of ethnology as the study of 'man's mental life.'" Boas was interested in the "fundamental psychic attitudes of cultural groups" and man's "subjective worlds."

In an obituary, one of a number she wrote, Benedict noted:

What [W. I.] Thomas called the "definition of a situation" Boas called, in its most striking manifestations, subjectively conditioned relations . . . attitudes that arise gradually by giving values and meanings to activities, as good or bad, right or wrong, beautiful or ugly, purposive are causally determined. . . .

He believed that the world must be made safe for differences. He spoke out therefore against all American efforts to set themselves up as arbiters of the world. In 1916, when the emotions of the last war were running high, he protested against any American who "claims that the form of his own government is the best, nor for himself only, but also for the rest of mankind; that his interpretation of ethics, of religion, of standards of living, is right." Such an American, he said, is mistakenly "inclined to assume the role of a dispenser of happiness to mankind" and to overlook the fact "that others may abhor where we worship." (Benedict 1942b)

In an obituary for Boas published in the *Nation* on January 2, 1943, Benedict describes Boas as valuing those societies and people who seek to respect and improve human endeavors and individuals. She expanded on these ideas in her 1941 Shaw Lectures on social synergy. She rejected both extremes regarding the nature-nurture argument and environment-genetic dispute in their multitudinous manifestations. With Boas, she held that both operate in human social and cultural life. Also with Boas, she sought to move toward an empirical means for studying that significant relationship. The Shaw Lectures contained her mature thoughts on the issue.

"THE PROBLEM OF ANTHROPOLOGY"

The first lecture in the series, "The Problem of Anthropology," published as "Anthropology and Culture Change" in the *American Scholar* (1942a), set the tone for the series. Benedict begins by giving a quick overview of the field of anthropology and its development. She indicates how anthropology moved from a search for a unilineal scheme of human development to a comparative view based on intensive fieldwork. Quickly, she moves toward the relationship between race and civilization and the role physical anthropology has played in exploring the issue.

Benedict notes that Franz Theodor Waitz indicated in 1859 that there was no evidence whatsoever of the Negro's racial inability to participate in the development of civilization. Similarly, she says there was no evidence in Waitz's work of any privileged leadership of whites in its development. As Boas had indicated on many occasions, every race has its share in the development of civilizations (see Boas 1906). Waitz also believed that every race has had its isolated peoples living simple lives. Benedict carries the argument further, noting that there is no pure race among civilized peoples, for civilization requires diversity, the mingling of people. Pure races, where they exist, are isolated, and they are not, in her words, leaders in high civilizations.

Interestingly, the discussion of diversity, lack of pure races, and civilizations leads to the topic of human nature. She states that much of what people perceive as human nature is, in fact, "cultural determinism." Indeed, cross-cultural studies demonstrate quite clearly that institutions, emotions, and attitudes vary with culture. Thus, it is necessary to add social order to heredity and the idiosyncrasy of an individual life to understand human activity. The addition, she is careful to note, of social order does not replace or negate heredity and idiosyncrasy; it supplements them and puts them into a more intelligible context. As Benedict elucidates, "But culture could make any specific inheritance or any episode in an individual's life either a matter of pride or humiliation" (1942a:246). No wonder Thomas's concept of the social construction of reality intrigued Benedict and Boas. In their hands, it becomes a path toward linking the individual and society, of enabling us to understand the context of a situation and unearth its social and individual meaning at the same time.

Benedict indicates that the earlier period of anthropology provided a great treasure trove of material containing detailed descriptions of earlier civilizations. Moreover, anthropologists were observing and regarding actual human behavior in real-life situations from numerous cultural settings. These curious anthropologists "raised questions about 'human nature'" (Benedict 1942a:243). They noticed that people reacted differently according to the sociocultural settings in which they found themselves. Adolescence was not always a time of storm and stress. Men were not always violent warriors, nor were women meek and mild: "The list of contrasts was endless, and the conclusion could not be avoided: a great deal of what had ordinarily been regarded as due to 'human nature' was, instead, culturally determined. Institutions, emotions and attitudes varied with culture, that body of conventions and values which is socially transmitted in every society and which distinguishes that society from all others which belong to a different tradition" (245).

Anthropology earned a reputation for being contentious, quarreling with so-called sociological and psychological laws based on studies confined primarily to Western cultures in the twentieth century. That time span was too limited geographically and historically to account for the possible range of cultural expressions in the human species. So significant is this fact that it forces those who seriously wish to understand human behavior to add the social order to heredity and "idiosyncratic incidents of individual life" (1942a:246) as factors in understanding human behavior. Therefore, Benedict notes that while heredity and idiosyncratic facts remain important, "culture could make any specific inheritance or any episode in an individual's life either a matter of pride or of humiliation" (246). She then gives a series of examples underscoring her point and leading up to what became her central concern: the presence or absence of aggression in society and its structuring. Along the way, she goes beyond what she terms explanations that are merely culturally relative (246). Interestingly, mere cultural relativity leads to skepticism and ignores fundamental questions of vast importance to anthropology. While necessary at arriving at these questions, in itself cultural relativity is not sufficient to do so.

At this point her argument takes a Durkheimian bent:

The fundamental problem in the study of society—like the fundamental problem in engineering or physiology—is still to learn the conditions which do bring about a designated outcome. We need desperately to know the positive conditions under which, for instance, social conflict and disintegration occur, and it is possible to study such conditions in society after society with the same scientific detachment with which one studies cultural relativity. We need to know what conditions are necessary for social cohesion and stability, and these too can be studied. It is a matter of phrasing the anthropological questions positively. (Benedict 1942a:247)

Benedict argues that the period of cultural relativity, including studies of diffusion, the measurement of human remains, and careful description, provided numerous examples that could be used to test ideas of which conditions bring about various outcomes. She further maintains that fieldwork and its holistic view provide the anthropologist with a vantage point for observation denied the sociologist and psychologist. The field anthropologist can see the entire society in motion, noting the gap between what people say they do or think and what they actually do in given situations. Moreover, anthropology has gone well beyond a single period or culture as a whole, providing a vast spectrum of human thought and behavior at the service of understanding the many ways of being human that have been recorded.

"HUMAN NATURE AND MAN-MADE CULTURES"

The themes stated in this first lecture, the only one she published, continue throughout the lecture series. Consequently, in the second lecture, "Human Nature and Man-Made Cultures," Benedict (1941c) picks up her central idea, the plasticity of human nature and the fundamental importance of culture in structuring human societies.[1] Some societies have norms very like those in Western cultures. However, others are quite different. In some, both men and women are mild and nonaggressive. Conversely, there are societies in which people are "ruthlessly aggressive." Benedict provides examples of a range of human behavior in various societies. Interestingly, she observes, "These differences were not due to climate or to hard living conditions or to race for they varied independently of such features. The problem to be investigated was: under which conditions does human nature in one society become a tumult of hatred and aggression and under which conditions in another society does it become able to live graciously and without attacking its fellows" (1941c:1).

At the root of Benedict's concept of synergy, both high and low, is the issue of how to build a peaceful society. Certainly, the coming world war and its threat to civilization occupied her thoughts. However, this question was a long-standing one with Benedict, as her papers make crystal clear. The role of anthropology in understanding and applying ideas to help move toward that peaceful society without violating its ethical foundations also concerned Benedict, as her published and unpublished work demonstrates. With Boas she boldly stated that democracy was not a panacea, and not all countries or societies were compatible with it. Societies could work for the good of all their people without being democratic societies in the American sense, a rather brave statement in the World War II period.

In her notes for the lecture, Benedict begins her explication of synergy through noting that one must take into account the "definition of the situation," bringing us back to W. I. Thomas again. Synergy does not force an act of another's will. She uses an example from the Cheyenne, noting that actions are not forced on individuals; instead, exchange is only possible with mutual consent. In sum, Benedict was investigating the conditions in which high synergy might be created as opposed to those of low synergy. Basically, she was attempting to discern the type of social structure that would aid peaceful and cooperative social solidarity in contrast with those that promote aggression and conflict.

Benedict next compares various societies regarding "institutionalized insecurities." In these societies, adults pass on aggression to individuals. She notes, for examples, the Ojibwa, Apache, Eskimo, and Pomo, later adding the Omaha and others to her discussion. In contrast to what we would now term *zero-sum games*, which Benedict described as low-synergy societies in which the interests of the individual and the collective were at opposite poles, she puts forward a key to understanding a high-synergy society. The key is the "interdependence of private & collective acts of thought, feeling & experience of individuals/and the social arrangements of a culture" (1941c:4).

In a chart comparing high- and low-synergy cultures, Benedict lists five key areas: distribution of goods and services, responsibility for advancement (upward mobility), religion, family, and child rearing. After comparing each type of society on each variable, she summarizes the material in an interesting fashion. For high-synergy societies, "humiliation is only for uncooperativeness or transgression" (1941c:8). The goal is affiliation and symmetrical nurturance. What is good for the individual is also good for the collective. However, in low-synergy societies, threats to individuals are constant throughout life. Aggression and retribution are primary means of social control, and blood feuds are common. Benedict expands these ideas while clarifying them in later lectures.

"INDIVIDUAL BEHAVIOR AND THE SOCIAL ORDER"

In the third Shaw Lecture, "Individual Behavior and Social Order," Benedict continues these thoughts, opening with this statement:

> But our very personal feeling about ourselves and our behavior needs much correction and it will not serve, as it stands, as a basis for a science of behavior. Not just the chance happenings of individual life, but also gross cultural facts have entered into one's experience. Last week I spoke of one of these great cultural contrasts. I spoke of societies with high social synergy, where their institutions ensure mutual advantage from their undertakings, and low social synergy where the advantage from any individual becomes a victory over another, and the majority who are not victorious must shift as they can. I spoke too of the differences the *structure* of society makes. (1941d:15)

Benedict stipulates that she is not ignoring the "constitutional factor." Certainly, our individual makeup is important, but it is not "a fixed entity." Culture sets limits on the expression of our abilities. Our constitutional makeup "may find its outlet in professional crime or the activity of robber barons, or it may find satisfaction in another society in organizing great give-aways" (1941d:15). Thus, we must take into account three factors in our experience in any society: heredity, the idiosyncratic incidents of a person's life, and the social order. However, we must also look at the interaction of a number of factors, including "all traditional institutions: child rearing and the economic order and the sexual arrangements and tabus. It is an illusion to seek for a single determinant" (16).

To illustrate her point, Benedict focuses on the interaction of the economic system with other aspects of society. It proves a significant platform from which to observe high or low synergy and the creation of aggressive or nonaggressive societies and individuals. She uses economics because she argues that whatever behavior is stabilized in any tribe is generally integrated into economic life. She employs two concepts to clarify her ideas, a funnel system and a siphon system.

A funnel system of economics is one that funnels wealth to the wealthy. However, some care is taken to keep necessary items in flux: "By these provisions primitive funnel societies often attain a comparatively high synergy; they provide that essential means of livelihood shall not be put into the funnel at all, and hence food, clothing and shelter cannot be diverted from the majority of the population to the man who is already rich. There is another mechanism which is found where the funnel system depends on exploited labor, and it is a mechanism with which we are all familiar because it was characteristic of feudalism at its height on the continent of Europe" (1941d:15).

In contrast, there is the syphon system, in which "wealth is constantly channeled away from the point of greatest concentration—from any point of concentration—and spread throughout the community" (1941d:17). People receive honor and prestige for spreading the wealth. Indeed, Benedict points out that goods are pooled even before they are given away. Those who refuse to share wealth are looked down upon. Indeed, in these societies one should give away something before another asks. It is important to avoid any sign of selfishness or hint of causing jealousy.

After discussing economics, Benedict turns to a discussion of religion: "Societies with high synergy construct religions in which they pray and dance and sing for benefits that are benefits to all the tribe. These may be rain or good crops or a run of salmon or many children or general health or ensuring the succession of the seasons" (1941d:18). Moreover, even personal benefits ultimately aid the community: "In tribes of high synergy amulets are used, not to harm another, but to strengthen oneself, and guardian spirits give power to win against tribal enemies, to cure the sick, and to name children—all of which are general benefits" (18).

In contrast, tribes exhibiting low synergy continue their zero-sum games in their religious lives. The belief that a benefit for one is a loss for another, the theory of the limited good, is clear in their religious practices. They "typically build their religious practices upon these privately owned supernatural powers, and use these according to the habits of aggression set up in their daily lives. They use them, if they are amulets, to bury in another's field and ruin the crops; if they are charms or spells, to bring starvation or small pox or elephantiasis or madness upon a fellow tribesman; if they are guardian spirits, to go at their command to kill a rival in combat" (1941d:18). The private ownership and selfish practices of their economic systems carry over into their religions, for we create our gods in our own images. Thus, one can buy powers, including the powers of sorcery. Life in these societies is hostile; everything, including religion, is a conflict. To succeed, one must bring others down and keep them from flourishing.

Hence, Benedict shows, using economics and religion, that social synergy is important in shaping psychological behavior: "In both these fields of life the culture creates situations where synergy is either possible or impossible, and the individual cannot carry on his individual life without reference to these created situations. The culture, as it were, builds up a maze where one must follow the passageways either to blind alleys or to the goal" (1941d:20). In other words, culture sets limits for individual expression. Benedict's term for this limitation is "character structure." It is the place where the social structure and individual constitution meet.

In societies of low synergy, it is easy for the dominance-submission element in character structure to become aggression, for one must ensure individual security at another person's expense. There are relatively few areas where people can work toward mutual advantage in such societies. It is important to emphasize how different cultures demand different responses. Benedict drives this point home in her conclusion.

The different character structures which are found in different cultures therefore are the result of the interaction of man's constitutional equipment with different sorts of cultural arrangements. Upon these latter will depend whether or not a person has a psychological "need" to accumulate property, or to work out a dominance-submission balance in all his human relationships, or to act aggressively against or remove his opponent. In social orders that give the opportunity, there is an equally genuine psychological "need" for generosity or peace-ableness. The psychological equipment of the human being is plastic; the individual introjects what experience comes his way. (1941d:22)

Unfortunately, the lecture on socializing the young child appears to be lost. It would be fun to speculate on its contents and attempt to reconstruct it. Alas, no one can write Benedict as well as Benedict can. Within the context of these lectures it is, however, fair to say that Benedict most likely continued her theme of the plasticity of human nature and the importance of cultural interpretation of actions in shaping behavior and meaning in members of society. The fifth lecture, indeed, lends credence to this belief.

"ANTHROPOLOGY AND SOME MODERN ALARMISTS"

Benedict opens the lecture discussing red herrings and true problems. She states that she is not excited about the concept of human nature: "I have said often in these lectures that human nature, from comparative study, is plastic and that all its triumphs have been due to this very plasticity. Human nature relies for its adjustment to the environment upon learned behavior and in this process reason and intelligence were born" (1941a:21).

Once again, Benedict is interested in the kind of social structure that will promote synergy, that is, the type of condition in which the gain of any one person is the gain of all. She wanted to get away from zero-sum games. As she states, "Human nature is in many societies almost spectacularly cooperative and these have been highly stable and satisfactory societies. It is change that is difficult" (1941a:21).

Along the way she has to pause a bit to discuss a major red herring: race. First, she notes that people do not inherit their social structures genetically from their race. Indeed, the only "pure races" existing are in backwaters. Next, she takes the time to explain a simple fact, one many anthropologists grow weary of reiterating: "The laws of genetics cover one's inheritance from one's actual ancestors, not from a race" (1941a:2). She goes on to dispute the concept of any master race, a point she would soon have to make against both bigoted U.S. senators and Hitler. Moreover, she asserts, civilization ignores racial boundaries.

Focusing on America, Benedict remarks that in America each new group wishes to be American until prevented. She advises, "Those who are working to promote race relations could take advantage of this if they would, and watch for occasions where the aliens could work shoulder to shoulder with the native born of the ward or the village or the city for better city administration, better schools, better housing—occasions when they would be working as citizens of America and not as a group singled out and labeled for their differences from other citizens" (1941a:3). Increasingly, in her later work, Benedict was turning to understanding American culture and society within an international context.

She was also concerned about the way in which an emphasis on diversity endangered the stability of American society, especially when that diversity separated people and created minorities. She presents a number of examples of minority groups, for example, women, the "Younger Generation" among them. Here she harks back to her work on continuities and discontinuities in societies, stating that there is a need to provide the minimal social conditions in which American values can be put into operation. In speaking of women as a minority she asserts that many gains are to be made from advancing women's needs.

Indeed, the equality of women is essential to moving toward the type of social structure that will promote synergy. In addition, Benedict promotes the rights of workers, rights that include organization and fair return for their labor. She says, "It is in any society a symptom of conflict which has its origins in the total social order, not in facts of sex or generations or race. We cannot get rid of our race problem by proving for instance, that the Jews are not a race" (1941a:4). These categories are excuses or symptoms of inequality. To combat them she advises the increase of areas where all citizens profit mutually and decrease discriminatory differences.

In sum, she asserts that special privileges lead to dictatorship and antidemocratic rule:

Special privileges and minority groups are two sides to the same coin and occur in societies with what I have called low social synergy. They are consequences of certain norms of the social order and I have been making the point that special privilege is not a sacred right and that minority groups are not written in the nature of things but are the outcome of cultural arrangements. . . . Instead, the more extreme a tribe's or nation's way of behaving, the more it will sacrifice to maintain it and the more extreme it will make it become. (1941a:5)

She provides the example of some Australian groups with no one to marry because their marriage rules are so stringent. Of course, they do marry, but every marriage is against their rules, and the spouses must hide until a child is born, which then allows them to be welcomed back into the society. Her point is that "those things which a society pursues most passionately are easily the most bizarre. They are the last things upon which that society will pass judgment. Just at those points where as reasonable men we should be most critical, we are bound to be least critical" (1941a:6).

"ANTHROPOLOGY AND THE SOCIAL BASIS OF MORALE"

Benedict presented the final lecture in the series on March 17, 1941. She presented her major thesis in this statement: "For morale includes on the one hand individual attitudes and behavior like zeal and loyalty and sacrifice, and on the other, social factors which hinder or reinforce such behavior. Whenever we use the word *morale* we imply that group conditions are inseparable from psychological behavior" (1941b:8). Benedict wishes to distinguish democratic morale from other types, since she is fully aware of events occurring in Nazi Germany. She ties democratic morale to synergy quite clearly: "It is attained when a person has reason to trust that he and all the rest of the group will further their own respective purposes by that course of action, but whether he has reason to believe this or not depends on sociological conditions which I have called social synergy" (9).

In this final lecture, Benedict notes that synergy means a "combined action." Moreover, it appears to be an ongoing process in her view, one that is "furthered by every extension of an area of mutual advantage and lowered by every curtailment of such an area" (1941b:9). Benedict ties together the entire lecture series by noting:

I have described in these lectures how such areas have been set up in religion and in economics when the goal sought was an advantage that accrued to all the group, not to one individual at the expense of another. I have showed how different architectural set-ups of society—atomistic, segmented, class societies, hierarchal societies—required different mechanisms for achieving synergy and how therefore the attainment of morale in the hierarchal set-up of city, county, state and nation has technical difference from attainment of morale between capital and labor or between nations. (1941b:10)

Unsurprisingly, Benedict points out how child-rearing practices enter into this scheme. Additionally, she argues that minority groups in societies result from low synergy, stating that psychological aggressions spread and flourish when conditions for high synergy are not met.

Attacking laissez-faire economics, which she notes leads to public losses, she states that synergy is attained when

private advantage becomes public gain and public gain becomes private advantage just insofar as respective advantages are channeled to reach all the participants in any enterprise. These are not identical advantages, for high social synergy exists often with inequality of wealth and always with inequality of prestige. But responsibility must be sociologically tied to wealth and to prestige, and wealth and prestige must be impossible without such responsibility, just as the classic feudal lord could not remain an overlord and put his serfs off the land. Until feudalism decayed such an irresponsible act was impossible for him if he was to maintain his position. (1941b:7)

In sum, the individual's good and that of the society should be synonymous. No advantage arises in putting "national welfare above personal desires" (1941b:11). Such a society, in which national welfare is placed above individual good, is one of low synergy and, she suggests, one that leads to tyranny. In fact, her general law of synergy notes that one's own advantage and the advantage of others in society are the same. She ends her talk with this thought: "In 1941, however, even the problem of achieving social synergy within any one nation is overshadowed by the problem of nation against nation. The civilization of which we are a part is rent by international warfare and its very existence is threatened. It is obvious to the most careless that the problem of social synergy transcends any one nation, however large and however distant from the seat of combat" (12).

CONCLUSION

The Shaw lectures provide some guidelines regarding general ideas regarding what is life affirming or life denying. Maslow and Honigman (1976:120) give some idea of specific cultures that are synergistic: among them are the Iatmul, a head-hunting tribe of New Guinea; the Zuni; the Arapesh of New Guinea; and the Balinese. Benedict's concept of synergy, based on Émile Durkheim's concept of social solidarity, sees high-synergy societies in which the desires of the individual and those of the society meet in a mutually advantageous form as promoting a unity of purpose that is nontyrannical and beneficial. She also makes clear that some form of democracy is involved in the highest form of synergy. However, she takes care to make clear that not all societies need be democratic in the same sense or to the same degree.

In the years remaining to her, Benedict became involved in various other projects and postwar efforts to use anthropology to promote peaceful goals. She gave some hints of where a fully developed theory of synergy might go but never published anything using the term, reverting to "social structure" and its varieties instead. Nevertheless, Maslow's work on the hierarchy of needs and self-fulfillment gives some idea of their discussions over the years on synergy. However, teasing out how much of Maslow's theory is Benedict's and how much is Maslow's is a project in itself. Basically, Maslow saw self-actualization as basic to synergy. He noted in his work that self-actualization was a means of promoting nonaggression and progress. Maslow's hierarchy of needs, which climaxed in self-actualization, noted that what is true in business is also true for individuals. The achievement of unselfishness is basically synonymous with his concept of psychological health (Maslow 1998:108–133; Takaki, Taniguchi, and Fujii 2016:462).

Finally, what matters is Benedict's resolution to use anthropology to advance humanistic ends and to provide the scientific means to do so. Her work on synergy cannot be understood without taking into account her work on race and Boas's own desire to combat through anthropological means attacks on human equality and dignity. She sought in her concept of synergy a means to combat threats to human freedom and dignity. It was a project worthy of a noble mind and profession.

NOTES

1. The article has been a difficult one to find, and it took a trip to the New York University Archives to discover it in the Sula Benet Papers in a file marked "R.B." I thank Laura Joanne Zeccardi and Angela M. Carreno for uncovering and copying the notes on the lecture for me. Many thanks to Dean Rogers of the Vassar University Special Collections for his patience and unfailing help.

REFERENCES

Banner, Lois W. 2003. Intertwined Lives: Margaret Mead, Ruth Benedict and Their Circle. New York: Vintage Books.

Bateson, Gregory. 1934. The Segmentation of Society. The First International Congress of Anthropological and Ethnological Science. London: Compte Rendu.

———. 1936. Naven. Cambridge: Cambridge University Press. 2nd ed., 1958.

———. 1949. Bali: The Value System of a Steady State. In Social Structure: Studies Presented to A. R. Radcliffe-Brown. Meyer Fortes, ed. Pp. 35–53. Oxford: Clarendon Press.

Bateson, Mary Catherine. 1989. Composing a Life. New York: Grove Press.

Benedict, Ruth, and Gene Weltfish. 1943. The Races of Mankind. New York: Public Affairs Committee.

Benedict, Ruth Bunzel, and Ralph Linton. 1940. Acculturation in Seven American Indian Tribes. New York: Appleton Century.

Benedict, Ruth Fulton. 1934. Patterns of Culture. Boston: Houghton Mifflin Co.

———. ca. 1937. Beyond Cultural Relativity. Chapter 1 for Columbia University Project 35. Unpublished manuscript. Ruth Benedict File, Research Institute for the Study of Man, New York.

———. 1940. Race: Science and Politics. New York: Modern Age.

———. 1941a. Anthropology and Some Modern Alarmists. Shaw Lecture 5. Vol. 58, p. 6. Ruth Fulton Benedict Papers, Vassar College, Poughkeepsie, New York.

———. 1941b. Anthropology and the Social Basis of Morale. Shaw Lecture 6. Vol. 58, p. 7. Ruth Fulton Benedict Papers, Vassar College, Poughkeepsie, New York.

———. 1941c. Human Nature and Man-Made Culture. Shaw Lecture 2, Research Institute for the Study of Man, New York.

———. 1941d. Individual Behavior and Social Order. Shaw Lecture 3. Vol. 58, p. 14. Ruth Fulton Benedict Papers, Vassar College, Poughkeepsie, New York

———. 1942a. Anthropology and Culture Change. American Scholar 11:243–248.

———. 1942b. Franz Boas: Obituary. American Sociological Review 8:223.

———. 1943. Obituary of Franz Boas. Nation, January 2.

———. 1946. The Chrysanthemum and the Sword: Patterns of Japanese Culture. Boston: Houghton Mifflin.

———. N.d. Contributions to Ethnology. Unpublished manuscript, Benedict to Maslow, 1939–1940, 32.8. Ruth Fulton Benedict Papers, Vassar College, Poughkeepsie, New York.

———. N.d. Obituaries, Franz Boas. Box 116.1. Ruth Fulton Benedict Papers, Vassar College, Poughkeepsie, New York.

Boas, Franz. 1906. Atlanta University Commencement Address. MSS B B61. Franz Boas Professional Papers, American Philosophical Society, Philadelphia.

Gatewood, John B. 1984. Cooperation, Competition, and Synergy: Information-Sharing Groups among Southeast Alaskan Salmon Seiners. American Ethnologist 11(May):350–370.

Grindal, B. T. 1976. The Idea of Synergy and Its Bearing on an Anthropological Humanism. Anthropology and Humanism Quarterly 1(1):4–6.

Kroeber, Alfred. 1948. Anthropology: Race, Language, Culture, Psychology, Prehistory. New edition. New York: Harcourt, Brace and Company.

Maslow, Abraham. 1998. Maslow on Management. With added interviews by Deborah Stephens and Gary Heil. New York: Wiley.

Maslow, Abraham, and John Honigman. 1970. Synergy: Some Notes of Ruth Benedict. American Anthropologist 72(April):320–333.

McElroy, Ann. 1985. Culture and Ethos. American Anthropologist 87(March):173–174.

Mead, Margaret, ed. 1961[1937]. Cooperation and Competition among Primitive Peoples. New York: McGraw-Hill.

———, ed. 1966[1959]. An Anthropologist at Work: Writings of Ruth Benedict. Boston: Houghton MiWin.

———. 1971[1928]. Coming of Age in Samoa. New York: Harper's Perennial.

Mead, Margaret, and Rhoda Metraux, eds. 1953. The Study of Culture at a Distance. Chicago: University of Chicago Press.

Sapir, Edward. 1924. Culture, Genuine and Spurious. American Journal of Sociology 29:401–429.

Takaki, Jiro, Toshiyo Taniguchi, and Yasuhito Fujii. 2016. Confirmation of Maslow's Hypothesis of Synergy: Developing an Acceptance of Self-ishness at the Workplace Scale. International Journal of Environmental Research and Public Health 13(5):462.

Thomas, W. I. 1923. The Unadjusted Girl. With Cases and Standpoint for Behavior Analysis. Boston: Little, Brown.

Thomas, W. I., with Florian Znaniecki. 1918. The Polish Peasant in Europe and America. Boston: Gorham Press.

———. 1958. The Concept of Social Disorganization Part II: Disorganization and Reorganization in Poland of The Polish Peasant in Europe and America II. New York: Dover Publications.

Waitz, Franz Theodor. 1877. Anthropologie der Naturvolker. Leipzig.

Young, Virginia Heyer. 2005. Ruth Benedict: Beyond Relativity, beyond Pattern. Critical Studies in the History of Anthropology. Lincoln: University of Nebraska Press.

JAMES M. NYCE AND EVELYN J. BOWERS

6

Continuity and Dislocations

A. I. Hallowell's Physical Anthropology

This chapter reviews the contribution A. Irving Hallowell (1892–1974) made to the study of human evolution and biological/physical anthropology (Shapiro 1967:608). Hallowell's work in human evolution bridges the pre- and postmolecular periods in biological anthropology and the evolutionary and postevolutionary periods in cultural anthropology. Because of this transition, some central elements important to our understanding of human evolution may have been lost, that is, those elements of human evolution that are difficult to quantify or to be "read" directly out of biology. Among these are the more ideational dimensions of culture—precisely the elements of culture that cultural anthropologists have focused on since Clifford Geertz. In biological anthropology, it is just these elements of culture that have largely been "given up on" or reduced to processes like cognition. Hallowell is important today because his vocabulary (e.g., "the behavioral environment") and his theoretical position on both self and culture offer a way to integrate past and present streams of evolutionary and cultural thought as it applies to ourselves. Hallowell's work on human evolution can provide an opportunity to revisit where we as anthropologists may have taken some wrong turns, and this could help strengthen evolutionary theory in biological and cultural anthropology.

This chapter has both historical and contemporary relevance because of the discipline's growing interest in the physiological basis of neuropsychology and human behavior. This turn in human behavioral studies will, however, have to be addressed (and critiqued) by anthropologists who are aware of the worldwide variation of human behavior. Otherwise, this research will be conducted by others who are much less aware of (or interested in) how much behavioral variation there is and how powerfully culture molds behavior (e.g., Diamond 1997, 2005; Wilson 1975, 1978).

THE BASIS OF HALLOWELL'S THOUGHT
ON HUMAN EVOLUTION

Hallowell (1972:52–53), like his teacher, mentor, and friend Frank Speck (1881–1950), was an Americanist trained in the Boasian four subfields at Columbia and the University of Pennsylvania. Speck was known primarily for salvage ethnography work among the Indians of eastern North America, although he did have students visit the Philadelphia Zoo to observe primate behavior (William A. Haviland to Evelyn Bowers, August 18, 2012). Hallowell, however, concerned himself only with the Northern Ojibwa and ethnological and theoretical problems that arose from his subarctic fieldwork.[1] The only exception to this was his work in the history of anthropology, the history of ideas and human evolution. Hallowell's papers on physical anthropology apply and elaborate on the theoretical perspective that developed out of his work among the Northern Ojibwa.[2]

Hallowell first published on the Ojibwa in 1926, and his interest in these subarctic people continued until his death.[3] It is not necessary to consider the contributions Hallowell made to Northern Ojibwa ethnography and ethnology here. There are appraisals of Hallowell's work by Fred Eggan (1967, 1976) and, more recently, Jennifer S. H. Brown and Robert Brightman (1988) and Brown and Susan E. Gray (Hallowell 2010). In addition, Regna Darnell (2006) has often written about the Department of Anthropology at the University of Pennsylvania, its history, and Hallowell (but see Kopytoff 2006). It was from Hallowell's work with the Northern Ojibwa that the themes that were to be important in his writings in physical anthropology emerged. What is striking is that none of the authors above have commented at any length on Hallowell's work in physical anthropology. At best we have this one sentence: Hallowell "further pioneered the study of human adaptation and evolution, combining the cultural and biological sides of Boasian four-field anthropology, a perspective that very few among his contemporaries were open to exploring" (Darnell 2001:243).

The four subfields of anthropology in Hallowell's time included an interest in human evolution, some of which had its basis in nineteenth-century discussions of the development of mind (see, e.g., Darnell 1988 on Daniel Brinton). At the time, the mid-twentieth century, Hallowell's crossover from Native American ethnology to human evolution was an unusual one. This is perhaps because of the short evolutionary "depth" then attributed to the New World under the Clovis hypothesis. Further, despite arguments over the relative age of human occupation in the New World, early humans such as Neanderthals and *Homo erectus* did not occur there. Further, Americanists (especially Boasians) saw little chance that evidence would emerge to link biology, unlike archaeology, and anthropology/ethnography anytime soon. The result is that most Americanists of Hallowell's generation seemed to feel little need to take up issues related to human evolution.

By 1929 Hallowell had carried out and published an anthropometric survey, "The Physical Characteristics of the Indians of Labrador." This was the only descriptive work in physical anthropology Hallowell was to complete and the only paper he published in this subfield for more than twenty years.[4] Still, physical anthropology was a large part of what he taught graduate students regardless of the course titles. Raymond Fogelson (email to James M. Nyce, October 12, 2012) believes Hallowell's continued interest in physical anthropology was inspired by Alfred Kroeber's work on animal behavior and what constituted the "threshold" of culture. The latter led William Haviland (Haviland to Evelyn Bowers, August 18, 2012) to recall students being assigned in the 1950s to read Boas's *Anthropology and Modern Life* (1940). Haviland notes too that Hallowell's social organization course started with primate social organization.

Regarding this two-term course, Benson A. Saler wrote, "We didn't get to human beings until the spring semester.... The fall semester we read ... the best available monographs on non-human animal social behavior" (email to James M. Nyce, October 10, 2012). In Hallowell's Personality and Culture course Haviland recalled that the class was assigned a paper on "the necessary and sufficient conditions for a human existence."[5] Haviland and Anthony F. C. Wallace (email to James M. Nyce, August 29, 2012) note that Hallowell was much interested in developing the field of primate behavior and, like Speck, had his students observe primates at Philadelphia's zoo. Hallowell stressed physical anthropology's importance even for students who were not committed to this subfield of anthropology. (Incidentally, according to the university's commencement programs from 1935 to 1963, Penn's Department of Anthropology only granted two PhDs in physical anthropology. One was Henderson's 1958 library study of Alfred Russell Wallace.)

The intellectual environment at Penn's Department of Anthropology supported Hallowell's interest in human evolution. When we polled Hallowell's former students and Penn colleagues for those in the department who shared his interest in the subject, the names that came up were Speck, Loren Eiseley, and Wallace. For example, Wallace collaborated with Sol Katz, a colleague and one of Penn's former graduate students in physical anthropology (Wallace 1978:214–215). Also, Wallace's variant of culture and personality, unlike others of the time, included the biological as well as the cultural and psychological (Wallace 1961). While those we asked did not mention Ward Goodenough, he too often talked about biological and cultural evolution in terms that came close to Hallowell's (for a recent example, see Goodenough 2002:435). But no one polled talked much about Hallowell and Carleton Coon or Wilton Krogman, Penn's physical anthropologists at the time. In fact, the only extended mention of Coon we obtained was not about Hallowell but rather about Sherwood L. Washburn's attack on Coon's 1960 Presidential Address to the American Association of Physical Anthropologists. Regarding this, however, Penn's "department was vigorously loyal to its own," that is, to Coon (Paul Kutsche, email to James M. Nyce, October 19, 2012).

Hallowell's lifelong participation in the Philadelphia anthropological community also helped maintain his interest in human evolution. In the Philadelphia area, anthropologists who published in physical, linguistic, archaeological, or cultural anthropology mixed socially, for example, during the Philadelphia Anthropological Society meetings. However, discussions of human evolution in the Philadelphia area were not limited to anthropologists; in fact, one important contributor to Hallowell's turn to human evolution was Grace A. de Laguna, a philosopher at Bryn Mawr (Dostal with Bhardwaj 2013).

Hallowell's interests, however, were to move away from his past work in subarctic ethnology. He was distancing himself from the naive empiricism and historicism that characterized most ethnographic work of the time and had begun to think about ideational elements of culture that few of his contemporaries had paid much attention to. Perhaps the first indication of this interest can be found in Hallowell's 1934 paper "Some Empirical Aspects of Northern Saulteaux Religion." Although its evidence came from the subarctic, the paper was concerned with a larger issue: how individuals adjust to different culturally constituted worlds and the psychodynamics involved in such adjustments.

What is remarkable is how Hallowell approached this issue given the position Boasians of the time took on history and culture. Hallowell, in this 1934 article, observes that the religious tradition among the Saulteaux is "the primary conditioning factor in the beliefs of successful generations of individuals and that in this sense their beliefs are but the impingement upon human minds of an arbitrary pattern, the result of historical circumstance" (1934:404).

While individuals interpret experience in terms of these cultural traditions or patterns, it is clear from this passage that the pattern is an arbitrary one, that is, that the pattern has no special value or meaning in itself. The Boasians took this one step further. For them, a pattern's structure or content could never be predicted in advance. Of course, the environment played some role in the diffusion and acceptance of these elements. However, for Boasians, history was more or less the mechanism through which a cultural assembly and/or its parts could be transmitted place to place and across time.[6] Further, Boasians at the time identified (and looked for) cultural "constraint" in customs, traditions, and material culture and primarily saw history as bringing cultural elements more or less by accident to or from one group to another (Darnell 1977:16–20; Stocking 1974:5–8).

Hallowell, however, was not content to leave history there. The rest of the passage reads: "Yet, in the experience of the believers themselves, the events of daily life and reflective thought offer recurrent proof of the objective truth of their beliefs" (Hallowell 1934:404). While religious traditions can be the result of certain historical events and acquired particular meanings over time, it is also clear from the rest of the passage that the individual can use the religious traditions to make sense of experience, and this, in turn, can help validate and legitimatize particular religious traditions.

What distinguishes Hallowell from his fellow Boasians is the central role he ascribes to the individual and where he locates culture, history, and tradition. (This led Hallowell ultimately to take up the issue of human evolution.) For Hallowell, in other words, his fellow anthropologists did not go "deep enough" when it came to culture. For example, Hallowell carefully distinguishes mind from the ideational. The second term does not refer directly to (nor can be equated with) the psychological or the symbolic. To try to avoid anachronism and presentism (which Richard Handler [2005] says is not necessary), one has to say a bit more here about what ideational means for Hallowell. For Hallowell, the term "ideational" is different from (and extends deeper than) the psychological or the symbolic. Further, when Hallowell does use the terms "psychological" and "psychology," the terms often have little to do what they mean popularly or in academia in America at the time. In brief, these terms encompass for Hallowell what we today might call something like the ideational constraints upon experience, that is, cultural epistemology and ontology. These for Hallowell were in no way residual categories—something to be addressed after we analytically exhaust the psychological and sociocultural. For Hallowell, it was the other way around: the understanding of the ideational (and how experience is informed by it) should be the central project for anthropology. Hallowell believed that it was as if we were looking by mistake through the wrong end of the telescope and so could not pick out those cultural factors that make social life possible, and even necessary, for those who live it.

It was his Ojibwa fieldwork (and a reality there that was as legitimate and meaningful as his own) that led Hallowell in this direction. (This fieldwork would lead Hallowell eventually to frame his work on human evolution in the manner he did.) The ideational for Hallowell is what structures experience, because it links the individual to a culture's folk epistemology and ontology. While Hallowell does not use these terms, it is individual agency and the ideational together that give culture for those who live within it both naturalness and objectivity. Hallowell's interest in this particular problem distinguishes him from most Boasian anthropologists (Stocking 1996), and Hallowell went on to develop these ideas about the individual and experience.[7]

As a result, Hallowell attempted to publish his ethnographic material so that it reflected Northern Ojibwa categories and understandings rather than our own (see particularly 1940, 1971a[1942]). This was not true, however, of the Hallowell manuscript Brown published after Hallowell's death (Hallowell and Brown 1991).[8]

Like Edward Sapir (Nyce 1977), Hallowell (1971b[1954]:88) was well aware that the discipline had its own set of conventions that guided not only the kind of research carried out but also how it was written up. Hallowell realized that these conventions were products of our literary and scientific traditions, and embedded in them were the biases and assumptions of our own culture. There are some parallels here to the critiques of ethnography that have been made recently by authors like James Clifford and George E. Marcus (1986). In particular, Hallowell (1972:58–59) believed that the traditional ethnographic form and its (explicit and implicit) categories made distinctions that the Northern Ojibwa themselves did not make or recognize.

To address these problems of ethnographic representation, Hallowell (1972:59) both borrowed from and modified Gestalt psychology's concept of the behavioral environment. This resulted in an analytic and interpretive device, Hallowell believed, that could represent those elements of culture, the felt, the internal, the perceived, and even the seemingly imaginary that for the individual represented experience. Hallowell defined the behavioral environment as "a frame of reference by which it may be possible to view the individual in another society in terms of the psychological perspective his culture constitutes for him, and which is the integral focus of his activities" (1971b[1954]:79). For Hallowell, this concept enables us "to approximate more closely . . . the kind of naïve orientation we unconsciously assume towards our own culture, but which is so difficult to achieve in the case of another" (88–89).

In brief, Hallowell used the construct of the behavioral environment because he felt it would provide the closest approximation in our own intellectual tradition to the ethnographic facts with which he was concerned. (Hallowell's at least 15-year commitment to his seemingly "off the track" Rorschach project with the Northern Ojibwa makes sense if we see it as another of his interpretive strategies. This one is intended to demonstrate with objective, numerical proof, i.e., Rorschach scores, the findings of his anthropology of experience.) But to go on, it is important to note here that Hallowell was more influenced by the German tradition of Gestalt psychology than by its North American clinical variants. This may be because Wolfgang Kohler, one of the founders of Continental Gestalt psychology as well as a primatologist, taught at Swarthmore College from 1935 to 1955. Kohler's combined interests (he was one of the few psychologists at the time who was also an evolutionist) may have encouraged Hallowell to link the concept of the behavioral environment to issues of culture and later human evolution.[9]

What Hallowell attempted to resolve in what he published on the behavioral environment was the tension between his increasing understanding of Northern Ojibwa thought and the means he had at his disposal to represent his understanding and analysis of these ethnographic facts. The use of this concept helped Hallowell address problems he saw that were both representational and interpretative. As Hallowell goes on to argue, "Viewing a culture from the 'inside' can be best achieved if we organize our data in a manner that permits us as far as possible, to assume the outlook of the self" (1971b[1954]:88–89). To do this, Hallowell believed that tradition and culture had to be studied from the perspective of the individual. This led Hallowell to the concept of self. As Hallowell refined the concept of behavioral environment as a means to arrange and present ethnographical facts, he also developed the concept of the self and discussed its theoretical implications for anthropology.

The self, as Hallowell used the term, is the self known to the individual and as such does not represent any "true" picture of the individual. The self is the construct through which the individual comes to know himself or herself, and for Hallowell that means through which "a human individual becomes an object to himself" (1971b[1954]:80). Having demonstrated that the self is in large measure culturally constituted and therefore cross-culturally variable (Hallowell 1971b[1954]; Spiro 1976:354), Hallowell does three things next.

First, he uses his Northern Ojibwa material to show how a culturally constituted self interacts with a particular behavioral environment. But Hallowell does not stop there. Second, he goes on to argue: "If it is possible to view the self as culturally constituted and known to the individual in the same frame of reference as we view the culturally constituted world in which the individual must act, this preliminary step may enable us to . . . define with more precision some of the constant and variable factors that structuralize the psychological field of behavior for the individual in different societies" (Hallowell 1971b[1954]:81). Third, Hallowell considers the self and the behavioral environment not just comparatively and synchronically but also diachronically. Hallowell first started to explore the latter in respect to his Ojibwa material. But he also began to consider the implications the self and the behavioral environment might have for how we understand cultural and human evolution.

THE BEHAVIORAL ENVIRONMENT, THE
SELF, AND HUMAN EVOLUTION

In 1949 Hallowell gave his presidential address "Personality Structure and the Evolution of Man" before the American Anthropological Association (Hallowell 1950). The subject on which he chose to speak may have surprised his colleagues, or they may have seen it as a logical extension of the work for which Hallowell was known. In any event, Hallowell saw his presidential address as a continuation of his earlier work on the Ojibwa. In an autobiographical sketch, Hallowell wrote, "All these investigations in psychology and culture inevitably led to a general consideration of the psychological dimension of human evolution" (1972:59). What Hallowell is making clear here is how important sociocultural factors like ideation were in human evolution. Hallowell went on to publish six more papers on this topic (1956, 1959, 1960, 1961, 1963, 1965).

Little attention has been given to these papers as a corpus (but see Spindler and Spindler 1975). What links the six papers is that they all make use of and share a common theoretical perspective that relies on the notions of the behavioral environment and the self. The argument Hallowell made in "The Self and Its Behavioral Environment"

(1971b[1954]) is the analytic basis of all the work he was to do on human evolution. This paper was Hallowell's first use of the trope of the self and the behavioral environment, which he would then go on to use to frame evidence and argument regarding the evolution of humans and culture.

Hallowell (1972) then argued for an approach to human evolution that was more inclusive than the one provided by physical anthropology and archaeology at the time. For this reason, his ideas are still relevant today. It is necessary, he believed, to consider all the dimensions that were important in the evolutionary process, not just those for which there is direct evidence (Hallowell 1963:441). One of the most important of these factors is, for Hallowell, the presence of social systems. From the earliest phases of human evolution, social systems formed the context in which behavioral and structural changes occurred (Hallowell 1965:52). These changes, Hallowell argued, did not occur all at once in human evolution at any single point in time. He also did not attempt to place them in any kind of absolute time frame.

Hallowell here was doing two things. First, he attempted to expand on what could be counted at the time as "direct evidence" (the fossil record); second, he brought into the debate what he considered equally "strong" evidence as the fossil record. The intent was to broaden the evidence (and theoretical) base in order to help us better understand human and cultural evolution. This meant for Hallowell that "the continuities as opposed to the discontinuities between man and the nonhuman primates" (1972:59) have to be considered. If the continuities were considered, it would be possible "to bring together as an integral whole the organic, physiological, social, and cultural dimensions of the evolutionary process as they relate to the underlying conditions necessary for human existence" (59). In this way, Hallowell thought he could help identify the factors responsible for human evolution.

Hallowell's position reminds us of the shift in evolutionary studies to the mosaic principle; that is, different characteristics and sets of characteristics do not evolve at the same rate (Hallowell 1965:31–32; Washburn 1951). Today biological anthropology uses modified variants of the Synthetic Theory of Evolution (see Dobzhansky 1937; Huxley 1942), like Washburn's "New Physical Anthropology" (1951), to see how genes, defined as DNA sequences, make traits via gene products and how changes in the frequencies of these DNA sequences in gene pools constitute evolution. In other words, how one conceptualizes what a gene is and the functions attributed to it (the role genetics had in the science of human beings) became central to the scholarly discourse on how evolution occurs in both nature and culture. When Hallowell was writing on the topic, Synthetic Evolution (Dobzhansky 1937; Huxley 1942) was becoming the primary theory in biological/physical anthropology.[10] This remained the case even after the Watson-Crick model of DNA redefined what is meant by a gene. The argument continues over how much of evolution concerns chance changes in neutral genes and how much is selective, as well as whether selection occurs primarily at the level of the gene, the individual, or the population (Fuentes 2009 and references therein; Jablonka and Lamb 2005). What Washburn wrote in 1950 provided some of the reasons for why Hallowell turned to the issue of human evolution when he did:

> There are three reasons why this is an appropriate time to discuss the origin of man. The first is the finding of abundant fossils of a new kind of missing link (Australopithecus) in South Africa. The man-like apes indicate an unanticipated stage in human evolution, which radically alters all current theories of human origins. The second reason is that through the work of numerous geneticists, zoologists, and paleontologists a theoretical framework is now available which is far superior to any previous theories. The third is the fact that evolutionary speculations can be experimentally checked to a far greater extent than has been realized in the past. It is the combination of new facts, new theories, and new hopes of proof that makes this an auspicious moment to reconsider the problems of human origins. (67)

Hallowell's work on human evolution appeared at a time when there was an almost unprecedented increase in knowledge, at least since Darwin, about human evolution. It was this intellectual capital Hallowell both made use of and critiqued in his work on human evolution.

Most social scientists of Hallowell's time believed that the capacity for producing and using culture was the result of some sudden all-or-nothing leap in primate development (Hallowell 1965:32).[11] This Hallowell challenged on the basis of how he thought humans and culture emerged and developed together: "Another way to put it is that some of the necessary, but not all of the sufficient, conditions for cultural development and psychological reorganization were present, not only in the earliest hominid phase, but even earlier. I have previously labeled this earlier grade of adaptation as *proto-cultural*" (1965:33, emphasis in original; see also 1961, 1963). The protocultural, Hallowell believed, included an incipient stable social system, with something like predictable social relations, some form of communication, the social transmission of habit, convention, and occasional tool use (33–34).[12] Hallowell writes that these are necessary preconditions to a cultural mode of adaptation, but it was not until symbolic or ideological systems emerged that evaluation, reflection, and self-orientation generally allowed the cultural mode of orientation to come into existence (1963:468, 483–488).[13]

One reason Hallowell took this approach to human evolution had to do with his friendship with Grace A. de Laguna, a philosopher at Bryn Mawr College. De Laguna had a long-standing interest in the differences between humans and other animals (Cassirer 1945). For example, in de Laguna's correspondence with her colleague Jose Ferrater-Mora, an important Catalan philosopher, we find many discussions that compare the philosophy of "nature" with "that of the human world, showing how each meets or crosses the other" (Ferrater-Mora 1962). Writing to de Laguna in 1963, Ferrater-Mora observes, "I am very interested to hear that you are working on the problem of time in connection with your plan to show the relationship of the philosophy of nature with the philosophy of man. You know how I feel about this plan. It is the *soundest* philosophical plan anyone could think of" (emphasis in original).

Ferrater-Moya (n.d.) then writes to her, "It has always seemed to me that it is a serious weakness of the existentialists (or of all philosophies . . .) that they have no way of dealing with the empirical 'fact' of evolution." This discussion of the philosophies of nature and humans has to do with where the line can be drawn when it comes to human society between what is "objective" in its properties and what emerges from history and ideology. In relation to the "facts" of human evolu-

tion, both Ferrater-Moyer and de Laguna believed this was an important philosophy project but one that was barely on the radar screen in
the academic philosophy of their time. But if we substitute the words
"biology" for "objective" and "ideology" for "ideation," it is clear that
Hallowell was thinking about human evolution along much the same
lines. In fact, de Laguna opens her 1966 collection of essays with a discussion of a paper, "Science Sets a Problem: The Role of Teleonomy
in Evolution." In her foreword she writes, "To my friend, Professor A.
Irving Hallowell, my thanks are due for the many evenings of anthropological conversation . . . and also for his . . . reading the completed manuscript" (de Laguna 1966:vii). A look at what de Laguna published in this
area and the dates of their publication shows how much their arguments
on human evolution owe to each other (de Laguna 1960, 1962, 1966).

Hallowell (1965:52) argued that changes in the central nervous system, integrated with the development of systems of symbolic reference,
were responsible for the psychological restructuralization in which ego
functions, and a sense of self-awareness assumed central importance
in human evolution. This is Hallowell's contribution to the study of
human evolution. To understand human evolution, he argued that we
had to factor in the self-awareness that emerged from the interaction
between neurology and the ideational, because it is from this interaction that something like a moral order emerged in which an individual
over time learned "to take the place of the other." Hallowell (1965:42,
52) believed this was a primary mechanism that enabled hominids
(hominins) to transcend the protocultural stage.[14]

Hallowell was trying to bring to the debate what he believed to be
critical elements of human evolution. These elements were being overlooked because they seemed too speculative, almost theological, to
the evolutionary community of the time. The field of human evolution was in the midst of taking a turn to biology, and the arguments
and evidence this "new" community regarded as "scientific" left little
room for those elements of hominin evolution Hallowell believed to
be primary mechanisms of human evolution. However, some biologists and psychologists (Alexander 1987; de Waal 1994, 2009; Roe and
Simpson 1964) and biological anthropologists (Fuentes 2009; Hrdy
1999, 2009) have once again returned to these issues.

Hallowell was too good an anthropologist not to recognize the value this turn to biology had (for the place biological anthropology has in Boasian anthropology, see Darnell 1982). But at the same time he saw that what biological anthropologists came to mean by culture was defined by the kinds of markers that left little room for what Hallowell believed culture to be. He was not alone here. According to Harry L. Shapiro, "It is curious that in spite of at least 150 years of exposure to the concept of culture as elaborated by its sibling sciences in anthropology, physical anthropology itself has remained remarkably unaffected by it" (1967:52).

For Hallowell, then, *Homo sapiens (sapiens)* is demarcated by a sociocultural system "characterized by two distinct and interrelated features: (1) a culturally constituted normative orientation, and (2) a psychological structuralization of the actors in these systems as *persons*" (1965:42, emphasis in original). Hallowell attempts to identify what is necessary for human order to emerge. He argues that a human social order is a moral order. In a human social order the notion of the self becomes important because of two of its attributes: (1) self-awareness (Hallowell 1971b[1974]:81–83) and (2) the experiential sense of continuity it gives the individual across time and space (92–100). These led, Hallowell argued, to self-evaluation (106–107). Self-judgment, Hallowell believed, is an important element of the moral order because it makes it possible for the individual to both introject (incorporate) norms and values and to assume responsibility for his or her actions. This is reminiscent of the ideas developed by primatologist Frans de Waal (1996), but Hallowell's work is not cited by de Waal. But to go on, Hallowell, always skeptical of analytical reduction, refused to define or equate moral order with single terms like "empathy" and "altruism."

When it came to culture, the distance between what could be "fact" and speculation, between science and "theology," increased as physical anthropologists began to affiliate more closely with biologists, geneticists, and other laboratory scientists. What worried Hallowell the most was the reduction here of culture to tangible markers, that is, to what could be easily dated or read out of the fossil record and other evidence bases. What physical anthropologists were learning to rule out as difficult to locate "in the record," were issues like morality and self-awareness, ones Hallowell believed were central to hominin evolution. It was Hallowell's insistence on the importance of culture as a moral order, the construction and elaboration of self, and that together culture and self so constituted, as both agent and agency, that for him "drove" hominins in the direction of being human.

WHAT CAN HALLOWELL CONTRIBUTE TO TODAY'S RESEARCH ON HUMAN EVOLUTION?

Today, the psychological and cultural elements of human evolution as Hallowell (1963:442–446) understood them have largely been neglected. The development of the self and self-awareness for Hallowell, as we have seen, was critical to human evolution. It is not clear yet whether the developing interest today in neurological evolution will ever address Hallowell's concerns with self and culture. Recently, though, some ideas like Hallowell's have been picked up under the rubric of "theory of mind" (Premack and Woodruff 1978). However, what falls under this rubric now may not be as inclusive as what Hallowell believed was central to human evolution. This recent work has tended to focus on the cognitive and individualist functions of mind (Fuentes 2009). This is far from Hallowell's interest in how self-evaluation, reflection, and organization have evolved together and become central to the development of culture and modern hominins.[15]

The early 1960s saw the publication of two landmark collections in behavioral evolution (for the role the volumes have played in evolutionary thought, see Vassiliki 2012). The second volume of Sol Tax's *Evolution after Darwin* (1960) contained several chapters devoted to behavioral evolution, while Washburn's collection *Social Life of Early Man* (1963) was devoted to the same topic. *Evolution after Darwin* emerged from the 1959 International Congress of Anthropological and Ethnological Sciences. This congress, during the centenary of Darwin's *On the Origin of Species*, focused on the Synthetic Theory of Evolution (Dobzhansky 1937; Huxley 1942). In the late 1950s, when the Watson-Crick model of DNA had given a new definition to the gene (Watson and Crick 1953), the relation of genes (and genetics) to behavior and culture to evolution was at the time unclear. In fact, Hallowell's work can be seen as a response to this intellectual "vacuum."

Hallowell was invited to give a paper to *Evolution after Darwin* (Tax 1960:vols. 2 and 3), and in Washburn's 1963 edited volume, two of Hallowell's (1960, 1963) papers on human evolution were published. While a number of contributors to the two books wrote about some of the broader concerns in human evolution, only Hallowell discusses the development of self-awareness in hominins and the implications it had for human evolution. The fact that Hallowell had been invited to take part in both of these high-profile conferences and their discussions (e.g., Tax's panel 4, "The Evolution of Mind" with Julian Huxley and Nikolaas Tinbergen) shows the value that some of his peers placed on Hallowell's physical anthropology. Another indication of the value others found in Hallowell's work is that his 1956 paper, "The Structural and Functional Dimension of a Human Existence," was published in the *Quarterly Review of Biology*—a flagship journal in biology. This leads us to ask: Why, since these publications, has there been so little interest in Hallowell's ideas on human evolution? The answer to this may lie in the "turn" the study of human evolution has taken, especially among American physical anthropologists, since the 1960s.

American physical anthropology barely survived World War Two. In part this can be attributed to the interruption in the training of anthropologists by the war and in part due to the misuse of physical anthropology by the Nazis (Jones 1993). Also, Jonathan Marks (2010) has to remind us that during this time the links between German and American physical anthropology were complex and often morally ambiguous. In the 1930s, Marks tells us, for example, that Earnest Hooton found it necessary "to distinguish publicly between (bad) German physical anthropology and (good) American physical anthropology" (2010:188). Regardless of the position one takes on issues Marks raises, the postwar survival of American physical anthropology can be attributed to three individuals (Paul Baker, Gabriel Lasker, and Sherwood Washburn) and its transition to biological anthropology with its emphasis on genes and metabolites. Of the three, it was Sherwood Washburn who trained the majority of America's anthropological primatologists and established the New Physical Anthropology.

Hallowell's work on human evolution gives time depth to a central tenet of Boasian anthropology, that is, that culture is somehow learned

(Boas 1940). Hallowell did not completely follow the party line. He believed that some necessary preconditions, both in biology and in the social order, are necessary for culture to emerge. Shortly after their publication, Hallowell's papers on human evolution were reviewed in the *American Anthropologist, American Antiquity*, and the *American Journal of Physical Anthropology*. Admittedly, the reviews are few in number, but they appeared in flagship journals and may say more about Hallowell's place in the physical anthropology of the time than the kinds (and number) of conferences he was invited to.

Eric R. Wolf, in his review of *Evolution and Anthropology: A Centennial Appraisal* (Meggers 1959), comments on "Behavioral Evolution and the Emergence of Self," Hallowell's contribution to this volume: "[While] this is not the only alternative view to the more usual conception of evolution . . . at least it eschews the old-fashioned biological analogy of organic growth that characterized our more usual developmental schemes" (1960:885). However, Wolf goes on to suggest that mechanics and communications theory could provide conceptual frameworks that would be just as useful as Hallowell's.

Hallowell's "Self, Society, and Culture in Phylogenetic Perspective" was published in *Evolution after Darwin* (1960), and Charles Erasmus (1961:384, 385) called Hallowell's paper interesting and stimulating. While Erasmus does not discuss Hallowell's paper at length, Erasmus does write that Hallowell's "emphasis on the importance of self objectification and ego-awareness in a developmental context is a step in the right direction" (387–388). Despite this, Erasmus spends much of his review discussing the issues raised by the volume's other papers. Even today, while there has been more discussion of things like brain size, much of this discussion focuses on cognition, and the term "cognition" still tends to be narrowly defined. Even ontology, an important area in biological anthropology that studies development over the life span, has paid little attention to cultural learning, although there is a growing interest in the evolution of mind, brain, and culture.

In *American Antiquity*, the reviewer places Hallowell's paper "among the more psychologically directed of the volume" (Haag 1961:439). Derek F. Roberts reviewed the same volume for the *American Journal of Physical Anthropology* and called the quality of the contributions uneven. He mentions several he thinks have some merit, but Hallowell's is not one of them (Roberts 1960:607). Roberts, an anthropologist and geneticist, would have believed that science does not progress primarily by argument but by testing predictions. Hallowell's evolutionary concern with "vague" and "untestable" elements would have clashed with Roberts's position on science.

The only positive reviews Hallowell received were from fellow cultural anthropologists Erasmus and Wolf. When taken as a whole, these reviews suggest that Hallowell's work on evolution was an outlier. What is exceptional about Hallowell's argument, even today, is the emphasis he places on culture as a moral order (1957:97; 1960:345–349; 1963:452, 458, 476). For Hallowell (1965:442–444), the transition from protoculture to culturally based adaptation requires a normative orientation and the psychological processes that support this transition. Considering the kind of research done on human evolution in the first two-thirds of the twentieth century, Hallowell's argument may have seemed too far removed from the evidence and consequently seems almost metaphysical. This in itself would have made Hallowell's position difficult for others to take seriously. There is, however, another and perhaps more central problem.

Hallowell's work on human evolution rests on a number of theoretical constructs such as normative orientation and the notion of self. The constructs Hallowell used to present his argument presuppose the importance of "self-awareness" and the psychological dimensions in human evolution. This is where Hallowell's position becomes problematic, for his argument seems more imposed on the evidence than derived from it. The mediation between fact and interpretation that generally characterizes scholarly argument does not occur here. Hallowell's work was also not seen as generating testable hypotheses, nor was it possible to link mind and ideation to brain at the time Hallowell wrote, because information that could connect the brain to genetics had yet to be published.

Hallowell's work on human evolution during his lifetime was seen as too speculative. When facts seemingly do not influence interpretive structure, and structure does not seem to either reflect or accommodate evidence, such arguments are often seen as biased, weak, or suspect. This is because they do not seem well connected to the facts they attempt to account for. This seems to be the case in Hallowell's work on human evolution, and this may be responsible for the little attention his work in this area has received. This is still true, even though neuropsychology is moving out of primatology and is beginning to have an impact on other subfields of anthropology.

Things may be different today. The behaviors that enable culture and self-awareness are starting to be researched again by anthropologists. For example, Sarah Blaffer Hrdy, in *Mothers and Others*, calls attention to the role alloparenting has in culture and society and notes that it is only possible because of our "aptitudes for theorizing about mental states and intentions of other people, our species' gift for mutual understanding" (2009:2). Here we return to issues Hallowell believed were central to hominin evolution.

Still, today's practitioners of anthropology's subfields are much like debutantes who are waiting to be invited to dance. However, if we, as anthropologists, could pick up on what Hallowell believed was central to the study of human evolution, we could now all join in the dance. This would reduce anthropology's ongoing specialization and spare the discipline from further irrelevance. As Hallowell argued, we need to learn to work together (again) on important higher-order issues. For example, what role do culture and self-awareness play in human evolution? If we turned our attention together to the questions Hallowell asked, this just might help us put the sacred bundle of anthropology back together again (Segal and Yanagisako 2005).

NOTES

This chapter makes use of archival material held by the National Anthropological Archives, Bryn Mawr College's Archives, Vassar College's Archives, the University of Pennsylvania Museum Archives, the University of Pennsylvania Archives, and the Bancroft Library Archives at the University of California–Berkeley. For Hallowell's "turn" to physical anthropology and his interactions with physical anthropologists of the time, two visits to Hallowell's papers at the American Philosophical Society and subsequent online key word searches of APA holdings provided little of interest. The same was true of the requests we sent to the journals and publishers of Hallowell's papers on human evolution.

We wish to thank here those colleagues and students of Hallowell who were kind enough to reply to our inquiries. We also want to thank *American Anthropologist's* editor, Michael Chibnik, and the three anonymous reviewers for their very helpful comments. Gail Bader, S. Homes Hogue, Dick Preston, Herb Stahlke read various manuscript drafts; they too, especially Gail Bader, deserve our thanks.

1. The differences in their work reflect not only the differences in the personalities, experiences, and interests of the two men but also changes in the interests and orientations within anthropology as a discipline (Darnell 1977; Nash 1977). Little attention has been paid to Speck, but Speck's obituary by Hallowell (1951) is informative. There is also the nice collection of papers Blakenship (1991) published on Speck years later.

2. It is curious that Hallowell (1972) does not mention the contributions he made to the history of anthropology and the history of ideas in the sketch he drew of his career. This sketch, however, makes it clear that his theoretical concerns and work emerged from his attempts to make sense of the ethnographic materials he had collected among the Northern Ojibwa (Hallowell 1972:55–57).

3. His MA thesis (Hallowell 1920) is concerned with an ethnological problem and uses Northern Algonkian material. Hallowell's dissertation (1924), published in 1926, also used North Algonkian ethnographic data. Since his death, one more or less complete manuscript dealing with the same area has been found (Fogelson 1976:xvi). Brown subsequently published this manuscript (Hallowell and Brown 1991).

4. Hallowell (1972:54) mentions a series of physical measurements he made among the Abenaki of eastern Canada that was never published. The relationship of this research to the paper he published in 1926 is not clear. Hallowell's material submitted for his Viking Medal notes that he also did field excavations in a French Mousterian site under George Grant McCurdy in 1925 and that he taught European archaeology for several years after he returned from France (Anon. 1956).

5. These models of behavior either presumed some innate basis à la Freud, among others, or borrowed something from the behaviorists; that is, behavior was entirely learned. In short, there was no consensus in American anthropology at the time as to what linked self to behavior.

6. Hallowell's dissertation, accepted by the University of Pennsylvania in 1921 and published in the *American Anthropologist* (1926), traces the development of one such religious tradition: bear ceremonialism. The

dissertation is a study of cultural traits and their diffusion and distribution. This was, for Boasians of the period, state of the art work in method and argument (Darnell 1977:16–20).

7. Hallowell (1972:56–57) was sympathetic with the culture-and-personality movement that emerged around this time, and a number of his papers employ theoretical perspectives that have come to be identified with this "school." Nevertheless, Hallowell considered his interests to be broader in scope and theory than many of those who have also been associated with the culture-and-personality school.

8. Hallowell, at the end of his career, wrote a monograph on the Northern Ojibwa for the Holt series. The manuscript was lost, and because of his failing health, Hallowell was unable to reconstruct it from his notes (Fogelson 1976:xvi). It would have been interesting in light of Hallowell's criticisms of conventional ethnographic form to see how he would have presented his Northern Ojibwa material if he had been able to. For a history of this manuscript and how it came to be published, see Hallowell and Brown (1991).

9. Wolfgang Kohler was director of the Canary Islands Anthropological Station from 1913 to 1920. In 1917 he published *Intelligenz-Prufung an Anthropoiden* (*The Mentality of Apes* [1921]). After criticizing the Nazi government in print, he left Germany in 1935.

10. A major factor in this change was the publication of volume 15 of the Cold Spring Harbor Symposium on Quantitative Biology, titled *Origin and Evolution of Man* (Demerec 1950).

11. Today we believe that the capacity for culture, the origins of language, and that part of human personality that is innate are governed by multiple genes in multiple pathways, subject to various epigenetic effects under differing selective pressures, varying in intensity over both developmental and geological time.

12. Geertz (1964) argued for this position, and Hallowell cited him: "The reigning social solution of the origin of culture problem has been what might be called the 'critical point' theory" (1965:33). He notes in that same paper that Geertz points out that the Australopithecus had an elementary form of culture. Hallowell argued that this shows that cultural development had been under way for some time and that the evolution of culture cannot be adequately explained in terms of critical point or saltatory hypotheses (31–33). Today, chimps' tool use is widely known. Also, given how Geertz has come to dominate what we think culture is,

it might be worthwhile to assess what Geertz left out of his definition of culture (and one could turn again to Hallowell here).

13. We now know that all higher primates are social, with the exception of the orangutan, and the development of the anthropoids from a pro-simian ancestor occurred over 55 million years ago. All known primates have innate communications: vocal, gestural, postural, and olfactory, including smiling, laughing, and crying. However, the link all these have to verbal language, humanity's primary mode of communication, is unclear. How old spoken language might be is still a matter of debate. Social transmission of group habits, including tool use, is established for chimpanzees, so it might be expected in our last common ancestor more than 6 million years ago. Stone tools are first seen at 2.5 million years ago. Still, Hallowell would remind us, none of these markers can clearly be equated with those elements of culture and self he believed were the most important, that is, made us the most human.

14. It is important to note that all the features of the protocultural stage were incorporated in this new level of sociopsychological integration (Hallowell 1965:42).

15. The emphasis on the normative and the notion of the person, which are culturally constituted but maintained mostly by internal, ideational processes, shows how much Hallowell's work on human evolution owed to his Northern Ojibwa studies and to the theoretical work that emerged from them. It is this emphasis that makes it difficult to take seriously Barkow's (1968) argument that Hallowell was a sociobiologist.

REFERENCES

Alexander, Richard D. 1987. The Biology of Moral Systems. New York: de Gruyter.

Anon. 1956. Citation. Bulletin of the Philadelphia Anthropological Society 9(2):2.

Barkow, Jerome H. 1978. Social Norms, the Self and Sociobiology: Building on the Ideas of A. I. Hallowell. Current Anthropology 19(1):99–118.

Blakenship, Roy, ed. 1991. The Life and Times of Frank G. Speck. University of Pennsylvania Publications in Anthropology 4.

Boas, Franz. 1940. Anthropology and Modern Life. New and rev. ed. New York: W. W. Norton.

Brown, Jennifer S. H., and Robert Brightman, eds. 1988. "The Orders of the Dreamed": George Nelson Cree and Northern Ojibwa Religion and Myth, 1823. St. Paul: Minnesota Historical Press.

Cassirer, Ernest. 1945. Letter of February 19 to G. de Laguna. Frederica de Laguna papers 1975-06, Special Collections, Mariam Coffin Canady Library, Bryn Mawr College.

Clifford, James, and George E. Marcus. 1986. Writing Culture: The Poetics and Politics of Ethnography. Santa Fe: School of American Research.

Darnell, Regna. 1977. Hallowell's "Bear Ceremonialism" and the Emergence of Boasian Anthropology. Ethos 5:13–30.

———. 1982. Franz Boas and the Development of Physical Anthropology in North America. Canadian Journal of Anthropology 3:101–112.

———. 1988. Daniel Garrison Brinton. Philadelphia: Museum of the University of Pennsylvania.

———. 2001. Invisible Genealogies: A History of Americanist Anthropology. Lincoln: University of Nebraska Press.

———. 2006. Keeping the Faith: A Legacy of Native American Ethnography, Ethnohistory, and Psychology. In New Perspectives on Native North America: Cultures, Histories, and Representations. Sergei A. Kan and Pauline Turner Strong, eds. Pp. 3–16. Lincoln: University of Nebraska Press.

de Laguna, Grace. 1960. The Lebenswelt and the Cultural World. Journal of Philosophy 57(25):777–791.

———. 1962. The Role of Teleonomy in Evolution. Philosophy of Science 29(2):117–131.

———. 1966. On Existence and the Human World. New Haven: Yale University Press.

Demerec, Milislav, ed. 1950. Origin and Evolution of Man. Cold Spring Harbor Symposia on Quantitative Biology, vol. 15. Cold Spring Harbor NY: Biological Laboratory.

de Waal, Frans B. M. 1994. The Chimpanzee's Adaptive Potential. In Chimpanzee Cultures. Richard W. Wrangham, William C. McGrew, Frans B. M. de Waal, and Paul G. Heltne, eds. Pp. 243–260. Cambridge MA: Harvard University Press.

———. 1996. Good Natured: The Origins of Right and Wrong in Humans and Other Animals. Cambridge MA: Harvard University Press.

———. 1999. Cultural Primatology Comes of Age. Nature 399:635–636.

———. 2009. The Age of Empathy. New York: Harman Books.

Diamond, Jared. 1997. Germs and Steel. New York: W. W. Norton & Company.

———. 2005. Collapse. New York: Viking.

Dobzhansky, Theodosius. 1937. Genetics and the Origin of Species. New York: Columbia University Press.

Dostal, Robert, with Kiran Bhardwaj. 2013. History of the [Philosophy] Department [at Bryn Mawr College]: The de Laguna Years (1907–1946). Electronic document, http://www.brynmawr.edu/philosophy/history2.html, accessed March 26, 2013.

Eggan, Fred. 1967. Northern Woodland Ethnology. *In* The Philadelphia Anthropological Society. Jacob W. Gruber, ed. Pp. 107–124. New York: Columbia University Press.

———. 1976. Ojibwa Ecology and Social Organization: Introduction. *In* Contributions to Anthropology: Selected Papers of A. Irving Hallowell. Pp. 313–316. Chicago: University of Chicago Press.

Erasmus, Charles. 1961. *Review of* The Evolution of Man (vol. 2 of Evolution after Darwin). American Anthropologist 63:383–389.

Ferrater-Mora, Jose. 1962. Letter of December 16 to G. de Laguna. Frederica de Laguna Papers 1975-06, Special Collections, Mariam Coffin Canady Library, Bryn Mawr College.

———. 1963. Letter of June 6 to G. de Laguna. Frederica de Laguna Papers 1975-06, Special Collections, Mariam Coffin Canady Library, Bryn Mawr College.

———. N.d. Letter to Grace A. de Laguna. Frederica de Laguna Papers 1975-06, Special Collections, Mariam Coffin Canady Library, Bryn Mawr College.

Fogelson, Raymond D. 1976. General Introduction. *In* Contributions to Anthropology: Selected Papers of A. Irving Hallowell. Pp. ix–xvii. Chicago: University of Chicago Press.

Fuentes, Agustin. 2009. Evolution of Human Behavior. New York: Oxford University Press.

Geertz, Clifford. 1960. *Review of* The Evolution of Man (vol. 2 of Evolution after Darwin). American Anthropologist 26:439–441.

———. 1964. The Transition to Humanity. *In* Horizons of Anthropology. Sol Tax, ed. Pp. 37–48. Chicago: Aldine Publishing Company.

Goodenough, Ward D. 2002. Anthropology and the 20th Century and Beyond. American Anthropologist 104(2):423–440.

Haag, William G. 1961. *Review of* The Evolution of Man (vol. 2. of Evolution after Darwin). American Antiquity 26(3):439–441.

Hallowell, A. Irving. 1920. The Problem of Fish Nets in North America. Master's thesis, University of Pennsylvania.

———. 1924. Bear Ceremonialism in the Northern Hemisphere. PhD dissertation, University of Pennsylvania.

———. 1926. Bear Ceremonialism in the Northern Hemisphere. American Anthropologist 28:1–175.

———. 1929. The Physical Characteristics of the Indians of Labrador. Journal de la Société des Américanistes de Paris 21:337–371.

———. 1934. Some Empirical Aspects of Northern Saulteaux Religion. American Anthropologist 36:389–404.

———. 1940. Spirits of the Dead in Saulteaux Life and Thought. Journal of the Royal Anthropological Institute 70:29–51.

———. 1950. Personality Structure and the Evolution of Man. American Anthropologist 52:159–173.

———. 1951. Frank Gouldsmith Speck 1881–1950. American Anthropologist 53:67–75.

———. 1956. The Structural and Functional Dimension of a Human Existence. Quarterly Review of Biology 21:88–101.

———. 1959. Behavioral Evolution and the Emergence of Self. In Evolution and Anthropology: A Centennial Appraisal. Betty J. Meggers, ed. Pp. 36–60. Washington DC: Anthropological Society of Washington.

———. 1960. Self, Society and Culture in Phylogenetic Perspective. In The Evolution of Man (vol. 2 of Evolution after Darwin). Sol Tax, ed. Pp. 309–371. Chicago: University of Chicago Press.

———. 1961. The Protocultural Foundations of Human Adaptation. In Social Life of Early Man. Sherwood L. Washburn, ed. Pp. 236–255. New York: Wenner-Gren Foundation for Anthropological Research.

———. 1963. Personality, Culture and Society in Behavioral Evolution. In Psychology: A Study of a Science, vol. 6. Sigmund Koch, ed. Pp. 429–509. New York: McGraw-Hill.

———. 1965. Hominid Evolution, Cultural Adaptation, and Mental Dysfunctioning. In Ciba Foundation Symposium on Transcultural Psychiatry. A. V. S. de Reuck and Ruth Porter, eds. Pp. 26–54. London: J. and A. Churchill.

———. 1966. The Role of Dreams in Ojibwa Culture. In The Dream and Human Societies. Gustave E. Von Grunebaum and Roger Caillois, eds. Pp. 267–292. Berkeley: University of California Press.

———. 1971a[1942]. The Role of Conjuring in Saulteaux Society. New York: Octagon Books.

———. 1971b[1954]. The Self and Its Behavioral Environment. In Culture & Experience. A. Irving Hallowell, ed. Pp. 75–110. New York: Schocken Books.

———. 1972. On Being an Anthropologist. In Crossing Cultural Boundaries: The Anthropological Experience. Solon T. Kimball and James B. Watson, eds. Pp. 51–62. San Francisco: Chandler Publishing Company.

———. 2010. Contributions to Ojibwa Studies: Essays, 1934–1972. Jennifer S. H. Brown and Susan E. Gray, eds. Lincoln: University of Nebraska Press.

Hallowell, A. Irving, and Jennifer S. H. Brown. 1991. Ojibwa of Berens River, Manitoba: Ethnography into History. Austin TX: Holt, Rinehart and Winston.

Handler, Richard. 2005. *Review of* Ruth Landes: A Life in Anthropology. Isis 96(10):143.

Heizer, Robert F. 1959. *Review of* Evolution and Anthropology: A Centennial Appraisal. American Antiquity 25:611–612.

Hrdy, Sarah Blaffer. 1999. Mother Nature. New York: Pantheon Books.

———. 2009. Mothers and Others. Cambridge MA: Harvard University Press.

Huxley, Julian S. 1942. Evolution: The Modern Synthesis. New York: Harper.

Jablonka, Eva, and Marion J. Lamb. 2005. Evolution in Four Dimensions: Genetic, Epigenetic, Behavioral, and Symbolic Variation in the History of Life. Cambridge MA: MIT Press.

Jones, Steve. 1993. The Language of the Genes. New York: HarperCollins.

Kohler, Wolfgang. 1921. The Mentality of Apes. London: Routledge.

Kopytoff, Igor. 2006. A Short History of Anthropology at Penn. Expedition 49(3):29–36.

Lewontin, Richard. 1974. The Genetic Basis of Evolutionary Change. New York: Columbia University Press.

Marks, Jonathan. 2010. The Two 20th-Century Crises of Racial Anthropology. *In* Histories of American Physical Anthropology in the Twentieth Century. Michael A. Little and Kenneth A. R. Kennedy, eds. Pp. 187–206. Lanham MD: Lexington.

Meggers, Betty J., ed. Evolution and Anthropology: A Centennial Appraisal. Washington DC: Anthropological Society of Washington.

Nash, Dennison. 1977. Hallowell in American Anthropology. Ethos 5:3–12.

Nyce, James W. 1977. The Relationship between Literature and Ethnography: The Example of Edward Sapir 1917–1922. Halifax: Congress of the Canadian Ethnological Society.

Premack, David, and Guy Woodruff. 1978. Does the Chimp Have a Theory of Mind? Behavioral and Brain Sciences 1(4):515–526.

Roberts, Derek F. 1960. *Review of* The Evolution of Man and Issues in Evolution (vols. 2 and 3 of Evolution after Darwin). American Journal of Physical Anthropology 21:607.

Roe, Anne, and George Gaylord Simpson, eds. 1964. Behavior and Evolution. 2nd ed. New Haven CT: Yale University Press.

Segal, Daniel A., and Sylvia J. Yanagisako, eds. 2005. Unwrapping the Sacred Bundle: Reflections on the Disciplining of Anthropology. Durham NC: Duke University Press.

Shapiro, Harry L. 1967. The Direction of Physical Anthropology. In The Philadelphia Anthropological Society. Jacob W. Gruber, ed. Pp. 47–54. New York: Columbia University Press.

Spindler, George D., and Louise Spindler. 1975. A Man and a Book. *Review of* Culture & Experience. Reviews in Anthropology 2:144–156.

Spiro, Melford E. 1976. Obituary of A. Irving Hallowell. American Anthropologist 78:608–611.

Stocking, George W., Jr. 1966. Franz Boas and the Culture Concept in Historical Perspective. American Anthropologist 68(4):867–882.

———. 1974. Introduction: The Basic Assumptions of Boasian Anthropology. In The Shaping of American Anthropology 1883–1911: A Franz Boas Reader. George W. Stocking Jr., ed. Pp. 1–20. New York: Basic Books.

———. 1996. Boasian Ethnography and the German Anthropological Tradition. In Volksgeist as Method and Ethic: Essays on Boasian Ethnography and the German Anthropological Tradition. George W. Stocking Jr., ed. Pp. 1–8. Madison: University of Wisconsin Press.

Tax, Sol, ed. 1960. Evolution after Darwin. 3 vols. Chicago: University of Chicago Press.

Vassiliki, Betty Smocovitis. 2012. The Biological Anthropology of Living Human Populations: World Histories, National Styles, and International Networks. Current Anthropology 53(s5):s108–s125.

Wallace, Anthony F. C. 1961. Culture and Personality. New York: Random House.

———. 1978. Basic Studies, Applied Projects, and Eventual Implementation: A Case History of Biological and Cultural Research in Mental Health. George D. Spindler, ed. Pp. 203–216. Berkeley: University of California Press.

Washburn, Sherwood L. 1950. The Analysis of Primate Evolution with Particular Reference to the Origin of Man. In Origin and Evolution of Man. Cold Spring Harbor Symposia on Quantitative Biology, vol. 15. Milislav Demerec, ed. Pp. 57–78. Cold Spring Harbor NY: Biological Laboratory.

———. 1951. The New Physical Anthropology. Transactions of the New York Academy of Sciences, Series 2, 16:577–578.

————, ed. 1963. Classification and Human Evolution. Viking Fund Publications in Anthropology, no. 37. Chicago: Aldine.

Watson, James D., and Francis H. Crick. 1953. Molecular Structure of Nucleic Acids: A Structure for Deoxyribose Nucleic Acid. Nature 171(4,356):737–738.

Wilson, Edward O. 1975. Sociobiology: The New Synthesis. Cambridge MA: Harvard University Press.

————. 1978. On Human Nature. Cambridge MA: Harvard University Press.

Wolf, Eric R. 1960. *Review of* Evolution and Anthropology: A Centennial Appraisal. American Anthropologist 62:884–885.

7

An Epistemological Shift in the History of Anthropology

The Linguistic Turn

Anthropology's venerable and unusual tradition of self-critique addresses its complicity with colonialism and has sought, moreover, to periodically reconstitute its political relevance by addressing social inequality worldwide (Asad 1980[1973]; Hymes 1969). Toward this end, anthropologists have absorbed the critical insights from allied disciplines and the broad parameters of nonpositivistic critique. One only has to think of Marx or the numerous anthropologists who have been influenced by the Frankfurt School and the multiple contemporary currents of Continental social theory more generally. In what follows, I explore the historical relation between the "linguistic turn" in social theory and the strides that anthropologists have made to understand the relation between rationality, power, and the representation of others, as I believe that much of the contemporary critical engagement with issues of representation depart from or, at the very least, are indebted to the continuing resonance of the linguistic turn.

While there is no question that anthropologists of various theoretical traditions made use of the study of languages and diverse cultures that would provoke considerable philosophical debate of both epistemological and ontological import, there is little that is uniform in the linguistic turn, taken broadly, other than to say that language is foregrounded. The range of theoretical approaches includes, albeit not exhaustively, the formalism of Saussure and Jakobson, which influenced Lévi-Strauss; diverse semiotic traditions (e.g., Lyotard 1984; Baudrillard 1975) that have been used, among other things, to critique Marxist materialism; the pragmatics of sociolinguistics (e.g., Hymes 1974; Labov 1972) as applied to important social and political themes, such as the virtues of "black English"; the wider applications of generative grammars and what they suggest about mind or perhaps brain (e.g., Chomsky 1998); and the implications of cognitive science for a digitalized construction of thinking (e.g., Conklin 1962; Tyler 1978). There are, moreover, the multiple influences of poststructuralism and postmodernism inclusive of Foucault and Bourdieu, not to mention the merging of Marx and Hegel in some versions of critical theory. This would, in turn, shape our present communicatively derived concern with representations of "others" and our challenge to antiquated notions of culture as bounded (Moore and Sanders 2014). Consequently, with the exception of Lévi-Strauss, who cannot be ignored historically, I will focus on ordinary language philosophy, hermeneutics, and poststructuralism for their enduring influences on contemporary cultural and social anthropology without, however, negating the importance of other currents in linguistic theory. This essay thus cuts selectively across the theoretical domains of analytical philosophy, with its emphasis on logical rigor and clarity of expression, and Continental philosophy, which has long focused on human experience and social meaning. While my primary objective is a selective historical rendering of the linguistic turn in relation to social and cultural anthropology, I argue, nonetheless, that many of the contributors to the linguistic turn operate with a notion of a speech community and discourse that is insufficiently attentive to the heterogeneity and permeable boundaries of speech communities. Thus contemporary and future engagements with language as a model for social interaction must be able to take up, as we have more generally with the concept of culture, "people on the move" who are positioned differentially both locally and globally. Contrary to what Ludwig Wittgenstein (1961) maintained, the limits of my language are not, and never have been, the limits of my world.

HISTORICAL BACKGROUNDS

The linguistic turn in philosophy, or, more generally, social theory, is associated with a number of theoretical innovations and political displacements that can be traced to the 1970s and 1980s. That is, expanding communicative opportunities through technology such as social media combined with, ironically, the decreasing political vitality of the public realm has foregrounded the importance of language.[1] As we well know, theory does not materialize in a social and political vacuum, and so we must pay attention to the conditions under which theory is developed. The linguistic turn, in short, brought to theory a view of social action as communicative with political implications for how power can manifest itself in social relations through hegemonic discourses (e.g., Bourdieu 1984; Foucault 1978). This surely challenges the reciprocity often associated with normative communicative exchange, what Jürgen Habermas (1984) refers to as nondistorted and distorted communication, and provides us with a strong cultural model for understanding inequality and the positioning of human agency. Moreover, the communicative model of social action provided, with its emphasis on human agency as both world and meaning creator, a strong challenge to positivistic and scientistic models in the social sciences and the dominion of instrumental rationality, of which the positivist disputes in German sociology are illustrative.[2]

It may seem, however, wrongheaded to argue for the novelty and perhaps importance of philosophy's linguistic turn to anthropology, especially in North America, where linguistics has been since the early twentieth century one of our four disciplinary subfields. One could reasonably assert that there is little that is novel for anthropologists due to the fact that the study of languages across cultures was already an established and theoretically diverse practice. Moreover, the study of indigenous languages in particular provided fertile ground for a number of important epistemological questions (such as the potential relation between differential grammars and alternative ways of understanding, conceptualizing, or "being" in the world) that would, in turn, have a measurable generative influence on the linguistic turn itself.[3] Benjamin Lee Whorf's (1956) often-cited discussion of Hopi grammar, with its lack of a future tense yet ability to account for the temporality of all events, is perhaps one of the more salient and well-known examples—as is the Sapir-Whorf hypothesis more generally—in that it raised doubts concerning the universality of time reckoning and thus the reputed objectivity of the world if rightly grounded in language.

Guy Deutscher (2010) argues, though, that it is remarkable that the

Sapir-Whorf hypothesis was so widely accepted, including its implications for linguistic relativism, among cultural anthropologists without ever being subject to empirical testing, a testing he argues that it cannot support. In his *Through the Language Glass*, he takes us through a wide range of theories that reputedly support linguistic relativity and the independence of language from world before concluding that language does shape our thinking largely through the habitual uses of other mother tongues. Although Deutscher's criticism of linguistic relativity is erudite and provocative, I believe that its empirical emphasis on questions such as color terms does not nullify the larger and important epistemological and, by extension, ontological questions that are raised through Sapir and Whorf. At the very least, even if unresolved, it forces us to not take for granted the relationship between language and world.

Although paradigmatically distinct from what became known above as linguistic relativity, Lévi-Strauss's linguistic formalism emphasized the universality of structuring principles that underlie and shape phenomenal experience and the categories we employ to describe the world. If we might so consider it epistemologically, Lévi-Strauss's view on language is analogous to Immanuel Kant's philosophy of knowing minus the transcendental ego. Compared to English colleagues such as A. R. Radcliffe-Brown, who thought of structures as empirical entities, Lévi-Strauss contended that structures were a deeper organizational and invariable property of mind that gave shape to the phenomenal world yet to which they were not reducible. Lévi-Strauss's views of language imaginatively derive from the Swiss linguist Ferdinand de Saussure and the Prague school of linguistics, especially Roman Jakobson, whom Lévi-Strauss came to know during the war years in New York. The innovation comes from Lévi-Strauss's application of language to culture and social relations rather than the more limited domain of contrasting phonemes. Consequently, opposites as deep and invariable organizational principles, such as hot and cold and male and female, are relational rather than individually substantive. This is important philosophically and anthropologically because it challenges essential notions of identity. Lévi-Strauss (1969) applied his unique structural perspective in his *Elementary Structures of Kinship* to explain the incest taboo by arguing for the primordial nature of exchange, of which language is exemplary. Thus for Lévi-Strauss, language is, as I believe it should be, at the very center of social life.

Lévi-Strauss articulated, likewise, through his monumental studies of mythology an important connection between the deep structuring principles of mind that underlie the variations of stories, phenomenal experience, that different peoples tell about themselves. That is, myths from various cultures and times are simply variations on select human themes shared in common. Although equally important for its emphasis on language, the general critique of Lévi-Strauss is that he rendered culture and meaning as epiphenomenal and produced a static notion of structure that was inattentive to social change and history (e.g., see Geertz 1973:chap. 13).[4]

While influences are often difficult to trace in a linear or determinative fashion, Lévi-Strauss did profoundly shape and serve as a source of reaction to anthropology's concern with language and structure. It is reasonable to assume, for example, that efforts to reconcile structure with agency (e.g., Bourdieu 1984; Giddens 1986; Sahlins 1985) in light of criticisms regarding social change and history are at least indebted to his legacy. Whether we agree or not with his views on language, there is little doubt that Lévi-Strauss's copious writing from early on emphasized the importance of language to solidifying social relations and what it means to be human more generally, a view not inconsistent with the linguistic turn itself.

The ordinary language philosophy of the later Wittgenstein as applied to social action and the ontological casting of hermeneutics inclusive of social action as text are arguably among the most influential figurations and take us in a direction quite distinct from Lévi-Strauss's formalism and digital rendering of mind (Ulin 2001). It is self-evident that I cannot address this breadth of theory here, so I will limit myself, as mentioned previously, to some of the diverse currents that are still very much engaging the attention of anthropologists, linguists, and philosophers. I will in particular discuss the influences of ordinary language philosophy and hermeneutics with respect to the ostensible linguistic turn in anthropology, a journey that takes me back to familiar ground. As we will see, the linguistic turn also has an importance for the various questionings of ethnographic writing whether in the version of text or literature. I will, moreover, suggest that Foucault and Bourdieu offer us continuity with the major themes of the linguistic turn while addressing issues of power, agency, and the body absent from ordinary language philosophy and hermeneutics.

ORDINARY LANGUAGE PHILOSOPHY

Not to be overlooked in examining the relationship between anthropology and the linguistic turn is philosopher Peter Winch's now classic, yet controversial, *The Idea of a Social Science and Its Relation to Philosophy*, a very short but important work published in 1958 that would give rise to the Anglo-American rationality debates of the 1970s, 1980s, and 1990s. Winch's book borrows significantly from the ordinary language philosophy of the later Wittgenstein (1965) in a novel application of language games to social action more generally. As Winch and others have pointed out, the later Wittgenstein departed significantly from his earlier work of the *Tractatus* by arguing that language should be understood as action, something we do, rather than as a platonic label that we attach to objects in the world. The meanings of words are thus dependent on the plurality of language games in which they are employed, thus suggesting that "playing" or "speaking" is more important than the formal rules of the game. In fact, we learn a language not by mastering a priori the rules or grammar but rather through saying things in different contexts.

Following the later Wittgenstein, Winch thought by analogy that if the meanings of words are based upon their use, why not then attribute the meanings of what people do to the language games or forms of life—interrelated language games—from which they obtain their sense? That is, the meanings and identities of human actions—what doing something amounts to—are based upon the language communities with which they are associated. Human actions are intrinsically communicative, a conclusion quite different from deep linguistic structures, comparative grammars inclusive of diverse worldviews, and the historical study of languages that had typified anthropological linguistics of the past.

Winch's refiguration of ordinary language philosophy as presented in

The Idea of a Social Science is accompanied by his sympathetic yet critical discussion of E. E. Evans-Pritchard's (1937) classic work on Azande witchcraft. Evans-Pritchard had addressed the rationality of witchcraft practices against the background of Lucien Lévy-Bruhl's argument in *The "Soul" of the Primitive* (1965) that indigenous belief systems are not rational because they fail reputedly to comply with Aristotelian categories of logic and nonidentity. For example, Lévy-Bruhl wondered how it was possible, as some indigenous healers or shamans contended, to claim to be both human and nonhuman without transgressing what appears to be the logic of identity. However, Evans-Pritchard demonstrated convincingly that Azande beliefs are just as logical as our own once the assumptions that inform witchcraft beliefs are understood. Azande reason, therefore, just as we do, an assertion that is hardly controversial among anthropologists today.

Winch was, however, ultimately critical of Evans-Pritchard's claim that although witchcraft beliefs are logical, there is no empirical evidence to support the existence of witches. According to Winch, Evans-Pritchard makes a category mistake in refuting the empirical existence of witches through rules of evidence typically associated with the language games of science, in which, he maintains, the Azande have no interest. Winch argues, to the contrary, that witchcraft practices among the Azande must be understood through language games from which they obtain their sense. As for the empirical existences of witches, for the Azande, the question has no epistemological or ontological import.

One could argue that Winch makes too much of Evans-Pritchard's assertion that Azande witches do not exist. I argued, for example, that Evans-Pritchard's refutation of witches has more to do with his Anglican religious views than his anthropology (Ulin 2001). Nonetheless, Winch's assertions about the relativity of science and its rules of evidence certainly generated considerable debate among contributors to the aforementioned rationality debates with respect to how we should make sense of human action and other cultures unlike our own. The debates are also important for what they suggest about the relation between the truth claims of science and the relativity of language.[5]

Not only did Evans-Pritchard's corpus of writings give rise through Winch to the Anglo-American rationality debates, but his 1962 work published as *Social Anthropology and Other Essays* also discloses a serious interest in hermeneutics. This may come as a surprise, given his more typical association with ecological perspectives on East African pastoralists and his direct connections to British structural functionalism more generally. However, Evans-Pritchard was deeply interested in the relationship between anthropology and history and believed that anthropology must be historical or nothing at all, a curious assertion for someone often associated with functionalism's ahistoricism and the synchronic view of social life.[6] Nevertheless, Evans-Pritchard was very much interested in the works of the late nineteenth- and early twentieth-century hermeneutic philosopher Wilhelm Dilthey. Dilthey is perhaps best remembered for his methodological distinction between the natural and human sciences. According to Dilthey (1988), the object of knowledge in the natural sciences is nature, and thus the experimental-empirical standards of science are suitable to determining the regularities and laws of that which was not created by humans. However, the object of knowledge in the human sciences inclusive of the social sciences and humanities is humankind, and therefore a distinct method is warranted that is well suited to understanding humanly created social meanings. It is the emphasis on understanding social meanings that most attracted Evans-Pritchard to the uses and importance of history to anthropologists.

HERMENEUTICS AND THE LINGUISTIC TURN

It would be somewhat of a stretch to directly link Dilthey's hermeneutics and Evans-Pritchard's later emphasis on history to the philosophical linguistic turn and its subsequent influence in turn on contemporary anthropology. However, both history and hermeneutics remained as connected and influential themes in the work of numerous anthropologists, Clifford Geertz (1973) perhaps most noteworthy, where language was central. The connection, though, to the contemporary scene departs from Dilthey but matures through the hermeneutics of Gadamer and Ricoeur, the later having had a direct influence on Geertz.

With Hans-Georg Gadamer, in his often-cited classic, *Truth and Method* (1975), we discover a novel application of Martin Heidegger's notion of "being" that both critiques the Western obsession with method and emphasizes the importance of language to the historicity of "being." Gadamer's approach to language has nothing to do with its empirical analysis, as, for example, with sociolinguistics or the afore-mentioned Deutscher (2010). Rather, Gadamer argues that it is not so much that we speak language as it is that "language speaks us." While he acknowledges the importance of speech acts, his point is that the language communities of which we are a part prefigure human consciousness concretely and historically. Although Gadamer's view of language suffers, as does that of Wittgenstein and Winch, from a now widely recognized provincial sense of language communities as bounded rather than porous, multiple, and transient. However, his argument moves questions concerning the centrality of language from that of epistemology, how an ego comes to know, to that of social being, the languages we speak mediate all existence. The idea of "a language community being in the world" thus displaces the independence of the Cartesian ego, singular or plural, and is world inclusive of the traditional subject and object dichotomy. For Gadamer, methods of any sort are not neutral or independent of the communities of which they are a part, therefore illustrating the superficiality of a now-antiquated but once-embraced methodological distinction between emics, the insider's view, and etics, the outsider's view.[7]

Gadamer does address the seeming incommensurability of language communities (the problem of understanding others and the implications for rationality) and the multiplicity of social beings that they suggest by arguing that the contact between language communities, whether in terms of different cultures or of the past, involves a "fusion of horizons." This metaphor seems appropriate in that the encounter of others unlike us, or the past as "other," involves a dynamic conceptual prefiguration that is subject itself to being refigured. One could argue that both knowing and being are historically configured, but I think that it is important to challenge untenable divisions between knowing and the world, a move that can be supported through an ontologically and dynamically formed conceptualization of language.

Gadamer's thoughts about language and social being do provide a significant bridge between history and anthropology, a concept best captured in David Lowenthal's *The Past Is a Foreign Country* (1985).

Lowenthal suggests that we should think about the past much as anthropologists think about other cultures. The strategy is one of defamiliarization. Gadamer's thoughts about language and social being likewise make explicable Evans-Pritchard's thoughts about history in relationship to his interest in the hermeneutician Dilthey. They set up a strong relationship between language; the meaning of lived experience, which also belongs to phenomenology; and a dynamic view of the past as a collective cofashioning of the present.

However, Gadamer is not alone among hermeneuticians who have influenced the linguistic turn in anthropology. Rather, because of Paul Ricoeur's influence on Clifford Geertz in particular, anthropologists tend to be more familiar with Ricoeur's copious writings than with those of Gadamer. Although Ricoeur has written numerous books that are known to anthropologists schooled in Continental philosophy (*The Conflict of Interpretations* [1974] and *Freud and Philosophy* [1970] are two examples), it is actually an essay published in *Social Research* that has been the most influential. It is in his "The Model of a Text: Meaningful Action Considered as a Text" (1971) that Ricoeur outlines a communicative view of social action along with a method, unlike Gadamer but like Dilthey, by which the social meanings of texts can be deciphered.

According to Ricoeur, there is an analogy between the fixation or objectification of an author's intentions in a text and the objectification of the plurality of meanings of actions in memory, oral accounts, and historical documents—all of which are, as we shall see, open to public negotiation. Ricoeur maintains that authors' intentions and the meanings of social actions have a fleeting character and would disappear without a trace were it not for their fixation in writing or action as text, metaphorically speaking. I bring our attention to two noteworthy points that by extension can apply to social action as text. First, by becoming fixed in writing, authors' intentions take on an independent existence as directed to potential readers or audiences. Second, because intentions can be divorced from those who produce them, they maintain their historicity as potential and variable audiences take them up in the future. On both accounts, divorcing intention from the author avoids the all too common erroneous idea that exploring meanings suggests getting inside the heads of authors or actors, a point that was strongly refuted by Geertz as well.[8] Ricoeur is not interested, therefore, in individual motivations, the "why" or intentions of social action, but rather their import or meaning, which he refers to as their "said." The point of Ricoeur's hermeneutics is to explore social meanings as independent of the intentions of social actors as these meanings are engaged, or read, by any potential audience inclusive of an anthropologist conducting field research. Ricoeur thus provides dynamism to social meanings, as they are never constant.

As noted above, Ricoeur's approach is methodological in that he brackets, much like Edmund Husserl's (1973) epoché, the external references of a text in order to explore the text's internal coherence, an initial methodological move not totally remote from Lévi-Strauss's analysis of myth. Once the internal dynamics of the text are apparent, Ricoeur believes that the external reference of the text should be restored. Again, while the formalism of Ricoeur's approach may be unsatisfactory, it does give us a historically sensitive way to explore the relationships between action and meanings without reducing the effort to internalized and subjective intentions in the heads of actors who are resistant to critical examination.

Geertz's adoption of Ricoeur's model of social action as a text has not been without criticism. William Roseberry (1982), for example, argued that Geertz's famous essay on the Balinese cockfight ignored the history of how the text itself was formed. Thus, according to Roseberry, Geertz is silent on the colonial context in which Balinese cockfighting is embodied. Moreover, if we take Derrida's (1967) suggestion on the deconstruction of texts, it is important to consider not only the text's inside but also the multiple voices that are relegated to the margins of history. Thus for Derrida, who has been very influential in terms of how anthropologists think about narratives, a critical reading requires that we examine what has been excluded from the narrative of the text itself.

Nevertheless, as we are no doubt aware, Ricoeur's emphasis on social action as a text would become, albeit with Wittgenstein's and Kenneth Burke's influence as well, central to Geertz's interpretive anthropology, which is devoted to exploring public meanings, a task as we know from Geertz that is never final or complete. While the connections are anything but linear, causal, or direct, there are links between linguistic philosophy and hermeneutics to an often-unrecognized interest of Evans-Pritchard in history and meaning, interpretive anthropology, and much of what amounts to the various critical "posts" of contemporary anthropology and social theory more generally.

ELECTIVE AFFINITIES

While the connection between Geertz and Ricoeur is self-evident as it was acknowledged by Geertz himself and illustrated by what Geertz has said about the model of the text, this connection likewise extends to Geertz's connection to the new cultural history and the more general affinity between anthropology and history based upon a shared communicative model (see Hunt 1989). It was often wrongly thought that anthropology and history had two distinct object-subject methodological domains, in that historians dealt with the past and anthropologists studied contemporary societies. This was, of course, further reinforced by British social anthropology's distaste for oral accounts as simply speculative (e.g., Radcliffe-Brown), even though their theoretical emphasis on synchrony was often at odds with their historical work on the indigenous states. Geertz's not so methodological idea of "thick description," actually borrowed from Gilbert Ryle but equally applicable to both the later Wittgenstein and Ricoeur, was meant to illustrate the sequence of meaningfully shared lived experience, life worlds phenomenologically speaking, that separates self and other yet serves as a metaphor of cross-cultural understanding. As Geertz reminded us, thick description is continuous but not circular, constantly reformulating our understanding of self and other. For Geertz, there was no comprehensive grasp of the other. Whatever problems we may have with Geertz in terms of his failure to discuss power and concretely positioned subjects (see Roseberry 1982), he nonetheless presented us with very vivid and lively ethnographic narratives, even if, regrettably, the dominant voice was his own.

The new cultural historians, and here Carlo Ginzburg's *The Cheese and the Worms* (1980) comes to mind, have likewise sought, and successfully so, to replicate thick description in their illuminations of past lives. Ginzburg's story of the 16th-century miller Menocchio and his struggles with the church are vivid and captivating. We learn much about what Menocchio read, thought, and said to explain his being brought in front of the Inquisitional courts. The reader feels very much transported to past times. Ginzburg's objective is less the rendering of fact and so much more the explication of meaning in its multiplicity.

POSTSTRUCTURALIST METAPHORS

One could argue, and rightly so, that although Geertz and thick description surely influenced anthropologists and historians in seeing the close affinity between ethnographic and historical writing, this influence was surely equaled, if not surpassed, through both Michel Foucault and Pierre Bourdieu. They are especially important to the linguistic turn because in distinct manners they have bridged the somewhat pedestrian schism between structure and meaning and agency while retaining the emphasis on language and discourse.[9]

Foucault has had, and continues to have, a very significant impact on scholars from both the humanities and the social sciences. Without going into extensive explanation, Foucault's key point of difference from Geertz and the hermeneutic philosophers is his addressing directly the issue of power in both subtle and demonstrative ways by likewise making language, in his case discourse, a central concern.

Foucault's early influences, like many scholars who have embraced communicative models, were phenomenology, specifically Merleau-Ponty, and Heidegger's ontology shared with the hermeneutician Gadamer, discussed previously. However, no single influence can capture Foucault's immense originality. His somewhat later encounter with Lacan, Bachelard, Saussure, and Althusser surely accounts for his displacement of subjectivity and challenge to universal configurations of reason. Quite contrary to the Cartesian emphasis on the self, Foucault proposes, not unlike Gadamer, that the self is a product of discourse or discursive practices, a view that likewise rejects foundations and essential origins.

The appeal to historians, especially social and cultural historians, is that Foucault directs our attention to shifts in discourses or discursive practices. Thus in his brilliant *The Birth of the Clinic* (1973), we learn how the "opening up" of corpses changed how we have come to talk about and regard the material body. Perhaps most important is Foucault's providing an alternative to a reductive application of Marxist ideology, too often seen as overdetermined by class interests or narrowly construed in terms of base and superstructure. Here it is *Discipline and Punish* (1978) that is instructive in terms of Foucault's celebrated idea of the "gaze" or "surveillance" that seems especially well attuned to our technological age and its characteristic dominion of technical reason. The gaze entails the observation of people inclusive of the internalization of hierarchical notions of control, thus suggesting a very close relation between power and knowledge. This is evident in the observation not only of inmates in the prison yard, which structures and controls a prison environment, but also of students in schools, where the educational environment is engaged in the making of citizens through disciplinary routines.

Foucault's emphasis on discourse and discursive practices was never drawn into the immediate company of the rationality debates discussed earlier. My own contributions, for example, came late to the debates focused on hermeneutics and critical theory's reformulation of the Marxist tradition. Nevertheless, Foucault's work is pertinent to questions of cross-cultural understanding and the reputed claims of rationality associated with other life worlds. The rationality debates were consistently concerned with the subject-object relation as a given of encountering other cultures. With Foucault, we have the option of regarding both subject and object and their relation as a product of history and discontinuities or breaks in discourse. Moreover, the social sciences more generally in constructing humans as the object of knowledge enable us to see the anthropological "gaze" not simply as one of potential reciprocity and understanding but, more specifically, as one of power. This is a very substantial insight that invites ongoing reflection on multiple and sometimes subtle means through which "others" are subject to disciplinary practices contoured by power, an insight that has not escaped the attention of a wide range of anthropologists from more classical Marxists to those from poststructuralism, postmodernism, and semiotics. Because language in multiple theoretical articulations cross-cuts virtually all of these theories, the theories themselves belong to the legacy of the linguistic turn or various reactions to it.

With respect to anthropology specifically, it could be argued that

Pierre Bourdieu has made an equal if not larger impact on the ethnographic research and writing of anthropologists and the raising of questions related to representation. I made, for example, extensive use of Bourdieu's concepts of cultural and social capital in trying to account historically, and against all too common arguments in favor of climate and soil, for why some wine-growing estates in France have reputations for better wines than those that are located in proximity (1996). The intentional and thus elective affinity between elite estates and their nostalgia for a former aristocracy resonate well culturally in establishing a privilege for château wines.

Likewise, anthropologist Philippe Bourgois (1996) appeals to Bourdieu in trying to explain the subaltern position of his drug-dealing informants in East Harlem, New York. Contrary to the popular media, Bourgois shows that his informants often tried to make a living in the legitimate economy before turning to the sale of drugs. However, they lacked the cultural capital that would have enabled them to negotiate the challenges they faced at Manhattan businesses. Through Bourgois, we see his informants not simply as victims but as reproducing inequalities and structures of power that undermine their senses of self-worth and dignity, a point that resonates widely with Wolf's critique of world systems theory and others who have sought to emphasize the importance of agency and resistance.

Like Foucault, Bourdieu regards social relations as communicative, but, unlike Foucault, he places an emphasis on human agency, and a differentiated human agency at that, apparent in his discussion of class differences and their cultural reproduction in *Distinction: A Social Critique of the Judgment of Taste* (1984). His emphasis on habitus, moreover, links rationality, dispositions, ways of thinking, power, and the body to the experience of collective life. Bourdieu's theory is distinct but not totally remote from the formal linguistics of Saussure and Lévi-Strauss in that he likewise places an emphasis on symbols as structured and the structuring of structures. Like Foucault, there is some potential to think productively about the central theme of the rationality debates, Azande witchcraft, through the concept of habitus. Habitus would enable us to think about witchcraft apart from dichotomies of objective and subjective and rational and unscientific and more in terms of dispositional practices. Furthermore, Bourdieu's articulation of habitus would enable us to recognize the relations between practice, bodies, and power, a perspective that was virtually absent in a good deal of debates about their rationality and veracity. Bourdieu, like Foucault, is a descendant of the linguistic turn who takes language and discourse in novel and empirically productive directions.

CONCLUSION

The linguistic turn that I have outlined and discussed here is selective and partial to my own interests, as is perhaps all historical reckoning and theoretical elaboration. I have largely steered clear of formal linguistics and semiotics, with the exception of Lévi-Strauss, because although they have contributed significantly to advancing the linguistic turn, I maintain that they have a very weak sense of a historical and differentiated agency. Rather, I believe that a dynamic sense of agency is critical and indispensable to how we should think about anthropology's enduring emphasis on marginalized and subaltern populations. This is not to say that semiotics has nothing important to contribute to understanding the multiple plays of power outside the labor process, and here I have Jean Baudrillard (1975) in mind; however, semiotics tends to remove the process of signification too far from the more concrete domain of praxis and the making of the material world (see Ulin 2001). While not a fault particular to semiotics, it is not especially productive to regard oppressed peoples as simply victims, as we should by now well understand how human cosubjects both reproduce and resist their own conditions of subordination (see Wolf 1999). I therefore leave the historical account of formal linguistics and semiotics to others.

Although there is a venerable tradition of language and linguistic theory of multiple sorts in the history of North American anthropology, this is quite distinct from the broader implications of the linguistic turn. That is, by equating action itself with communicative practice, the linguistic turn entails an important epistemological if not ontological shift with enduring historical implications. I have touched on only a few of the salient influences that admittedly have shaped my own work while out of necessity have given little attention to others. A more comprehensive review would necessarily address Marxist permutations as found in Bakhtin and contemporary formulations of the communicative casting in Habermas's communicative theory of society. While Habermas has been peripheral to most anthropologists, his work on instrumental rationality in relation to the depoliticization of the public domain is surely important to anthropology's concern with local and global relations. These theoretical formulations, taken collectively, offer differentially historically sensitive and dynamic figurations through which to narrate the plurality of "lived experience and life worlds" mediated through collective and individual agency, what Hannah Arendt (1958) distinguishes as the "power over" and the "power to." As mentioned previously, this has had significant contemporary implications for how we think about the complexities of representing "others" and the shifting terrain of culture itself. For that reason alone, communicative paradigms and tropes of communication (Fernandez 1991) are likely to continue their constructive and critical engagement with shifting and new emergent theoretical paradigms.

Finally, it is important to acknowledge that iterations of the linguistic turn seem to reproduce speech communities as bounded, the very problem that plagued the traditional anthropological concept of culture. The problem of bounded culture is not resolved but rather reproduced in notions of self and other and how to bridge that gap of understanding. This is true with the ordinary language philosophy of the later Wittgenstein as it is with hermeneutics and ostensibly fused horizons. Rather, we must be especially attentive to agency as differentially positioned and to borders and boundaries as permeable and shifting. Such an undertaking will require new metaphors of social interaction and perhaps recognizing that if language is at the center of social life, it is also in the mix of power and the multiplicity of our material lives.

NOTES

1. I have long believed that what Habermas (1984) refers to as the depoliticization of the public domain and the colonization of the life world through instrumental rationality have a lot to do with our emphasis on language in social theory. Habermas is not alone in asserting that the potential to engage each other in mutual communicative exchange about what is important to social and political life is what makes the public realm vital and democratic.

2. The positivist disputes in German sociology (1976) largely but not exclusively involve debates between Karl Popper and Jürgen Habermas over the nature of science and rationality as applied to understanding and explaining the social world.

3. Of course it should not be overlooked that the ethnographic research of anthropologists provided sufficient grounds for philosophers to argue about cultural relativism even if philosophers have wrongly concluded that anthropologists believe that "anything goes."

4. Geertz is by no means alone in his critique of Lévi-Strauss. Moreover, the criticisms of Lévi-Strauss are also applicable to a structuralism more generally that had its height of popularity during the 1970s and 1980s.

5. This is an enduring issue in the philosophy of science and of some concern to anthropologists who insist that ethnographic research and writing should seek to emulate the standards of the natural sciences. For Winch, all statements about the nature of reality inclusive of science are relative to the language games of which they are a part.

6. There are numerous reasons why structural functionalism was synchronic. The reason that is most pertinent to history was the fact that many indigenous societies of the colonial era were not literate and thus relied on oral accounts to talk about the past. Radcliffe-Brown, for one, was distrustful of oral accounts because he saw them as subject to embellishment, and therefore they were not reliable. This has, of course, changed today in that oral histories are taken seriously.

7. It is well known that the emic and etic perspective derives from the distinction in language between phonemics and phonetics. It was widely believed that what makes sense for language in terms of distinguishing the idiosyncratic from the general rules also applied to the study of social life by distinguishing local views from those of outsiders. The outsider's perspective was privileged because it was seen as more objective. The distinction falls apart with hermeneutics in that insiders' and outsiders' views are both negotiated and mediated.

8. Current Supreme Court Justice Clarence Thomas has declared that he is a constitutional textualist, which means that he believes we can know what the authors of the Constitution intended. This goes quite contrary to what Ricoeur argues and seems to suggest that we can get inside the heads of our constitutional authors—a very improbable exercise.

9. One can easily devote much more attention to Foucault and Bourdieu than I have done here. My discussion is necessarily truncated and largely designed to show where the linguistic turn has taken us.

REFERENCES

Adorno, Theodor, et al. 1976. The Positivist Dispute in German Sociology. New York: Harper Torchbooks.

Arendt, Hannah. 1958. The Human Condition. Chicago: University of Chicago Press.

Asad, Talal, ed. 1980[1973]. Anthropology and the Colonial Encounter. New York: Humanities Press.

Baudrillard, Jean. 1975. The Mirror of Production. St. Louis: Telos Press.

Bourdieu, Pierre. 1984. Distinction: A Social Critique of the Judgment of Taste. Cambridge MA: Harvard University Press.

Bourgois, Philippe. 1996. In Search of Respect: Selling Crack in El Barrio. Cambridge: Cambridge University Press.

Chomsky, Noam. 1998. On Language. New York: New Press.

Clifford, James, and George E. Marcus, eds. 1986. Writing Culture: The Poetics and Politics of Ethnography. Berkeley: University of California Press.

Conklin, Harold C. 1962. Lexicographic Treatment of Folk Taxonomies. International Journal of American Linguistics 28(2):119–141.

Derrida, Jacques. 1967. Of Grammatology. Baltimore MD: Johns Hopkins University Press.

Deutscher, Guy. 2010. Through the Language Glass: Why the World Looks Different in Other Languages. New York: Metropolitan Books / Henry Holt and Company.

Dilthey, Wilhelm. 1988. Introduction to the Human Sciences: An Attempt to Lay a Foundation for the Study of Society and History. Princeton NJ: Princeton University Press.

Evans-Pritchard, E. E. 1937. Witchcraft, Oracles and Magic among the Azande. Oxford: Clarendon Press.

———. 1962. Social Anthropology and Other Essays. New York: Free Press.

Fabian, Johannes. 1983. Time and the Other: How Anthropology Makes Its Object. New York: Columbia University Press.

Fernandez, James W., ed. 1991. Beyond Metaphor: The Theory of Tropes in Anthropology. Stanford CA: Stanford University Press.

Foucault, Michel. 1973. The Birth of the Clinic: Archaeology of Medical Perception. London: Tavistock Publications.

———. 1978. Discipline and Punish: The Birth of the Prison. New York: Pantheon.

Gadamer, Hans-Georg. 1975. Truth and Method. New York: Seabury.

Geertz, Clifford. 1973. The Interpretation of Cultures. New York: Basic Books.

Giddens, Anthony. 1986. The Constitution of Society: Outline of a Theory of Structuration. Cambridge: Polity Press.

Ginzburg, Carlo. 1980. The Cheese and the Worms: The Cosmos of a Sixteenth-Century Miller. Baltimore MD: Johns Hopkins University Press.

Habermas, Jürgen. 1984. The Theory of Communicative Action. Vol. 1: Reason and the Rationalization of Society. Boston: Beacon Press.

Hunt, Lynn, ed. 1989. The New Cultural History. Berkeley: University of California Press.

Husserl, Edmund. 1973. Cartesian Meditations: An Introduction to Phenomenology. The Hague: Martinus Nijhoff.

Hymes, Dell, ed. 1969. Reinventing Anthropology. New York: Random House.

———. 1974. Foundations in Sociolinguistics: An Ethnographic Approach. Philadelphia: University of Pennsylvania Press.

Labov, William. 1972. Sociolinguistic Patterns (Conduct and Communication). Philadelphia: University of Pennsylvania Press.

Lévi-Strauss, Claude. 1963. Structural Anthropology. New York: Basic Books.

———. 1969. Elementary Structures of Kinship. Boston: Beacon Press.

Lévy-Bruhl, Lucien. 1965. The "Soul" of the Primitive. London: George Allen and Unwin.

Lowenthal, David. 1985. The Past Is a Foreign Country. Cambridge: Cambridge University Press.

Lyotard, Jean-François. 1984. The Postmodern Condition: A Report on Knowledge. Minneapolis: University of Minnesota Press.

Moore, Henrietta L., and Todd Sanders, eds. 2014. Anthropology in Theory: Issues in Epistemology. Oxford: Wiley Blackwell.

Ricoeur, Paul. 1970. Freud and Philosophy: An Essay on Interpretation. New Haven CT: Yale University Press.

———. 1971. The Model of a Text: Meaningful Action Considered as a Text. Social Research 38(3):529–562.

———. 1974. The Conflict of Interpretations: Essays in Hermeneutics. Evanston IL: Northwestern University Press.

Roseberry, William. 1982. Balinese Cockfights and the Seduction of Anthropology. Social Research 49(4):1013–1028.

Sahlins, Marshall. 1985. Islands of History. Chicago: University of Chicago Press.

Tyler, Stephen A. 1978. The Said and the Unsaid: Mind, Meaning and Culture. New York: Academic Books.

Ulin, Robert C. 1996. Vintages and Traditions: An Ethnohistory of Southwest French Wine Cooperatives. Washington DC: Smithsonian Institution Press.

——. 2001. Understanding Cultures. 2nd ed. Perspectives in Anthropology and Social Theory. Boston: Blackwell Publishers.

Whorf, Benjamin Lee. 1956. Language, Thought, and Reality. Cambridge MA: MIT Press.

Winch, Peter. 1958. The Idea of a Social Science and Its Relation to Philosophy. London: Routledge and Kegan Paul.

Wittgenstein, Ludwig. 1961. Tractatus Logico-Philosophicus. London: Routledge and Kegan Paul.

——. 1965. The Blue and Brown Books. New York: Harper and Row.

Wolf, Eric. 1999. Envisioning Power: Ideologies of Dominance and Crisis. Berkeley: University of California Press.

8

Westermarck and the Diverse Roots of Relativism

Cultural relativism is arguably an older concept than institutionalized anthropology. There are foreshadowings of it in the work of Herodotus, Protagoras, Sextus Empiricus, Johann Gottfried Herder, and Wilhelm von Humboldt. However, the genealogy of the concept in modern American anthropology may, as Regna Darnell shows (2001:39, 40), be correctly traced back to Boas's 1889 article, "On Alternating Sounds," which drew attention to the ethnocentrism that can result when scholars from our speech community apperceive one sound in another supposedly primitive language as two alternating sounds (e.g., Inuit *mv* as *m* and *v*) and claim that speakers of that language don't follow consistent rules of pronunciation (see also Boon 2010 for an excellent discussion). Relativism was developed in various ways in the work of Boas (notably, *The Mind of Primitive Man*), Sapir, Benedict, Mead, Whorf, and Herskovits. It has persisted in the work of more recent scholars, including Clifford Geertz and his "anti-anti-relativist followers."

Most of us are familiar with the role of cultural relativism in the American tradition, but we are less aware of its presence in other anthropologies. Notably, Rodney Needham (1972) and Stanley Tambiah (1990) have claimed that relativism was a major theme in the writings of the much misunderstood Lucien Lévy-Bruhl, with whose work E. E. Evans-Pritchard engaged in his writings about the mishaps that beset Azande granaries. Perhaps the most neglected version of relativism in anthropology was promulgated by the Finnish, Swedish-speaking philosopher and anthropologist Edward Westermarck, one of Malinowski's teachers, who wrote a book called *Ethical Relativity* in 1932 that was the culmination of more than forty years' work. Curiously, Westermarck's writings advocated ideas that today are associated with individuals who vigorously attack relativism, namely, sociobiologists and evolutionary psychologists. His relativism was Darwinian, whereas Boas's was grounded in the German idealist tradition (see Kluckhohn and Prufer 1959).

Relativism, whatever we may prefer to think and feel as relativist anthropologists, has frequently been attacked both within and outside our discipline. Opposition to something they call(ed) relativism may be said to unite E. O. Wilson, Mary Daly, Paul Johnson, Marvin Harris, Pope Benedict, Richard Dawkins, Frances Mascia-Lees, Derek Freeman, and Robin Fox. Are all members of this unlikely band actually opposed to the same "thing"? This incongruous band of antirelativists includes Christians, secular feminists, religious feminists, cultural materialists, sundry opponents of "postmodernism," and supporters of sociobiology and evolutionary psychology. The relativisms that most of them oppose have a theoretical foundation that is different from Westermarck's, inasmuch as most are not Darwinist and some are antipositivist.

Perhaps there is a vagueness, indeed a relativity, about relativism that needs to be noted before we proceed further. Obviously, Richard Feinberg (2007) is quite correct when he says that there is "no such thing" as cultural relativism, because it is in fact many things. He himself distinguishes between contextual, empirical, and epistemological relativism (Feinberg 2001, 2007). In an important article that appeared thirty years ago, Melford Spiro (1986) distinguished between descriptive relativism, normative relativism (including both cognitive and moral/ethical relativism), and epistemological relativism. In an encyclopedia article on moral relativism, Emrys Westacott (n.d.) distinguishes between descriptive relativism, cultural relativism, ethical nonrealism, ethical noncognitivism, metaethical relativism, and normative relativism. He manages to fit Ruth Benedict into three of these pigeonholes.

These distinctions do not reflect a form of mindless nominalism.[1] It is important to know what kind of relativism one is writing or talking about. Moral relativism, the subject of this article, is only one important aspect of cultural relativism in anthropology. While most cultural relativists are explicitly or implicitly moral relativists (at least to some degree), a moral relativist such as Westermarck may not be concerned with the relativity of other aspects of culture. Linguistic relativism and cognitive relativism are other important traditions. Linguistic relativists (Whorfians and neo-Whorfians) may not necessarily concern themselves with the relativity of norms and ethics. The words "relativity" and "relativism" only came into general usage in anthropology in the 1920s, and there may be room for disagreement as to when and in whose writing anthropological relativism first appeared. There are many nonanthropological relativisms and relativities that need not be cross-cultural, and sometimes they are confused with cultural relativism. When Richard Dawkins attacks cultural relativism, is he attacking sociocultural anthropologists, postmodernists in general, or advocates of the "strong program" in the sociology of science? He is probably most concerned with all those who claim that knowledge in the hard sciences is not specially privileged.

Many anthropologists would endorse Spiro's typology of weak and strong forms of cultural relativism, even though only a minority might endorse his conclusions. The key variable in his analysis was the degree of cultural determinism one is willing to accept. One does not have to be an extreme cultural determinist to accept that many ideas, institutions, norms, practices, customs, modes of socialization, utterances, and so on differ widely from culture to culture, but they usually make sense within the cultural context(s) in which they are found. This is descriptive or contextual relativism, a position that most anthropological traditions would endorse.

Normative relativism, according to Spiro, implies that radical differences in the ways people think about the world or in the ways they judge right and wrong mirror radical differences (sometimes incompatibilities) between cultures. Epistemological relativism is a strong form of relativism for which Spiro had particular disdain. It assigns no power to human nature and sees each human as a tabula rasa on which disparate cultures, reflecting different histories and divergent worldviews, inscribe a specific pattern. According to Spiro, this form of particularism and determinism (rooted, we should note, in some of the writings of Benedict) was most notably present in the writings of Geertz and Michelle Rosaldo.

All forms of strong cultural relativism have obvious implications for the tasks anthropologists perform. The most obvious is that it is not always easy, and sometimes it may be impossible, to cross the gap between cultures. A strong relativist position may involve a slippage between stating that a custom is right *within* a culture (it fits, it is understandable within a context) and that it is right *for* a culture (adapted from Williams 1972:20–25). This implies a stance of tolerance (at the very least) or justification.

In my view, ethical relativism, as a particular form of cultural relativism, may encompass both weak and strong positions. A weak ethical relativism will demonstrate that societies exhibit differences as to the kinds of actions they approve or suppress, but these differences may be attributed to environmental factors or issues of factual knowledge. The issue of a fundamental difference in social values may not be raised. For strong ethical relativists, however, differences in moral norms and judgments, in the ways different peoples define and react to misconduct, may reflect underlying differences in core values. Such a position is opposed to any objectivist (moral realist) stance that supports the existence of universal moral standards or truths. If the weak ethical relativist may find it a little difficult to pass judgment on the moral standards of members of some other cultures, the strong ethical relativist might find it impossible, because there would be no scale of comparison. Westermarck, we shall note, supported a version of the strong position, but with important qualifications.

The most explicit Boasian writing on cultural relativism was the work of Melville Herskovits, and his most important writings on the subject were republished in a collection that appeared shortly after his death (Herskovits 1972[1956]).[2] Herskovits, like many of his contemporaries such as Benedict, seemed at times to espouse a strong relativism, but, confronted with the rise of Nazism, he was forced to state where he thought relativism's limits lay. On the one hand, he stated: "While the fact that every culture has an accepted code governing attitudes and conduct has been empirically established, the absolute worth of any of these codes, except for a given society in terms of its own culture, is amenable to no such empirical valuation" (Herskovits 1972[1956]:89). This assertion would imply that criticisms of other cultures' moral standards could not be made from an objective standpoint, indeed, that there might be no meaningful way of making them. On the other hand, just a few pages later we find a qualification of this argument that indicates that understanding the other's moral standards and behavior does not necessarily imply tolerance of them, particularly when the other is not merely inhumane, according to the standards of one's own culture, but also intolerant of difference:

> Most frequently the question posed is, "Granting the validity of each people's ways of life, and the respect to be accorded these ways by peoples whose values are different, what should we do in the face, let us say, of the Nazi policy of extermination of the German Jews?" The question has unending variants. It is asked about the Soviet work-camps, about the headhunters of Borneo, about the lynching of Negroes in the United States....
>
> These are questions not easy to answer, but not because they pose problems that lie outside the philosophical dialectic of cultural relativism or of practical solutions. To espouse a philosophy based on the scientific findings of cross-cultural study does not imply unilateral tolerance of ideas other than one's own. If one must respect, one must also be respected. What we face is the gigantic task of dealing with man's inhumanity to man. (Herskovits 1972[1956]:93, 94)

Nearly a quarter century earlier Westermarck had attempted his own solution to the problem philosophers have dubbed the *argumentum ad Nazium* (Hocutt 1986; Ressler 2008). The expression is derived from Leo Strauss's phrase *reductio ad Hitlerum*. To understand that solution, we must first gain some understanding of some brilliant albeit flawed pioneering work in moral anthropology.

THE MORAL ANTHROPOLOGY OF EDWARD WESTERMARCK

Recently, David Shankland (2014a) compiled the first edited volume about Westermarck to appear in thirty years. Its title is simply *Westermarck*. There are nine essays, including one that is coauthored; of the ten authors, three are well-known anthropologists (Shankland, who is director of the Royal Anthropological Institute, Maurice Bloch, and Arthur Wolf), two are sociologists, and five are philosophers. The essays cover many details of Westermarck's academic life and some of his most important ideas, but some aspects of his work on sexuality, including his views on homosexuality, are omitted. Two essays by philosophers (Timothy Stroup, editor of a 1982 volume on Westermarck, and Camilla Kronqvist) address the allied themes of subjectivism and relativism in Westermarck's work. These excellent essays are best read by scholars already familiar with Westermarck's writings. Inasmuch as their authors are philosophers, they do not always ask the same questions as anthropologists. Over the years a number of authors, Arthur Wolf being the most prominent, have discussed Westermarck's ideas about incest, but few anthropologists have had anything to say about other aspects of his work. Didier Fassin's important *Companion to Moral Anthropology* (2012) contains a couple of mentions of Westermarck. Fassin tells us that Westermarck did some interesting work, but his contribution was omitted from an article on the founders of moral anthropology because that work has had little influence in the social sciences. On the other hand, in an essay on relativism in Fassin's volume, Richard Schweder tells us that Westermarck was "arguably the deepest and most philosophically sophisticated moral relativist and subjectivist in the history of anthropology" (2012:91). However, Schweder's discussion of Westermarck is basically confined to quoting a passage about moral absolutes. Christer Lindberg (2008:161–164) also has a brief but useful discussion of Westermarck in Henrika Kuklick's *New History of Anthropology*. Lastly, Kuklick herself was beginning work on a project about Westermarck shortly before her untimely death and gave a paper on biology and culture in the work of Westermarck at a session I organized on anthropological relativities for the 2009 AAA.

In our 2004 book, *Irregular Connections*, Harriet Lyons and I discussed Westermarck's significant roles in deconstructing and demolishing Victorian myths about "primitive" sexuality. In the *History of Human Marriage* (1891), which was based on his 1889 doctoral thesis, Westermarck examined the existing ethnographic record in the exhaustive fashion typical of practitioners of the Victorian comparative method, sorting out the wheat of truth from the chaff of rumor. Not all primitive societies were promiscuous. There was enormous variance. Monogamous pair bonding could be found just about everywhere, along with rules prohibiting incest. Rules permitting premarital sex should not be confused with promiscuity, nor should so-called secondary marriage customs among Australian Aborigines. There was no evidence that primitive societies routinely treated women in a worse way than civilized peoples. There was no evidence that matriliny routinely preceded patriliny, nor was it likely that there were societies that did not acknowledge the role of the father in paternity. Many of these arguments had been advanced by others (e.g., Charles Staniland Wake [1889] and Carl Nicolai Starcke [1888]), but never before had they been advanced ensemble in so convincing a fashion. Westermarck claimed that he had begun his thesis as a convinced follower of the British theorists of "mother right" (John Ferguson McLennan [1865], John Lubbock [1870], and Edward Burnett Tylor [1889]), but the facts he had discovered had dissuaded him. Under the influence of Darwin, he may have exaggerated the role of monogamy and male jealousy among higher primates and humans, but it is important to note that he was a supporter of women's rights who believed that there was an urgent need to reform divorce laws in most European societies.

Westermarck was a thoroughgoing atheist who was convinced that Christianity had not exercised a beneficial, improving effect on sexual morality. He became an ally of two English anthropological critics of sexual repression, Havelock Ellis and Ernest Crawley. Westermarck's skeptical attitude toward the dictates of Victorian morality may reflect his own concealed problems. Westermarck taught philosophy in Finland for more than thirty years while holding a position in sociology at the London School of Economics. From the late 1890s right through to the 1920s he also spent summers in Morocco, where he had done fieldwork. It was rumored that in Morocco he was free to be a homosexual, whereas in London in the decades after the Wilde trial and also in Finland that would have been impossible. Because Westermarck was very discrete and a very proper gentleman, we learn little from his autobiography except that he formed emotional ties with some male friends. So our evidence is of the type that X told Y that Westermarck was homosexual, or specifically, for instance, that Malinowski told Raymond Firth, who repeated the remark to J. Ihanus in London in the 1980s. All of this is relevant in that in his two-volume magnum opus, *The Origin and Development of the Moral Ideas* (*Moral Ideas* hereafter), a work addressed to anthropologists and sociologists as well as philosophers, Westermarck advanced the idea that moral truths and judgments that modern societies assume to be universal and absolute are not such at all and that in other cases it seems obvious that there is no consensus (Westermarck 1906, 1908). One example of the latter is human sacrifice, found often in some societies, seldom in others, and usually justified by the need to find a surrogate victim to appease or supplicate powerful forces in times of danger. We might deplore human sacrifice, but some peoples that practice it might deplore our willingness to "sacrifice" our young people in battle. An example of the former is the treatment of homosexuals. In most societies they are not respected, but Christian Europe is particularly harsh in its attitudes toward them. Westermarck reviewed the ethnographic record extensively, pointing out some of the cases (like the *berdaches*) where homosexuals played valued ceremonial roles, as well as societies with single-sex institutions that tolerated or condoned single-sex mating when members of the opposite sex were unavailable (including the relationship of some Islamic teachers with their scribes in Morocco, as well as ancient Sparta). In his opinion, all humans had bisexual capabilities at the outset of adolescence, albeit heterosexual instincts usually prevailed. There were some humans, however, in whom homosexual drives dominated most of the time and others who were willing to engage in same-sex relations in the absence of the opposite sex. In *Moral Ideas* Westermarck very rarely if ever used words such as "relativity" and "relativism" to describe these arguments (a search of the PDF of volume 2 revealed that neither word was used in the book). However, very similar material is used again in his late work, *Ethical Relativity* (1932), a book primarily addressed to philosophers. "Relativity" and "relativism" by then were terms in common usage, no doubt thanks to Max Planck and Einstein, although they were sometimes deployed some decades before their use in physics. Westermarck may have been the first scholar to use the phrase "ethical relativity" (Stroup 1980:32 after Stace 1967:249). Once one applies a label to something, it more readily becomes something good to think.

I am therefore suggesting that in Westermarck's writing the *emergent practice of relativism*, the rigorous deployment of the comparative method to demonstrate that the ethnographic record did not support Victorian moral absolutism as manifested in theoretical formulations of primitive promiscuity and moral evolution, preceded the explicit *naming of ethical relativity as the core theoretical concept* by as much as four decades. The impetus for the move to relativism perhaps had some connection with personal factors in Westermarck's life and his professed humanism, but he would have argued that his positions were based on critical reading and analysis that overthrew theoretical formulations that he himself had initially accepted (variations of the matrilineal theory).[3]

It must also be noted that relativism and concomitant egalitarian beliefs were not overnight creations. Westermarck still talked of "lower races"—he did not defy convention in this regard. While he rejected reports that primitives were oversexed, he gave credence to reports that they were sexually inactive at some points of the year because of poor environmental circumstances and that they had a rutting season. In similar fashion, Robert Lowie and some other senior Boasians were not at first sure that primitives and moderns had the same degree of intelligence. Even in 1932 the self-described relativist Westermarck, just like Malinowski, still utilized a received vocabulary that might make twenty-first-century anthropologists cringe just a little.

Westermarck became interested in ethics in the late 1880s. His first interest was in dilemmas about such matters as the degree of kindness a bad man should receive (von Wright 1982[1965]:38). According to G. H. von Wright, the famous Finnish philosopher who consulted relevant archival records in Finland, Westermarck proved able, after some early theoretical forays that were false trails, to revise, refine, and develop the core of his ideas about moral judgments between 1895 and 1897. Westermarck delivered a paper to the Philosophical Society in Helsinki, revised it in London, and eventually published it in 1900 in *Mind* with the title "The Predicate in Moral Judgments" (von Wright 1982[1965]:45–48). The ideas expressed in this paper were further refined in the next few years by Westermarck's own fieldwork in Morocco and by his contact with some prominent British academics, including the psychologists James Sully and Alexander Faulkner Shand.

Moral judgments are the product of emotions or sentiments (groupings of emotions) of disapproval and approval occasioned by the actions and perceived actions (and the personalities that produce them) of other members of one's group. Emotions of disapproval are more common than those of approval. Obviously, not all such reactions are moral. Revenge may not be moral at all. Gratitude is not necessarily moral. A feeling of approval or disapproval of somebody's actions becomes moral because an impartial, disinterested third party would have the same reaction as me to those actions of which I approve or disapprove. That person might be guided by reason and by the advice of others embedded in custom. Although the source of moral judgments and/or concepts is ultimately emotional, the individual(s) who makes the judgment may be guided by rational considerations (or rationally grounded beliefs) toward his reaction, and the judgment itself is refined by the reasoning process, does not reflect personal bias, and should conform to custom. There is something in the *actor's* performance that evokes the moral reaction by a disinterested party. One should note the distinction Westermarck makes between judgments of disapproval/approval phrased in the language of duty—the actions are "right" or "wrong"—and judgments of gratitude with predicates such as "good" (see Kronqvist 2014:132–134; Nielsen 1982:126). Retributive emotions, varying from resentment and aggression to cooperation and altruism, contribute to the survival of the species (Stroup 1982b:117).

Inasmuch as moral concepts and judgments are based on emotions, they cannot be based on any body of universal, absolute truths, because emotions cannot be described as true or false. However, every community perceives its morality as grounded in objective truth. Westermarck's subjectivist position fits into the broad taxon that Westacott (n.d.) describes as ethical nonrealism.

Very obviously, many questions are unresolved in Westermarck's theory of moral judgments and concepts, such as the boundaries between emotions and reason, the individual and the social, and the existence of a biologically rooted altruistic sentiment. For all that, the theory may be no more flawed than other theories of moral judgment.

The *relativism* intrinsic to Westermarck's position is evident throughout *Moral Ideas*, but it is obviously explicit in *Ethical Relativity*, a book that is freer of evolutionist baggage. The first part of the book consists of a protracted attack on ethical absolutism and universalism in many forms (utilitarian, evolutionary, and Kantian). The rest of the book is concerned with Westermarck's own views.

Nobody, he argues, has proved the existence of any god or universal principle that would stand as the guarantor or standard of all moral concepts everywhere. At first sight the considerable variation between many moral rules in different societies on issues such as infanticide, notions of guilt, shame, and responsibility might seem both clear evidence of the absence of universal moral standards and clear support for a strong relativist claim about differences in fundamental values. However, such a claim might not be secure, because one might very conceivably explain the variation by differences in facts and the interpretation of facts, rather than by differences in values. Society A might not treat infanticide as a major crime, whereas society B might see it as a major offense.

It could be argued that both societies accepted as a universal principle the imperative of preserving human life, but society A accepted an exception in cases where there was not enough food to sustain the population. Similarly, society A might condemn suicides, but society B might venerate those who committed suicide to save the lives and honor of their compatriots. Society A might hold that it was fair to punish someone for a murder for which he was knowingly responsible but not for a death that was involuntarily caused. Society B might expel or shun a person who is held responsible for an involuntary death (perhaps by disease, perhaps after a taboo action) because he or she has polluted the community and is being punished by the gods. Here differences in the allocation of responsibility reflect differences in religious belief and a lack of scientific knowledge in society B, but neither society A nor B believes that people should suffer for causing the death of others unless they are in some way responsible.

In Westermarck's view, the absolutist position could be disproved in one set of cases only. Societies differed in the extent and inclusiveness of their moral universe, and this difference was due to variation in sentiments. One had full ethical responsibilities only toward those one considered to be human. As human communities expanded with the development of civilization, the altruistic sentiment was necessarily extended. Accordingly, it became possible to make statements such as "all men are brothers" and to extend compassion toward animals. There are inconsistencies in Westermarck's position, because he does at times seem to imply that larger, modern societies are better because of the extension and development of the altruistic sentiment, whereas at other times he clearly emphasizes that he is talking of a mere difference.

Despite his disbelief in the existence of ethical absolutes and universals, Westermarck did not believe that moral concepts were totally random. This was because all humans were members of the same species, and there were some moral issues that all societies had to tackle, such as theft and homicide, however they were conceived. All humans shared basically similar drives and sentiments such as sympathy and altruism, whatever the variance in norms caused by changing circumstances, reason, and custom.

Westermarck's emphasis on drives, emotions, and sentiments reflected his Darwinian allegiance and his friendship with the psychologists Sully and Shand. Doubtless through Westermarck's influence, Malinowski also utilized the ideas of Shand. The mixture of Darwin, early social psychology, sociology, ethnographic insights based on comparative analysis, and fieldwork, to which we could add a close reading of Hume and Adam Smith, produced the unique mélange that entertains the reader of *Moral Ideas* and *Ethical Relativity*. Inasmuch as structural functionalism was based on Durkheim's sociological method, and the Boasian tradition in the United States rejected all forms of biological reductionism as well as the presentation of data typical of the old comparative method ("among the Wotjobaluk . . . but among the Narrinyeri"), Westermarck's anthropology went so far out of fashion that his contributions have been neglected until recently.

It must be noted that there are echoes of Westermarck in the work of contemporary evolutionary psychologists such as Steven Pinker (in *The Better Angels of Our Nature*), inasmuch as Westermarck's ideas about the expansion of altruism somewhat resemble Pinker's ideas about the historical movement toward more peaceful societies. However, Westermarck's argument does not depend on the application of Hobbesian notions about the State of Nature, does not see Leviathan as a solution, does not rely on dubious statistics, and does not use extreme cases to distort the ethnographic record. Westermarck is not in Pinker's index.

We have observed that Westermarck was able in part to escape the accusation that strong ethical relativism causes moral nihilism by pointing to the commonalities that all humans share. However, like Herskovits many years later, he recognized all the conundrums that relativism creates. His answer was that honest relativism was a better strategy than an absolutist (or objectivist) lie or half-truth. One could view the customs of others and one's own group more clearly from a relativist standpoint. The tolerance that resulted was often desirable, and Westermarck always worked to diminish ethnocentrism. But how did he deal with behavior that most of us would find intolerable, such as Aztec human sacrifice, the Ruandan genocide, and the Holocaust?

We are back to the *argumentum ad Nazium*, a phrase that is almost anachronistic in Westermarck's case. As Mark Ressler (2008) has also noted in an excellent paper, Westermarck set out his position on the *argumentum* in an admirably clear way:

> I think that ethical writers are often inclined to overrate the influence of moral theory on moral practice, but if there is any such influence at all, it seems to me that ethical subjectivism, instead of being a danger, is more likely to be an advantage to morality.
>
> Could it be brought home to people that there is no absolute standard in morality, they would perhaps be on the one hand more tolerant and on the other more critical in their judgments. (Westermarck 1932:59 as quoted in Ressler 2008:5, 6)

For example, if I want to confront a custom I do not like in another culture, I will be more successful, given that emotion depends on cognition, if I understand that custom's psychological basis and historical roots, rather than if I merely state that the custom is what its practitioners consider moral. Westermarck was of course asking how we would understand and intelligently explain such a custom rather than outlining the practical steps we might take and the cultural knowledge we would need to persuade others to understand the error of their ways (cf. Harriet Lyons's [1981] first article on clitoridectomy). This is a good insight, although it is partly ruined by Westermarck's reference to "ignorance and superstition, as well as sentimental likes and dislikes" later in the same paragraph. As an atheist, Westermarck found it increasingly difficult to adopt a relativist attitude personally toward religion in any society.

My concern in this chapter has been to call attention to an alternate path toward relativism in anthropology and to recall the nearly forgotten figure who cleared it. I have suggested that Westermarck's relativism, like that of the Boasians, was based on strong, ethnographic comparison but that it was also personally and politically motivated. Westermarck's biological reductionism offered him a partial way out of the apparent aporia presented by ethical relativism. Otherwise, his contribution was to suggest that relativism led to a more honest and productive approach to cross-cultural moral dilemmas because it encouraged both tolerance and criticism, where appropriate. For those interested in such approaches, he pointed the way to an ethnographically informed evolutionary psychology, a pathway that may never be taken.

NOTES

I am grateful to Dr. David Shankland for drawing my attention to the website that includes his plenary address to the June 2014 meeting of the ASA. It is an impressive introduction to Westermarck's life and work, as well as a call for an overdue reevaluation of his contribution to social anthropology.

I first wrote on this topic for a session I organized for the 2008 AAA meetings. I have revised my ideas substantially since that time because the leisure of retirement has enabled me to undertake a slower and more informed reading of the original sources. This is therefore a very different paper from the one I wrote then.

1. Such lists appear to be de rigueur in papers on relativism in recent times. When I first wrote down my own list, I had forgotten the one that appears in Geertz's (1984) well-known paper on "anti-anti-relativism."

2. Herskovits's relativism in most respects accords with Franz Boas's teachings, but through his tentative explorations in ethical relativism (as outlined in this text) he may have ventured into areas Boas preferred to avoid. Herbert Lewis (2001:451, 461) states that Boas denied being an ethical relativist because he believed in certain "fundamental truths" that were common to all mankind. According to John Webber Cook

(1999), Boas (unlike Westermarck, who did not believe in moral universals) was not a true relativist but merely someone engaged in a pragmatic critique of ethnocentrism. However, as I stress, dissimilar varieties of relativistic theory follow some years after engagement in quite similar critical practices. Benedict, arguably, was an ethical relativist, but her "patterns" of culture involved so much more than moral values (Edel [1982] makes this point very clearly).

3. In similar fashion, Boasian relativism existed for years before Herskovits began to theorize about it. The use of ethnography to counter ethnocentric ideas about matriliny, representational and abstract art, "primitive" and modern thought, and "primitive" and modern languages was from the 1890s on a key aspect of the Boasian tradition. However, Herskovits's key essays date to the 1940s, 1950s, and 1960s.

REFERENCES

Bloch, Maurice. 2014. Westermarck's Theory of Morality in His and Our Time. *In* Westermarck. David Shankland, ed. Pp. 116–123. Canon Pyon: Sean Kingston Publishing.

Boas, Franz. 1889. On Alternating Sounds. American Anthropologist 2(1):47–54.

———. 1911. The Mind of Primitive Man. New York: Macmillan Company.

Boon, James. 2010. On Alternating Boasians: Generational Connections. Proceedings of the American Philosophical Society 154(1):20–30.

Cook, John W. 1999. Morality and Cultural Differences. Oxford: Oxford University Press.

Darnell, Regna. 2001. Invisible Genealogies: A History of Americanist Anthropology. Lincoln: University of Nebraska Press.

Edel, Abraham. 1982. Westermarck's Formulation of Ethical Relativity, in Twentieth Century Perspective. *In* Edward Westermarck: Essays on His Life and Works. Timothy Stroup, ed. Pp. 99–121. Helsinki: Philosophical Society of Finland.

Fassin, Didier. 2012. Introduction: Toward a Critical Moral Anthropology. *In* A Companion to Moral Anthropology. Didier Fassin, ed. Pp. 1–18. Chichester, West Sussex: Wiley, Blackwell.

Feinberg, Richard. 2001. Introduction: Schneider's Cultural Analysis of Kinship and Its Implications for Anthropological Relativism. *In* The Cultural Analysis of Kinship: The Legacy of David M. Schneider. Richard Feinberg, ed. Pp. 1–31. Urbana: University of Illinois Press.

———. 2007. Dialectics of Culture: Relativism in Popular and Anthropological Discourse. Anthropological Quarterly 80(3):777–790.

Geertz, Clifford. 1984. Distinguished Lecture: Anti-anti-relativism. American Anthropologist 86(2):263–278.

Herskovits, Melville. 1972[1956]. Cultural Diversity and World Peace. *In* Cultural Relativism: Perspectives in Cultural Pluralism. Frances Herskovits, ed. Pp. 71–96. New York: Random House.

Hocutt, Max. 1986. Must Relativists Tolerate Evil? The Philosophical Forum 17(3):188–200.

Ihanus, Juhani. 1999. Multiple Origins: Edward Westermarck in Search of Mankind. Frankfurt am Main: Peter Lang.

Kluckhohn, Clyde, and Olaf Prufer. 1959. Influences during the Formative Years. *In* The Anthropology of Franz Boas. Memoir No. 89 of the American Anthropological Association. Walter Goldschmidt, ed. Pp. 4–28. San Francisco: American Anthropological Association.

Kronqvist, Camilla. 2014. The Relativity of Westermarck's Moral Relativism. *In* Westermarck. David Shankland, ed. Pp. 124–144. Canon Pyon: Sean Kingston Publishing.

Lewis, Herbert S. 2001. The Passion of Franz Boas. American Anthropologist 103(2):447–467.

Lindberg, Christer. 2008. Anthropology on the Periphery: The Early Schools of Nordic Anthropology. *In* A New History of Anthropology. Henrika Kuklick, ed. Pp. 161–172. Oxford: Blackwell.

Lubbock, Sir John. 1870[1978]. The Origin of Civilization and the Primitive Condition of Man. Edited and with an introduction by Peter Rivière. Chicago: University of Chicago Press.

Lyons, Andrew, and Harriet Lyons. 2004. Irregular Connections: A History of Anthropology and Sexuality. Lincoln: University of Nebraska Press.

Lyons, Harriet. 1981. Anthropologists, Moralities and Relativities: The Problem of Genital Mutilations. Canadian Review of Sociology and Anthropology 18(4):499–518.

McLennan, John F. 1865[1970]. Primitive Marriage: An Inquiry into the Origin of the Form of Capture in Marriage Ceremonies. Edited and with an introduction by Peter Rivière. Chicago: University of Chicago Press.

Needham, Rodney. 1972. Belief, Language and Experience. Oxford: Basil Blackwell & Mott.

Nielsen, Kai. 1982. Problems for Westermarck's Subjectivism. *In* Edward Westermarck: Essays on His Life and Works. Timothy Stroup, ed. Helsinki: Philosophical Society of Finland.

Pinker, Steven. 2011. The Better Angels of Our Nature: Why Violence Has Declined. New York: Viking.

Ressler, Mark. 2008. Relativism and Tolerance Revisited. http//www.mark.ressler.com/doc/Relativism-and-tolerance-Revisited.pdf.

Schweder, Richard A. 2012. Relativism and Universalism. In A Companion to Moral Anthropology. Didier Fassin, ed. Chichester, West Sussex: Wiley-Blackwell.

Shankland, David, ed. 2014a. Westermarck. Occasional Paper No. 44 of the Royal Anthropological Institute. Published in association with the Anglo-Finnish Society. Canon Pyon: Sean Kingston Publishing.

———. 2014b. Westermarck, Moral Behaviour and Ethical Relativity. Plenary Address, ASA Conference "Anthropology and the Enlightenment." Edinburgh, June 2014. Yearbook of the Centre for Cosmopolitan Studies, 2014(1). http://ojs.st-andrews.ac.uk/index.php/ycs/article/view/953/771.

Spiro, Melford E. 1986. Cultural Relativism and the Future of Anthropology. Cultural Anthropology 1(3):259–286.

Stace, Walter T. 1967. Man against Darkness and Other Essays. Pittsburgh PA: University of Pittsburgh Press.

Starcke, Carl Nicolai. 1888[1976]. Die primitive Familie in ihrer Entstehung und Entwicklung. Leipzig: Brockhaus. English edition [1976]: The Primitive Family and Its Origin and Development. Translated and edited by Rodney Needham. Chicago: University of Chicago Press.

Stroup, Timothy. 1980. Westermarck's Ethical Relativism. Ajatus 38:31–71.

———, ed. 1982a. Edward Westermarck: Essays on His Life and Works. Acta Philosophica Fennica, vol. 34. Helsinki: Philosophical Society of Finland.

———. 1982b. Soft Subjectivism. In Edward Westermarck: Essays on His Life and Works. Pp. 99–121. Helsinki: Philosophical Society of Finland.

———. 2014. Looking Backwards and Forwards. In Westermarck. David Shankland, ed. Pp. 106–115. Canon Pyon: Sean Kingston Publishing.

Tambiah, Stanley. 1990. Magic, Science and Religion, and the Scope of Rationality. Cambridge: Cambridge University Press.

Tylor, Edward Burnett. 1889. On a Method of Investigating the Development of Institutions Applied to Laws of Marriage and Descent. Journal of the Anthropological Institute of Great Britain and Ireland 18:245–272.

Von Wright, Georg Henrik. 1982[1965]. The Origin and Development of Westermarck's Moral Philosophy. Anthony Landon, trans. In Edward Westermarck: Essays on His Life and Works. Timothy Stroup, ed. Pp. 25–61. Helsinki: Philosophical Society of Finland.

Wake, Charles Staniland. 1889[1967]. The Development of Marriage and Kinship. Edited and with an introduction by Rodney Needham. Chicago: University of Chicago Press.

Westacott, Emrys. N.d. Moral Relativism. *In* Internet Encyclopedia of Philosophy. James Fieser and Bradley Dowden, eds. University of Tennessee at Martin. http/www.iep.utm.edu/moral-re/.

Westermarck, Edward. 1901[1891]. The History of Human Marriage. 3rd ed. London: Macmillan.

———. 1906 and 1908. The Origin and Development of the Moral Ideas. 2 vols. London: Macmillan.

———. 1929. Memories of My Life. London: George Allen and Unwin.

———. 1932. Ethical Relativity. New York: Harcourt, Brace and Company.

Williams, Bernard. 1972. Morality: An Introduction to Ethics. New York: Harper and Row.

Wolf, Arthur P. 2014. Westermarck and the Westermarck Hypothesis. *In* Westermarck. David Shankland, ed. Pp. 96–103. Canon Pyon: Sean Kingston Publishing.

OLGA GLINSKII

9

Heritage Gatherers

*Peasant-Mania Ethnography and Pre–World
War I National Awakeners of Ukraine*

The decades leading up to the First World War were marked with profound concerns over the identities and loyalties of the peasantry in
eastern Europe.[1] Particularly after the revolutions of 1848 swept across
Europe, the looming question of uncertain allegiances of the peasant
masses came to be one of the most pressing issues for the pre–World
War I revolutionaries, the national awakeners, and the ruling elite in
both the Russian and Austro-Hungarian Empires. In this formative
context, Ukrainian national developments are inextricably intertwined
with their Polish and Russian counterparts, on the one hand, and pre–
World War I empires and dynastic loyalties, on the other.

In one of the most useful formulations of the reconfiguring and
reimagined identities and shifting allegiances in pre–World War I eastern Europe, Paul Robert Magocsi (2002b:38–54) places Ukrainian
national developments within the larger European context of enduring dynamic encounters between the hierarchical framework of multiple loyalties, on the one hand, and mutually exclusive identities, on the
other. This embattled coexistence of ideologies persisted, albeit under
different circumstances, under Soviet rule and even endured after the
Soviet collapse, with rather extraordinary consequences.

Magocsi points to the pre–World War I heritage-gathering ethnographic practices of local intelligentsia as integral to the newly emerging
conceptions of national culture and the reconfigurations of the relationship between nation(s) and empire(s). Other prominent scholars
of nationalism in eastern Europe have also pointed out the importance
of such activities in the decades leading up to the great war in what Eric

Hobsbawm and Terence Ranger (2012[1983]) term the "invention of tradition" on a massive scale. Indeed, Ernest Gellner's (1998) culminating account of a life-long fascination with Bronisław Malinowski's formative experiences in pre–World War I Habsburg-ruled Galicia features the foundational role of eastern European scholarly ethnography of peasant life on emanating national "awakenings." While the awakeners themselves did not always identify with the cultures they examined (Hroch 1985), a number of ethnographers actually converted from one national identity to another. In short, the emerging national consciousness of the vicarious awakeners was in an unprecedented state of flux. One could start out identifying as a Pole and then shift to a Ruthenian or "Little Russian" identity, or switch from an "exclusively" Ukrainian to the Pan-Slavic orientation propagated within the Russian Empire.

The dynamic state of flux is perhaps epitomized in the infamous fight between Malinowski and his compatriot and closest friend, Stas Witkiewicz, on Malinowski's research trip to Australia. The two were very close during Malinowski's youth in Habsburg-ruled Galicia, where they attended Jagiellonian University in the heyday of Krakow's Young Poland movement and spent their summers in the small mountain town of Zakopane, the epicenter of the Galician wave of the nationally inspired populist movement known as "peasant mania."

When news of the war reached the two friends in Australia, Stas abandoned the research expedition to fight in the war. Curiously enough, he chose to fight on the side of the Russian army. While this is often explained away by the fact that Stas was a Russian citizen by virtue of being born in Warsaw, which was part of the Russian Empire at the time, his decision seemed quite strange. It greatly upset not only Malinowski but also many of their patriotically minded Polish friends in Krakow and Zakopane and had devastating consequences for Stas's relationship with his father, who never spoke to his son again.

In a curious way, Stas embodies the key issues regarding the ongoing reconfigurations of groups and their contested and competing identities in the volatile pre–World War I climate of eastern Europe. His poignant letter to Malinowski reveals tremendous existential angst regarding competing identities and questions of national, historical, familial, and dynastic loyalties abruptly intensified by the war:

That handful of riflemen fighting for a piece of Galicia in alliance with the Germans . . . is a tragic monstrosity. The soldierly honour which makes them stick to Austria and fight on the German side could in itself be a beautiful thing but under the present circumstances it's just horrible. Thus in our abnormal situation merits turn into crimes against the spirit of the nation. Being quite alone with my thoughts about Russia and the need to take its side against the Germans I've lived through some awful moments pondering this question. . . . Right now the conscience of a Pole is a terrible thing. (Witkiewicz 2000[1914]:274)

At first glance we might take the "abnormal situation" that turns merits into crimes to mean the war. However, the collective historical "conscience of a Pole" had been in anguish since the bemoaned partitions of the Polish-Lithuanian Commonwealth, which erased the "historical" Polish nation from the maps of Europe and inspired continuing uprisings and insurrections well into the second half of the nineteenth century. Stas goes on to elaborate on the riflemen movement of nationalist militia groups in Galicia, who nonetheless chose to fight on the side of the Austrian army when the war broke out. He says he understands them but does not agree with their actions, and he describes his alienation from friends and family because of his decision to fight in the Russian army and his frustration that Malinowski did not seem sympathetic to his predicament.

While Malinowski (1989[1967]:34) declared the fight to be the *finis amicitiae* (end of friendship), the "Stas problem," as he sometimes referred to it in his diary, continued to torment the young ethnographer for some time, not only as the loss of a dear friend but also as something indicative of the overarching issues surrounding the outbreak of the war. Though Malinowski never explicitly tackled the subject of nationalism until his final publication, *Freedom and Civilization* (1944), the issue concerned him deeply. In another work, he points to his pre–World War I Galician past as the context under which he learned about nationalism, offers gratitude and praise to the Habsburg solutions to pre–World War I nationality problems, and identifies his childhood home as the "cradle of modern European nationalism":

It might be useful to define Central and Eastern European nationalism—which is also the nationalism of Ireland and of Turkey, of India and of modern Africa—in terms which I learnt, not so much as a student of anthropology and of social science, but above all as a Pole, brought up in the classical home, indeed the cradle of modern European nationalism. To us pre-war Poles, nationality meant allegiance to the language, the traditions, the customs and the ideas of our fore-fathers, as distinct from any political obligations and loyalties. By two at least of the powers who had divided and annexed our territory and absorbed our population, the whole political machinery of the State was directed toward de-nationalization. . . .

The free exercise of our own language, our own religion, of our own domestic institutions; self-government in local affairs of the village, the town and the province, was to the pre-war Pole a political paradise. Something of the kind we had within the old Austrian Empire, and I should like to put it here on record that no honest and sincere Pole would have given anything but praise to the political regime of the old Dual Monarchy. Pre-war Austria in its federal constitution presented, in my opinion a sound solution to all minority problems. (Malinowski 1935:viii–ix)

In *Language and Solitude* (1998) Ernest Gellner posits that the nationalist-inspired eastern European populist style of ethnography must have influenced Malinowski's development of his famous methodology, as well as his notion of "culture as unity." Gellner argues that Malinowski partially rejected and partially incorporated Polish neo-Romanticism into the empirical functionalist approach and outlines the efforts of Polish intelligentsia in the pre–World War I Austro-Hungarian province of Galicia to record and codify peasant ways of life. Considered as exemplars of the "purest" form of national culture, peasant "traditions" were meant to form the basis for the new nation-state and the national system of education (Gellner 1998:130). Often a specific region—like the small mountain town of Zakopane, where Malinowski spent the summers of his youth—was selected as the embodiment of the national culture and presented as a distilled and unified basis for national identity. Taking this further, I try to contextualize the developments of pre–World War I ethnography on territories of present-day Ukraine by offering a selective look at the ethnographic practices of the "peasant-mania" intelligentsia in the Russian and Austro-Hungarian Empires.

Known as *khlopomania* (Russian) or *chlopomania* (Polish), the populist movement came about as the sons of the demoted nobility entered university life in Kiev. This newly developing generation of intellectuals began to offer scholarly formulations for a "return" to their Little Russian peasant folk roots (Berestenko and Shamara 2012; Katchanovski et al. 2013:256; Magocsi 2010:390). A similar movement later became popular among the intelligentsia of the Young Poland movement in the Austro-Hungarian province of Galicia. The peasant-mania intelligentsia propagated love for the "folk" and began living among the peasants in the countryside and participating in village lifeways and traditions as part of a process for understanding and developing their own national identity. The founding members relied on reflexive ethnography to facilitate a kind of self-conscious shift in ethnonational identification.

PEASANT MANIA IN THE RIGHT BANK OF THE RUSSIAN EMPIRE

After the final partitions of the Polish-Lithuanian Commonwealth (1795), the Right Bank territory of present-day Ukraine (Kiev, Volhynia, and Podolia provinces) became part of the Russian Empire. The local peasantry remained under the control of the mostly Polish gentry, whose enduring memories of the partitions galvanized insurrections against tsarist rule.

The terms "Ukraine" and even "Little Russia" had no official meaning in the imperial context of the early nineteenth century. As Orthodox Christians and "descendants" of the medieval Kievan Rus', the local Little Russian population was seen as inherently part of what later came to be called the "all-Russian nation" and was treated differently from the Catholic Poles. For the local Little Russian intellectuals, participation in something like a Ukrainian public sphere meant simultaneously being a part of the all-Russian cultural and scholarly life. Indeed, prominent Ukrainian academics like Mykhailo Maksymovych, Osyp Bodians'kyi, and later Mykola Kostomarov all held chairs in Russian imperial universities (Bilenky 2012:6–7). The imperial government varied its policies toward Polish citizens, ranging from cultural autonomy allowed by Alexander I to the repressive policies that followed the infamous November 1830 uprising.

In this context, Ukrainian or Little Russian cultural developments were simultaneously enmeshed in fluctuating relationships with St. Petersburg, on the one hand, and the Polish gentry and intelligentsia, on the other. For a time, St. Petersburg regarded the Little Russian cultural revival as a promising counterweight to Polish nationalist aspirations and uprisings. However, this benevolent outlook changed after another Polish uprising in 1863, which caused all apparent manifestations of separatist activities to be banned. In the aftermath of the failed Polish uprising of November 1830, thousands of Polish officers and soldiers and most of the active intellectuals of the insurrection migrated to France, making Paris the center of Polish émigré political activities over the next two decades (Miłosz 1969:197–198).

In response to the November insurrections, tsarist efforts to reduce the influence of the Polish gentry in the Right Bank led to a number of governmental decrees that improved conditions for local serfs and revised the regulations of gentry privileges. In effect, the changes revoked the noble status of sixty-four thousand Polish or "Polonized" nobility between 1840 and 1845 (Berestenko and Shamara 2012:48; Magocsi 2010:389).

Disillusioned with the failures of the insurrection and stripped of noble status and estates, a large number of the demoted gentry turned to life and work among the townspeople and the peasants in the countryside. While members of the émigré Polish intelligentsia became convinced that lack of peasant support was the reason for the failure of the November insurrections, the demoted gentry of the Right Bank worked to understand local peasant traditions, language, and culture. Their efforts eventually resulted in a populist movement called *khlopomania*, or "peasant mania."

The founding members of the *khlopoman* movement who came to identify as Ukrainians include ethnographers Tadei Rylsky, Borys Poznans'kyi, Kostiantyn Mykhal'chuk, and the most famous of them, Volodymyr Antonovych, who eventually became the first professional historian of Ukraine at the University of St. Vladimir in Kiev. His student Mykhailo Hrushevskyi, a national historian and politician, became chair of Ukrainian history in Lemberg/Lwow, Galicia, and is considered to this day to be one of the most important contributors to Ukrainian nation building.

The emergence of peasant mania was a movement away from elite conceptions of history and society in favor of peasant ways of life. The *khlopomany* articulated a rejection of a Polish national identity that was deeply vested in the memories of the commonwealth and inseparably tied to noble status. Theirs was an articulation of a kind of Romantic humanism in the ardent rejection of the vast social inequality and class differences between the enserfed peasants and the nobility. This reorientation of identity relied in part on claiming the legacy of Kievan Rus' by drawing a line of continuity chronologically prior to the Polish-Lithuanian Commonwealth control of the territory. For Polish Catholics, this realignment required a return to the Orthodox Church. Moreover, as the sons of demoted Polish gentry came to identify as Ukrainians, they also made lasting scholarly contributions toward developing a specifically Ukrainian identity.

As national awakeners, Antonovych and his compatriots relied on ethnography and self-reflection to advocate for a reflexive embrace of a Ukrainian past. Borys Poznans'kyi's observations provide one of the most compelling illustrations of this:

> The ritual of everyday life, as a result of local living circumstances, is not easily susceptible to change. The Polonized Rusyn-Ukrainian, forced to change his language and to adopt the Catholic faith, could not internalize entirely the manner of Polish everyday life and retained even to this day his Old Rus' past. Disregarding the fact that Ivananko, Buhaj, Khmil', Jarmolenko, and Jarysh, with the adoption of Catholicism and immersion into contemporary Polish culture, became Ivanivsky, Buhajevsky, Khmilnevsky, Jarmolynsky, Jaroshynsky, and so on, [they] nonetheless continued to eat borsh, lemishku, varenyky. . . . Similarly, as in the past, they continued to kiss three times, and in response to the greeting "Christ is risen!" from Ukrainian peasants, they replied with "Indeed, He is risen!" in Ukrainian, because the Polish language has no required reply. (My translation of Borys Poznans'kyi 1913:68, quoted in Berestenko and Shamara 2012:52)

The members of the *khlopomania* movement adopted a Ukrainian identity, changed their names from Polish to Ukrainian forms, and converted from Catholicism to Eastern Orthodoxy. To get a better sense for the role of reflexive ethnography in such "conversions" of identity, I offer a bit of background on Antonovych and the sociopolitical and historical circumstances under which Włodzimierz Antonowicz came to be Volodymyr Antonovych, the famous Ukrainian historian, ethnographer, political activist, and founder of the modern Ukrainian civic movement.

Antonovych was born into a noble family with strong Polish sentiments but no land. They belonged to a distinct segment of Polish society in the Right Bank that did not have the social standing of the landed nobility and instead provided them with positions as lawyers, teachers, governesses, and the like (Bilenky 2013:177). Antonovych was an avid reader of French Enlightenment philosophers, whom he credits for providing the foundation for his outlook on life and subsequent "discovery" of things Ukrainian:

> I was brought up on literature, mainly French. In the advanced classes I managed to read many works of Montesquieu, Rousseau, Voltaire and other encyclopedists, under whose influence my outlook on life took shape. Every person I met in gentry society, every axiom of that society left me with an impression of something unexpected and archaic. I began to consider how the general principles of theoretical democracy might be applied to my native grounds. The democratic element in the area turned out to be the peasantry. Here again there arose the question of nationality. But my knowledge of things Ukrainian was almost nil.... I never heard a word about the Brotherhood of [Saints] Cyril and Methodius or about Taras Shevchenko. Nevertheless, the facts spoke for themselves. Applying my weak knowledge of things Ukrainian to general French democratic theory, I discovered Ukrainism all by myself. The more I studied and read and acquainted myself with history, the more I became convinced that my discovery was not an idle invention. At the university I imparted my ideas to my comrades. At first they looked on them as incomprehensible and almost mad. Then gradually there appeared

people who shared my ideas, and an entire circle was formed, the so-called *khlopomany* (peasant-lovers). (Antonovych 2013:217)

Antonovych and his *khlopomany* friends spent a lot of time traveling on foot around the countryside dressed in peasant clothes and studying peasant lifeways, traditions, and local mythology. In his recollections of his ethnographic travels, Antonovych imparts that the more time he spent among the peasantry, the more he felt to be a part of them. He became more and more opposed to the Polish nobility, whose interests he saw as incompatible with those of the peasants. Antonovych saw his ethnographic travels as a tool to see the peasantry "as it really was":

At the end of the fifties there arose in our circle the idea that it was shameful to live in a land and not know it or its population. We decided to devote our entire vacation, from [the] beginning of April to the end of August, to traveling on foot about the land. There is no doubt that we profited from our travels, but in gentry society the belief developed that we were going about teaching the peasants to massacre the landlords. To be sure, this belief was utterly false, but in the course of our travels we did become quite well acquainted with the people's outlook on life. The people appeared before us not as the gentry pictured it, but as it really was. We saw its very strong natural logic and its highly developed ethics, which were reflected in a readiness to help and in a friendly attitude to everyone in need. We accomplished our journey on foot, in peasant cloaks, and everywhere we were taken to be country boys. We did not conceal that we were students, but this term was incomprehensible to the people at the time. Sometimes we were asked what we did, and we replied that we studied. Most often the result was that we were considered doctor's assistants, for the most understandable field was medicine. Over three vacations we covered nearly all the Right Bank and new Russia: Volhynia, Podilia, the Kyiv region, the Kholm region, and most of the Katerynoslav and Kherson regions. It would take a very long time to recount our travels, and I have probably forgotten the greater part of what occurred. We usually obtained permission from peasants to spend the night with them. Not once did our hosts agree to take payment for a night[']s lodging or for supper. We observed this on our first trip and stocked up with crosses, icons, rings of St. Barbara and the like, which, when we left a night's lodging, we distributed as gifts to the children. It often happened, especially in New Russia, that we joined with a wagon train and spent several days with it. (Antonovych 2013:218)

Eventually, the prolonged contact of *khlopomany* with the peasantry caused enough anxiety among the gentry to bring about serious accusations of massacre instigations. They were summoned to stand trial, but because his fellow peasant lovers were away at the time, Antonovych appeared in court by himself. He describes the proceedings in great detail in his memoirs (Antonovych 2013:221–232) and recalls being called a communist. Similar accusations were made against Borys Poznansky, who actually began living in a peasant village: "He married a peasant girl from the area and began to live entirely in a folk manner. His good relations with the peasants and the considerable influence that he managed to acquire attracted the attention of the neighboring landowners. Denunciations of a massacre came showering down" (Antonovych 2013:229).

Although Antonovych was able to defend himself in court, partly with the help of a sympathetic ally he acquired among the accusing Polish nobility, other members of the gentry continued to view the activities of *khlopomany* as suspicious. The fears of the nobility foreshadowed the 1870s populist movement of *narodniki* (populists), intelligentsia who took up "going to the people" to incite peasant uprisings. Antonovych makes a point in his memoirs to distance the activities of the *khlopomany* from those of *narodniki*; however, the general fears of a peasant revolt were quite pervasive and not unfounded. After all, the Polish uprising of 1846 in neighboring Galicia in the Austro-Hungarian Empire was crushed not by the imperial army but by the peasantry, who rose up and massacred their Polish lords in the name of the emperor, thus foregrounding the importance of securing peasant loyalties.

PEASANT MANIA IN AUSTRO-HUNGARIAN GALICIA

Leading up to the first half of the nineteenth century, the Habsburg-ruled province of Galicia was relatively similar to the Right Bank in that the hierarchy of multiple loyalties prevailed as the orienting framework for conceiving identity categories within the empire. The majority of the population were peasants, roughly divided into the Roman Catholic Polish side in western Galicia and the Greek Catholic Ruthenian (Ukrainian) side in eastern Galicia. They remained under control of the Polish nobility, who viewed the partitions of the Polish-Lithuanian Commonwealth as a tragic dismantling of the Polish nation that led to Polish insurrections against Habsburg rule. The gentry primarily identified with Polish high culture. Ruthenian Greek Catholic landowners often identified as Poles, spoke Polish, and regarded the Ruthenian vernacular as "peasant speech."

While there was some sense of a distinct Ruthenian culture, it was primarily identified in terms of religious differences. For the most part, the Ruthenian peasants were seen as Poles *genre Rutheni* who happened to differ in their local vernacular and Eastern rite Catholicism.

After the partitions of the Polish-Lithuanian Commonwealth, the Eastern rite Uniate Church was abolished and "returned" to Orthodoxy in the commonwealth territories in the Russian Empire (Magocsi 2002b:113). At the same time, Vienna sought to increase the status of the Uniate Church and renamed it Greek Catholic as part of an overall effort to actively differentiate the local peasant populations of eastern Galicia from the peasants in the Right Bank of the Russian Empire. Similarly, newly developed ethnonyms became officially recognized as imperial bureaucratic categories. The German terms *Ruthenen* and *ruthenisch*, proposed by the Greek Catholic bishop, Mykhailo Levits'kyi, were officially adopted by Vienna in 1843 instead of the parallel German terms *Russienen* and *russinisch*, which were deemed too close to Russian (Kamusella 2008:383).

More generally, Vienna's civilizing mission (Wolff 2010) in the province of Galicia had two important consequences for the developments of ethnonational identities in the region leading up to World War I. The implementation of the Enlightenment-based reforms of Maria Theresa and Joseph II soon after Galicia became part of the Habsburg Empire drastically improved the conditions of the local serfs. Education reforms called for compulsory elementary schools in the local vernacular, which led to questions of linguistic differentiation and standardization. While

the term *Ruthenian* was often used to refer to the East Slavic populations of Galicia (Hann and Magocsi 2005:ix) and their local vernacular, figuring out exactly what the Ruthenian "language" was turned out
to be a rather complicated task that was often approached in terms of
what it wasn't, that is, not Polish, not Church Slavonic, not suitable for
scholarly publications. The language question soon offered a platform
for developing notions of ethnic, historical, cultural, and folk identity
categories that were central to the intelligentsia's efforts to define the
national identity of the Galician peasant masses. Furthermore, as the
emperor's subjects, the peasant serf populations acquired rights that
allowed them to take their feudal lords to court. This turned out to be
one of the crucial factors in securing peasant loyalties to the emperor.

It is important to point out that while the Ruthenian peasants were
more or less "seen" as Ruthenian-vernacular-speaking Greek Catholic
Poles by the Polish gentry, the peasants of Galicia in general did not
see themselves as Polish. This became glaringly apparent during the
1846 Polish insurrection. To combat the insurrection, Austrian authorities sought out the help of Jakub Szela, a peasant leader who taught
the serfs how to take their lords to court. Under Szela's leadership, the
serfs rose up and massacred their noble lords, citing Habsburg loyalty
(Davies 2005:108–109; Hahn 2001:173–174; Magocsi et al. 1974:134–135;
Wolff 2010:141–146).

As Eric Hobsbawm (1996[1962]:124–125, 137) observes about this
pivotal moment within the overarching context of pre-1848 revolutionary developments in Europe, the 1846 massacres underscored the
grand disconnect between the intelligentsia and the peasant masses.
The peasantry did not support the intelligentsia's revolutionary efforts.
Moreover, the 1846 serf rebellion and subsequent massacre of their
Polish nobles meant that peasant passivity would not last.

The massacre foregrounded the imperative to secure peasant loyalties
and gain the tactical advantages enjoyed by the emperor and the church,
both of whom were more than willing to utilize peasant support against
the revolutionary aspirations of the gentry. In the words of Hobsbawm,
the question for the gentry intellectuals was "not whether to seek alliance with the peasantry, but whether they would succeed in obtaining
it" (1996[1962]:125). The close connection of nationalist ideals to the

middle class and the gentry made them suspect to the poor and the peasantry, so much so that even the agrarian reform promised by the Polish revolutionaries was not enough to sway peasant loyalty (137).

Two years later, Vienna was quick to capitalize on peasant loyalties in the context of the 1848 revolutions. With memories of the 1846 Galician massacre, the provincial governor, Franz Stadion, forbade the landowners to free peasants on their own authority while lobbying for Vienna to grant him the power to abolish serfdom in Galicia. When he succeeded in April 1848, he explicitly pointed to his political motivations to "secure the loyalty of the servile rural population to the government, and deprive the supporters of Polish nationality this important means of gaining the support of the rural population for their interests" (Franz Stadion quoted in Hahn 2001:178). Stadion also openly encouraged Ukrainian national development as a counterweight to Polish aspirations in Galicia (Magocsi 2002b:71).

After the events of 1848, a kind of performative linguistic shift came about in eastern Galicia, particularly among university students in Lwow. Ostap Sereda (2001:202–203) observes the development of Ruthenian "national awareness" throughout Galicia's public sphere with the dramatic increase of Ruthenian and later Ukrainian literary and political periodicals that were guided by the Right Bank intelligentsia in the Russian Empire. Sereda offers several poignant quotes from students and activists in Lwow that reveal their self-conscious shift toward using Ruthenian, rather than Polish, as the means of communication in the 1860s Lwow public sphere. Yet as Benedict Anderson pointed out, the extent to which the urban and rural masses participated in the "new vernacularly imagined communities" varied across the board and depended a great deal on the "relationship between these masses and the missionaries of nationalism" (1991[1983]:80). The memories of the 1846 massacres continued to linger in Galician historical imaginations and in the persisting anxieties of the intelligentsia over the vast disconnect between them and "the people." In this context, the late nineteenth-century pursuit of both Polish and Ruthenian/Ukrainian nationalism turned to organic work among the peasant masses (Magocsi 2002b:29–30; Wolff 2010:195–196).

Organic work became the slogan for positivism among the Polish intelligentsia in Galicia. As the pragmatic alternative to the failed insurrections, it aligned with a kind of reorientation toward an "inclusive" provincial Galician identity as an administrative whole in accordance with Vienna's administrative imperial efforts to "know the land." Larry Wolff (2010) observes the positivist spirit of the numerous works documenting the "organic coherence" of Galicia. These include Hipolit Stupnicki's 1853 *Das Konigreich Galizien und Lodomerien, sammt dem Grossherzogthume Krakau und Herzogthume Bukowina: In geographisch-historisch-statistischer Beziehung* (The Kingdom of Galicia and Lodomeria, together with the Grand Duchy of Krakow and the Duchy of Bukovina: In geographical-historical-statistical relation, 1853), a "topographical-geographical-historical" account of the province. In it, Stupnicki enumerates various ethnographic types within the Austrian province: "No land of the Austrian monarchy is inhabited by such different peoples as Galicia. Poles, Ruthenians, Germans, Armenians, Jews, Moldavians, Hungarians, Gypsies." He goes on to say that although the customs of the peasants vary throughout Galicia, they are "collectively still very coarse" (quoted in Wolff 2010:195).

By the 1870s both the customs and the physical traits of the peasantry had been closely scrutinized and delimited by anthropological, ethnographic, and archaeological works produced by members of the intelligentsia in both the Russian and Austro-Hungarian Empires. In Galicia such works are exemplified by the 1876 encyclopedic volume, *The Physical Characteristics of the Populations of Galicia*. Written by two medically trained anthropologists, Jozef Majer and Izydor Kopernicki, the volume offered a "scientific" representation of the coherence of the province. This anthropometric project of "observations of living people" was sponsored by the Anthropological Commission of Jagiellonian University. Before conducting the research both authors took part in the Polish insurrections of the previous decades, Jozef Majer as a doctor in the 1830–31 November insurrection, and Izydor Kopernicki in 1863. After his involvement in the 1863 insurrection, Kopernicki was "let go" from Kiev University, spent time studying and publishing abroad, and moved go Krakow, Galicia, in 1871, where he became one of the founding figures of the discipline of anthropology at Jagiellonian University (Wolff 2010:236–238).

A closer look at Kopernicki is worthwhile for a number of reasons: his time at the Jagiellonian University closely coincides with Lucian Malinowski's, Bronisław's father and a prominent Slavic linguist who was thoroughly enmeshed within contemporary Galician politics of ethnonational and linguistic delimitations. More importantly, given Bronisław Malinowski's developing interest in anthropology during his time at Jagiellonian University, it would be hard to imagine that he would have been unaware of the work done by one of the founding figures at his own university. While numerous scholars have discussed Malinowski's relationship with Sir James Frazier's anthropological approach (Kubica 1988:95; Malinowski 1954[1926]:94; Stocking 1994:241), it may be worthwhile to consider what can arguably be seen as Malinowski's rejection of Kopernicki. This is especially interesting in the context of Kopernicki's early anthropological career among the Right Bank intelligentsia in Kiev during the *khlopomany* movement and his participation in the 1863 Polish insurrections.

Izydor Kopernicki studied medicine in Kiev and received his degree in 1849, after which he became a military physician for eight years and served in the Crimean War. In 1857 he came back to Kiev and produced his first scholarly work: *Preliminary Observations of Craniological Research on the Structure of Slavic Skulls* (1861). According to his obituary, he pioneered early research in Slavic craniology, developed the collection of skulls at Kiev University, and even invented his own cranial measuring device (Antonovych 1891:463). In 1863 he took part in the Polish insurrections against tsarist rule, after which he left the Russian Empire. In 1871 he moved to Jagiellonian University in Krakow, where he worked on a fourteen-volume anthropological collection of reports on the various populations in Galicia. The collection includes a great deal on South Rus' populations, particularly Galician and Carpathian mountaineers (Gorale). He also published his ethnographic work among Gorale populations in *O góralach ruskich w Galicyi: Zarys etnograficzny według spostrzeżeń w podróży, odbytej w końcu lata 1888r* (On the Rus' Highlanders of Galicia: An overview of ethnographic observations of late summer 1888; see Wolff 2010). His work among the Gorale continued to be appreciated by the Ukrainian intelligentsia of the Right Bank. In his obituary published in *Kievskaja Starina* (Kiev antiquity) in 1891, he is praised for scientific objectivity and the determination to publish the results of his work contrary to the prevalent scholarly views on the subject of Gorale national "origins":

> Kopernicki collected and analyzed vast amounts of [anthropological] material for the distinct differentiation of ethnographic types: Polish and Rus' (Rusinskago), despite the strong insistence at the time among Polish intellectuals, especially in Galicia, that those types are identical. Accordingly, his descriptions of the Russian (Russkikh) Gorale exactly determine their tribal belonging to the South Russian type, whereas the works of his predecessors on this subject . . . mixed them with groups of Western Polish Gorale, and muddled the issue so much that the reader would easily assume that the entire Western territory of the Carpathians was inhabited by various Polish types. (V.A. 1891:464–465, my translation)

Kiev Antiquity was a Russian-language monthly scholarly periodical published by the Ukrainian intelligentsia *hromada* (community) in Kiev. The obituary could very well have been written by Volodymyr Antonovych, who was one of the founders of the periodical, contributed to it regularly, and possibly had a relationship with Kopernicki during his time in Kiev. Interestingly enough, the obituary makes no mention of whether or not Kopernicki identified as a Pole or of his involvement in the 1863 Polish insurrections, only that he was "let go" from the university in 1863. It does, however, make reference to Kievan Rus' as Kopernicki's motherland. If the obituary was indeed written by Volodymyr Antonovych, we can read this as a kind of claiming of Kopernicki as "Ukrainian."

The relevance of Kopernicki's work as a "scientific" acknowledgment of a South Rus' identity for Gorale populations is particularly important given the intellectual climate of pre–World War I Galicia and the organic work of the Polish intelligentsia's efforts to record and codify the peasant ways of life as the "purest" exemplars of national culture from which to form the basis for the new nation-state and the national system of education (Gellner 1998:130). For the intellectuals of Krakow's Young Poland, the traditions, lifeways, and folk culture of the Gorale in the small mountain town of Zakopane were seen as embodiments of Polish national culture, and Zakopane became the epicenter for the Galician wave of "peasant-mania."

THE GORALE OF ZAKOPANE AND YOUNG POLAND'S "PEASANT MANIA"

The "discovery" and codification of Zakopane peasant culture are emblematic of late nineteenth-century appeals to vernacular traditions by urban and academically trained elites, artists, and writers across Europe. Zakopane Gorale lifeways were seen as natural expressions of Polish peasant national culture. Malinowski and his close friend Stas Witkiewicz spent a lot of time in the small mountain town that became the epicenter of Young Poland's peasant mania and the "summer capital" of Krakow's intelligentsia. It was in Zakopane that Malinowski encountered the Gorale as the first "natives" and later wrote about them in his diary as the "semi-savage Carpathian mountaineers" (Malinowski 1989[1967]:169 in Thornton and Skalnik 1993:11).

Stas Witkiewicz's father pioneered the development of the "Zakopane style" of design based on the region and greatly contributed to the broader intellectual fascination with the Gorale mountaineers. With the help of other artists and architects and Gorale craftsmen, Witkiewicz Sr. went about recasting the "raw materials" of the Tatra region as an elite architectural style of villas and summer houses for wealthy and patriotically minded members of the Polish intelligentsia (Crowley 2001:105–110).

The "return" to peasant ways of life among Krakow's Young Poland intellectuals is epitomized by the marriages of Polish intelligentsia to peasant women. This second wave of peasant mania was memorialized in the play *Wesele* (The wedding) by Stanislaw Wyspianski (1869–1907), the most famous modern Polish dramatist in the avant-garde of the Young Poland movement. The play is based on the sensational wedding of Wyspianski's friend Lucjan Rydel, a Krakowian poet, to a peasant woman in a nearby village (Segel 1960:76-90; Young 2004:64). Wyspianski was also briefly married to a peasant woman.

As Wyspianski's most famous play, *Wesele* strikes a number of thematic, national, and political chords in prewar Galicia, especially among the Young Poland intelligentsia. Through the use of symbolism and fantasy, it presents a commentary on the failures of the intelligentsia's expectations for providing leadership to the peasants. With the wedding itself as the symbol for the mythic union of the intelligentsia and the peasantry, the wedding guests represent different segments of Polish society. In the play, the host of the wedding has a dream that the legendary bard Wernyhora orders him to prepare the peasants for an uprising and gives him a golden horn with which to summon the countryside. The host sends one of the groomsmen out with the horn and awakens to find the peasants arming and gathering in preparation. He tells everyone at the wedding to prepare for the uprising, but when the "awakener" groomsman returns, it turns out he lost the golden horn, and instead of preparing for an uprising, everyone continues to dance at the wedding (Gerould 1984:176–179).

The more sinister scenes of the play are interposed with fantasy encounters with ghosts from Polish history. Wyspianski plays on the lingering traumatic memories of the massacres of 1846 with an appearance of the ghost of Jakub Szela, the infamous leader of the peasant revolt (Wolff 2010:187, 280–281). The lingering specter of the events of 1846, thoroughly entrenched in Galician historical memory, served as the perfect symbol for the ambivalent relationship between Galicia's intelligentsia and the peasantry. It also echoed the post-1848 European revolutionaries' anxieties over the looming questions of how to approach the peasantry.

While Poland's mythical historical past remained a constant theme throughout Wyspianski's works, the neo-Romantic symbolism of plays like *Meleager* (1898), *Protesilaus and Laodarnia* (1899), *Achilleis* (1903), and *The Return of Odysseus* (1905) was often inspired by Greek tragedy. Obsessed with Poland's historical destiny, the tragedy of the partitions, and Polish nationalist insurrections against foreign rule, Wyspianski modernized Greek mythology and a Greek-style chorus in his plays to comment on the national, political, and societal issues of pre–World War I Galicia and the Right Bank (Gerould 1984:176–179).

Wyspianski's Homeric paraphrases as dramatic variants of the history of Poland presented a fusion of a Romantic philosophy of history that simultaneously offered a critique of Polish Romantics.[2] Poland's historical destiny, the plight of the Romantics, and folk lifeways and traditions in Wyspianski's plays are combined with elements of Nietzsche's ethical philosophy and Wagner's drama (Wachocka 2007:196–197). Wyspianski was the most famous playwright of the Young Poland movement during Malinowski's time in Krakow, and his plays epitomize key issues that Malinowski himself engages in his first serious scholarly work, a critical essay on Nietzsche's *Birth of Tragedy*.

It was during this time, which Malinowski later called his "Nietzsche period" in his unpublished diaries, that he began to develop his charter function of myth (Thornton and Skalnik 1993:13). In it, Malinowski (1993[1905]:74) rejects Nietzsche's Apollonian-Dionysian opposition and argues that both elements are always present and coexisting. He takes up *tragedy* as the most profound combination of the Apollonian-Dionysian union and lays out a "positive research plan" in which he argues that to understand any myth, it must be situated within the context of its appropriate culture to know how "tragedy functions."

For the elite intelligentsia of Poland, the "birth of tragedy" still lay in the partitions of the Polish-Lithuanian Commonwealth, more tragically amplified by the massacres of 1846 in the vast disconnect between the "national awakeners" and the "peasant masses." We can see peasant mania as a kind of Apollonian-Dionysian mythological union witnessed by Malinowski among the Young Poland intelligentsia and memorialized in Wyspianski's *The Wedding*. The mythic figure of the ethnographer-anthropologist at work in the Galician context of the peasant-loving intelligentsia's use of ethnography in "ethically subordinating the present to the past" (Malinowski [ca. 1905] in Thornton and Skalnik 1993:70) was perpetually haunted by the violent specter of the 1846 disconnect between the nationalists and their proverbial "folk."

While the pre–World War I context of "peasant manias" in the Russian and Austro-Hungarian Empires offers insight into the ways ethnography could be amenable to co-optation for nationalist purposes, it continues to have the potential for elucidating the complex negotiations in contemporary politics of ethnonational identities. In selectively drawing on Ukrainian nationalist developments among other Slavic nationalisms, I have tried to examine the roles of ethnographers and anthropologists in crafting, delimiting, and contesting the parameters of ethnolinguistic identities leading up to the pivotal moment of the

Great War. The extent to which Malinowski was directly influenced by any of these figures remains purely speculative, of course. I would argue, however, that their activities illustrate the prevalent trends, anxieties, and complexities of the ambiguous and shifting national identities that were amplified by the realities of the war during the most formative years of Malinowski's youth (Ellen at al. 1988; Gellner 1998; Thornton and Skalnik 1993). Moreover, in illustrations of the complexity in delimitations of national and territorial parameters of the present-day nation-states that began to take shape in the decades leading up to the war, I have tried to develop a sense of a dialectical history through which Ukrainian nationality was formed. In light of the ongoing crisis in Ukraine, I hope this approach offers a critique of the post–World War I reliance on nationality as a "natural" principle for restoring world order.

NOTES

1. Such concerns with the national consciousness of the nineteenth-century peasantry were certainly not limited to eastern Europe alone. For instance, Eugen Weber's (1976) work, *Peasants into Frenchmen: The Modernization of Rural France, 1870–1914*, points to the eve of the war as the historical moment when peasants "turn into Frenchmen" (see also Himka 1988).

2. For example, *The Legion* (1900) is a polemic against Poland's foremost Romantic poet, Adam Mickiewicz, who appears as Brutus in Rome, kills Caesar (the symbol for the cult of Napoleon), and releases an old woman (the symbol for freedom), who runs into the crowd and is soon brought back dead. The play depicts the catastrophic results for Poland in the collapse of the Romantic era's mystical messianism (Gerould 1984:76). *The November Night* (1904) is comprised of ten scenes that are thematically united by the history of the 1830–31 November insurrections. Polish political ideas are symbolized by Greek gods intermixed among the human insurrectionists. *Akropolis*, the apex of powerful symbolism of classical figures, features animated statues and figures from tapestries and paintings of Wawel Cathedral that have replaced human beings in enactments of classical and biblical scenes (Gerould 1972:176–179). (In the final scene, the resurrection of Christ-Apollo represents the defeat of death—yet another one of Wyspiansi's obsessions that also makes an appearance in Malinowski's essay on Nietzsche.)

REFERENCES

Anderson, Benedict. 1991[1983]. Imagined Communities: Reflections on the Origin and Spread of Nationalism. London: Verso.

Antonovych, Volodymyr (possibly as V.A.). 1891. Izydor Stanislavovych Koernicki. Kievskaja Starina (Kiev antiquity) 12:462–465.

———. 2013. Selected Writings. In Fashioning Modern Ukraine: Selected Writings of Mykola Kostomarov, Volodymyr Antonovych, and Mykhailo Drahomanov. Toronto: Canadian Institute of Ukrainian Studies Press.

Berestenko, O. V., and S. O. Shamara. 2012. Natsional'nyj renesans "khlopomaniv" v istoriji pol'sko-ukrajins'kykh samovyznachen' (sotsial'no-psykholohichne doslidjen'ja) (The national renaissance of the "khlopomans" in the history of Polish-Ukrainian self-determinations [social and psychological research]). Visnyk Cherkas'koho Universitetu: Istorychni Nauky, 47–61.

Bilenky, Serhiy. 2012. Romantic Nationalism in Eastern Europe: Russian, Polish, and Ukrainian Political Imaginations. Stanford CA: Stanford University Press.

———, ed. 2013. Fashioning Modern Ukraine: Selected Writings of Mykola Kostomarov, Volodymyr Antonovych, and Mykhailo Drahomanov. Toronto: Canadian Institute of Ukrainian Studies Press.

Crowley, David. 2001. Finding Poland in the Margins: The Case of the Zakopane Style. Journal of Design History 14(2):105–116.

Davies, Norman. 2005. God's Playground: A History of Poland. Vol. 2: 1795 to the Present. Oxford: Oxford University Press.

Ellen, R., E. Gellner, G. Kubica, and J. Mucha, eds. 1988. Malinowski between Two Worlds: The Polish Roots of an Anthropological Tradition. Cambridge: Cambridge University Press.

Gawroński, Franciszek. 1912. Włodzimierz Antonowicz: Zarys jego działalności społeczno-politycznej i historycznej. Lwów: Gebethner i Ska.

Gellner, Ernest. 1998. Language and Solitude: Wittgenstein, Malinowski and the Habsburg Dilemma. Cambridge: Cambridge University Press.

Gerould, Danel. 1984. Wyspianski, Stanislaw (1869–1907). In The McGraw-Hill Encyclopedia of World Drama. New York: McGraw-Hill.

Hahn, Christopher, and Paul Robert Magocsi, eds. 2005. Galicia, a Multicultural Land. Toronto: University of Toronto Press.

Hahn, H. H. 2001. The Polish Nation in the Revolution of 1846–49. In Europe in 1848: Revolution and Reform. Dieter Dowe, ed. New York: Berghahn Books.

Himka, J. P. 1988. Galician Villagers and the Ukrainian National Movement in the Nineteenth Century. London: Macmillan.

Hobsbawm, Eric. 1996[1962]. The Age of Revolution: 1789–1848. New York: Vintage Books.

Hobsbawm, Eric, and Terence Ranger. 2012[1983]. The Invention of Tradition. Cambridge: Cambridge University Press.

Hroch, Miroslav. 1985. Social Preconditions of National Revival in Europe: A Comparative Analysis of the Social Composition of Patriotic Groups among the Smaller European Nations. Ben Fowkes, trans. Cambridge: Cambridge University Press.

Kamusella, Tomasz. 2008. The Politics of Language and Nationalism in Modern Central Europe. Basingstoke: Palgrave.

Katchanovski, I., Z. E. Kohut, B. Y. Nebesio, and M. Yurkevich, eds. 2013. Khlopomany. In Historical Dictionary of Ukraine. 2nd ed. Lanham MD: Scarecrow Press.

Kubica, Grazyna. 1988. Malinowski's Years in Poland. In Malinowski between Two Worlds: The Polish Roots of an Anthropological Tradition. R. Ellen, E. Gellner, G. Kubica and J. Mucha, eds. Cambridge: Cambridge University Press.

Magocsi, Paul Robert. 2002a. Historical Atlas of Central Europe. Seattle: University of Washington Press.

——. 2002b. The Roots of Ukrainian Nationalism: Galicia as Ukraine's Piedmont. Toronto: University of Toronto Press.

——. 2010. A History of Ukraine: The Land and Its Peoples. 2nd ed. Toronto: University of Toronto Press.

Magocsi, P. R., J. W. Sedlar, R. A. Kann, C. Jevich, and J. Rothschild. 1974. A History of East Central Europe: The Lands of Partitioned Poland, 1795–1918. Seattle: University of Washington Press.

Malinowski, Bronisław. 1935. Preface to The Cassubian Civilisation by F. Lorentz, A. Fischer, and T. Lehr-Splawinski. London: Faber.

——. 1954[1926]. Myth in Primitive Psychology. In Magic, Science and Religion and Other Essays. Garden City NY: Anchor Books.

——. 1989[1967]. A Diary in the Strict Sense of the Term. Stanford CA: Stanford University Press.

——. 1993[1905]. Observations on Friedrich Nietzsche's "The Birth of Tragedy." In The Early Writings of Bronislaw Malinowski. R. Thornton and P. Skalnik, eds. Cambridge: Cambridge University Press.

——. 2014[1944]. Freedom and Civilization. Mishawake IN: Better World Books.

Miłosz, Czeslaw. 1969. History of Polish Literature. London: Macmillan.

Nazaruk, O., and O. Okhrymovych. 1908. Khronika rukhu ukrains'koi aka-demichnoi molodizhi u Lvovi (An outline of the Ukrainian Academic Youth Movement in L'viv). In Istorychnyi ohliad zhyttia v students'kykh ukrains'kykh organizatsiakh (Historical overview of the lives of Ukrainian student organizations). Z. Kuzelia, ed. L'viv: Naukove Tova-rystvo Imeni Shevchenka (Shevchenko Scientific Society).

Segel, Harold. 1960. "Young Poland," Cracow and "The Little Green Bal-loon." Polish Review 5(2):74–97.

Sereda, Ostap. 2001. "Whom Shall We Be?": Public Debates over the National Identity of Galician Ruthenians in the 1860s. Jahrbücher für Geschichte Osteuropas 49(2):200–212.

Skalnik, Peter. 1995. Bronislaw Kasper Malinowski and Stanislaw Ignacy Witkiewicz: Science versus Art in the Conceptualization of Culture. In Fieldwork and Footnotes: Studies in the History of European Anthro-pology. Han F. Vermeulen and Arturo Alvarez Roldan, eds. London: Routledge.

Stocking, George. 1994. Maclay, Kubary, Malinowski: Archetypes from the Dreamtime of Anthropology. In The Ethnographer's Magic and Other Essays in the History of Anthropology. Madison: University of Wiscon-sin Press.

Thornton, Robert, and Peter Skalnik. 1993. The Early Writings of Bronislaw Malinowski. Cambridge: Cambridge University Press.

Wachocka, Ewa. 2007. Polish Modernist Drama. In History of the Literary Cultures of East-Central Europe. Vol. 3: The Making and Remaking of Literary Institutions. M. Cornis-Pope and J. Neubauer, eds. Amsterdam: John Benjamins Publishing Company.

Weber, Eugen. 1976. Peasants into Frenchmen: The Modernization of Rural France, 1870–1914. Stanford CA: Stanford University Press.

Witkiewicz, Stanisław Ignacy. 2000[1914]. Listy do Bronisława Malinows-kiego (Letters to Bronisław Malinowski). Daniel Gerould and Michał Klobukowski, trans. Konteksty: Antropologia Kukltury, Etnografia, Szyuka (1–4):240–291. http://www.konteksty.pl/numery/37,148-251.

Wolff, Larry. 2010. The Idea of Galicia: History and Fantasy in Habsburg Political Culture. Stanford CA: Stanford University Press.

Young, Michael. 2004. Malinowski: Odyssey of an Anthropologist 1884–1920. New Haven CT: Yale University Press.

10

Adopting Western Methods to Understand One's Own Culture

*Social and Cultural Studies by Vietnamese
Scholars of the French Colonial Era*

While studying Vietnamese intellectuals of the colonial era, I was struck by what an extraordinarily dynamic period it was, not only in terms of art and literature (fairly well documented already) but also in the intellectual and scientific spheres. My thesis (titled "The Beginnings of Anthropology in Vietnam: A Study of First-Generation Authors") therefore sought to answer the following question: Under which conditions and with what results did the science of anthropology enter Vietnam? It was far from self-evident that this science, still in its infancy, should be of interest to Vietnamese thinkers, considering the Institut d'Ethnologie (at the Sorbonne in France) wasn't founded until 1927.

The term "anthropology" is used here to refer to the study of peoples in its widest sense as defined so excellently in the work of Marcel Mauss. In contrast to the term "ethnology," "anthropology" broadens the concept of "otherness" from a merely external view of "ethnic" to include an internal social study as exemplified by Vietnamese authors examining their own society. One also has to bear in mind how, at the time, boundaries between the new social sciences were blurred; for instance, although the official terminology of the École Française d'Extrême-Orient (EFEO) defined Nguyễn Văn Huyên as an *annamitisant* (expert on Annam), Paul Mus referred to him as a geographer and sociologist; Nguyễn Mạnh Tường called him a sociologist, ethnologist, and philologist; and later, Georges Condominas considered him an ethnologist. Here I have followed the definition given in the *Dictionnaire des sciences humaines*, which states that anthropology is the "discipline that uses ethnographic and ethnological data to establish general laws of social organization in our own and among archaic and traditional societies" (Gresle et al. 1994:17).

In this analysis of the introduction of anthropology to Vietnam, I shall therefore examine Vietnamese authors who studied and wrote about people, culture, and society in Vietnam or elsewhere during the colonial era. In this context, I will focus specifically on the assimilation of Occidental scientific thinking and methods, which enabled some Vietnamese to see humanity in general and their own society in particular through new eyes. First of all, let's explore how this new field of "Vietnamese studies" became established during the French colonial era.

THE FIELD OF VIETNAMESE STUDIES (1862–1945): A DYNAMIC APPROACH

To understand how Vietnamese scholars conducted their research, I applied Pierre Bourdieu's concept of the "field" of study to their work. In this context, the Vietnamese work is no longer isolated from that of French and other Western authors as it was in a number of studies that differentiated between "ethnic" and "national" (a distinction that was created afterward) to account for particularities of scientific research. On the contrary, it is now clear that the meaning of a discourse and its very existence must be sought in the relation it bears to other discourses of its time (Foucault 1966).

The concept of the "field" also enables us to grasp the dynamic nature of the discourse; it is like a "force field," where a magnet is subject to the opposing forces of the negative and the positive poles. As in the sociological arena, between the "poles" of the dominant and the dominated, the "positions" occupied by the "agents" are defined by each other. In describing these positions, we describe a certain structure of social reality: "The fields appear to contemporary understanding as structured spaces of positions. . . . The structure of a field is a factor of the relationship of strength between the agents or institutions that are engaged in the struggle—or, if you prefer, of the distribution of the specific capital that, having been accumulated through previous struggles, steers future strategies" (Bourdieu 1980:116).

While each field is independent, with its own rules, it is equally linked to other social fields that can influence its evolution. For instance, in the colonial context, the scientific field is particularly sensitive to impacts from the political field, as we shall see in several instances. Hence the field is not a stable, fixed area with well-defined boundaries; instead, it is constantly in flux. This tension between the positions and between the agents must be fully grasped in order to understand the evolution of the whole—in contrast to, for example, Edward Said's viewpoint.

From this perspective, the sociological and cultural studies of Vietnamese scholars belong to the specific field of Vietnamese studies, which I define as having four stages between 1862 and 1945. This field of Vietnamese studies first made its appearance during the presence of the French administration. In the first period (1862 to the end of the nineteenth century), research was closely linked to the requirements of the conquest and then to the establishment of the colonial administration. The majority of relevant publications at this time were the work of the French military, administrators, colonists, and missionaries. A few Vietnamese authors—notably, Pétrus Trương Vĩnh Ký and Paulus Huỳnh Tịnh Của—added to this store of knowledge with works of lexicography, popular literature, history, and geography.

In the second period (1898–1928), the EFEO, founded in 1900, became the center. This institution was created primarily in response to developments in science, but it also supported the drive to "conquer the hearts" of indigenous people and justified the colonizers' "civilizing mission." The EFEO formed part of general government services in Indochina, but its scientific functions (notably, control of who could be proposed for membership and subsequently nominated by the governor-general) were entrusted to the metropolitan and scientific Académie des Inscriptions et Belles Lettres. The EFEO's official mandate was to bring together under one roof all the research in social sciences and humanities that had been done in Indochina and to exert its scientific authority over members of local organizations such as the Société d'Études Indochinoises, founded in 1883 in Saigon, and the Association des Amis du Vieux Hue, founded in 1913.

This was a period of huge turbulence in Vietnamese society. Armed resistance having failed, modernizing academics recommended that the country should open itself up to the West and learn from the outside world in order to modernize its society. Subsequently, a new cohort of intellectuals of the Franco-indigenous school began to publish the first studies of Vietnamese society. These appeared primarily in the magazines *Đông Dương tạp chí* (1913–19) and *Nam Phong* (1917–34), which were edited by brilliant teams with a mastery of several cultures (Vietnamese, Chinese, and French).

The third period (1929–39) is characterized by the Vietnamese mastery of scientific research. Within the EFEO, Vietnam was elevated to the status of assistant by the memorandum of 7 October 1929 and obtained full scientific membership by the decree of 29 July 1939. This last measure was taken in the context of the approaching World War II and of Japanese propaganda contesting French authority over Indochina (*Journal Officiel* 1939:2576). At the same time, there were structural failings within the EFEO that meant that, for various reasons, Vietnamese studies were neglected in favor of research into the more noble cultures of China and India.

These factors led to a number of Vietnamese obtaining research posts within the EFEO. Up until 1945 the Vietnamese group consisted of four assistants (Nguyễn Văn Tố, Nguyễn Văn Khoan, Trần Văn Giáp, and Nguyễn Thiệu Lâu) and one member (Nguyễn Văn Huyên, who joined the EFEO in 1938 and was made a temporary member in 1939). This rise by Vietnam to the higher reaches of scientific endeavor occurred simultaneously with a real Franco-Vietnamese collaborative effort, embracing both friendly relations and exchanges and more formal cooperation. The Indochinese Institute for the Study of Humankind was founded in 1938 as a result of a "spontaneous initiative" by a collective of French and Vietnamese from the EFEO and the Faculty of Medicine.

Equally important, on the part of the Vietnamese there was a real desire to seek understanding about humankind and to appropriate Vietnam as a subject for study in order to gain expertise about the country and then to diffuse this information. This strong desire was driven by the high stakes that were specific to the field of Vietnamese cultural studies, including the definition of an identity and the construction of a new national culture. The debate during the 1930s between academics and intellectuals about *quốc học* (national studies) is an example of this.

From 1940 to 1945 the Vietnamese position strengthened. Nguyễn

Văn Huyên was elected a permanent member of the EFEO in June 1941. Georges Coèdes, the EFEO's director, applauded his "incomparable advantage of having a personal and native experience of Vietnamese society," which enabled him to "conduct his studies at a deeper level than would be possible for European researchers" (1944:v). Here is a case of Vietnamese skills being recognized by the highest scientific authority in the field. On the Vietnamese side, the prospect of approaching independence stimulated researchers to unite implicitly around the "common purpose of cultural liberation as a precondition for political independence" (Trinh Van Thao 1997:107). This is exemplified not only by the magazines *Thanh Nghị* and *Tri Tân* but also by the work of Đào Duy Anh and the translation of scientific terms by Hoàng Xuân Hãn.

After 1945 political events hastened the transformations that were under way in the field of Vietnamese studies. The Japanese *coup de force* of 9 March marked the end of the EFEO's colonial period. A few months later, the independent Vietnamese Institute of the Far East (Phương Đông bác cổ học viện) was created to develop research projects and train young Vietnamese scholars. This institute and the University of Vietnam, which also teaches researchers, were the starting points for the country's current research institutions. These institutions are the tangible outcome of a long process of learning from the scientific thinking and methods brought in from the West.

LEARNING TO DO SCIENTIFIC RESEARCH

The dominant position of the EFEO led to it being considered the place where Vietnamese intellectuals were "manufactured." However, the archives are insufficient to give us a full picture of the process that they went through to learn how to conduct research. We have to look farther afield within the mass of information that has been produced, including not only official accounts, reports, articles, theses, and so on but also journals and memoirs. In my thesis, I made an analysis of this literature, which I called the "corpus of Vietnamese anthropology." I exhaustively appraised some works by Vietnamese authors on humanity and society while merely referring to others, since there is a considerable variation in the quality of these works. This great number of sources enabled me to build up a picture of where research was being done and disseminated and where the scientists' training and networking were taking place in order to understand the process they went through to learn how to do scientific research.

Where Research Was Being Done and Disseminated

It is notable that the official institutions hold only a limited number of Vietnamese compositions—this applies not only to the EFEO and the Institut Indochinois pour l'Étude de l'Homme (IIEH, 1938–45) but also to the Conseil des Recherches Scientifiques (1928–45) and the Conseil de Recherches et Études Historiques, Juridiques et Sociales (CREHJS, 1943–45). Some Vietnamese scholars practiced scientific research as part of their studies at the universities and *grandes écoles* in France; an exhaustive search of the *Catalogue of University Theses* turned up a total of 307 theses submitted by Vietnamese between 1911 and 1945 (252 in medicine, 4 in pharmacy, 43 in law, 4 in humanities, and 4 in science). Among these, several relate to humanity and society, such as, for instance, Nguyễn Văn Huyên's 1934 humanities thesis in Paris and Vũ Công Hòe's 1937 medicine thesis in Hanoi titled "Suicide in Annamite Society."

Research was also carried out and disseminated through scholarly societies in Vietnam. Among these, the Société d'Études Indochinoises (SEI, 1883–1945) and the Association des Amis du Vieux Hué (AAVH, 1914–45) are the best known, but the Geographical Society was also notable for its conferences and its journal, in which, for instance, Phạm Quỳnh published his 1930 essay "The Tonkinese Peasant Described through the Oral Culture."

Cultural reviews also published a great number of Vietnamese works. Apart from *Đông Dương tạp chí* and *Nam Phong,* worthy of particular mention are French magazines *Est* (1939) and *Indochine* (1940–45); Vietnamese-language *Đông Thanh* (1932–34), *Tri Tan,* and *Thanh Nghị* (1941–45); and the bilingual bulletin of the Société d'Enseignement Mutuel du Tonkin (BSEM, 1920–38). These Vietnamese magazines saw themselves as the hub for coordinating studies on Vietnam.

Several newspapers carried frequent columns relating to cultural and scientific life in Indochina, for instance, *l'Echo Annamite* and *Avenir du Tonkin.* In his newspaper *Annam Nouveau,* Nguyễn Văn Vĩnh published high-quality articles such as the series on Annamite cus-toms and institutions (February–September 1931), which Pierre Gou-rou cited copiously in his *Peasants of the Tonkinese Delta*. Other peri-odicals of a more or less specialized nature—for example, the *Bulletin Économique d'Indochine*—would also occasionally publish articles by Vietnamese authors.

Authors and private printers published a great deal, though only a part of this corpus is known today. Worth mentioning are Trần Trọng Kim's *Summary History of Vietnam* (1920) and *Confucianism* (1930–33) and Nguyễn Văn Ngọc's *Proverbs and Popular Songs* (1928) and *Tales of the Southern Country*.

Research and publication occurred in many different contexts. A lot of knowledge was displayed, for instance, through the works of the art schools and the skilled artisans under local administration; in such ways, learning was passed on. Let's look at traditional art: according to Louis Bezacier, who wrote *Drawings of the Monuments of Northern Vietnam* (1959), artists from EFEO and students of the École des Beaux-Arts de l'Indochine made several drawings of pagodas and temples; however, none of these drawings was published before 1945 (apart from the ones of the *temple du génie tutelaire* in Đình Bảng village), and many were destroyed in the war.

This summary of where Vietnamese research and publication were taking place shows the need for further work to be done to chroni-cle and log the existing corpus. Study of their contents and possibly their reprinting could be extremely useful for contemporary scholars, as demonstrated by the translation and publication of the works of Nguyễn Văn Huyên in Vietnamese a few years ago. Now let's look at the places where scientific research was being taught and try to deter-mine how this learning proceeded.

Centers of Learning

Despite its objective of training subordinate technical staff, the Franco-indigenous school undoubtedly contributed to the growth of genera-tions of Vietnamese intellectuals. There were some brilliant students eager to learn from passionate and competent teachers, as exemplified by the well-known relationship between Pierre Gourou and Võ Nguyên

Giáp, who would go on to become General Giáp of the battle of Điện Biên Phủ. Đào Duy Anh, however, in writing of the school, highlights "new knowledge and methods that the foreign teaching should necessarily and objectively bring to bear" (Đào Duy Anh 1989:20). We can thus consider the Franco-indigenous school as the primary center of learning for the thinking and methods of scientific research.

Higher education in Indochina produced an intellectual elite with skills and qualifications on a par with their French colleagues. The editorial team of *Thanh Nghị* was mainly made up of young graduates of the University of Indochina in Hanoi. As for the École Supérieure de Pédagogie of Hanoi, the literary critic Đặng Thai Mai wrote: "In the fields of Vietnamese, Chinese, and French literature, alongside the primary goal of training future schoolteachers of literature and literary history, the École also sought to teach students methods of research. Analysis of the texts was used as a vehicle for familiarizing us with the stages of research: research and writing of the bibliography, analysis of existing studies as a basis to establish the focus of your own work. As far as I'm concerned, that was the most important thing" (1997:291).

Studying the biographies of the authors, however, shows that most of them are autodidacts. The following confession by Phạm Quỳnh is revelatory:

> Although I was the top laureate [of the College of Interpreters' diploma], the only Chinese characters I knew were the two that made up my name and surname. In the exam, one test consisted of translating a text in Chinese characters into French. The sum of my knowledge enabled me to obtain half a point! Thankfully I did not score zero, or I would have failed the exam; I wrote a page of French text that was completely different from the Chinese! ... Following this experience, when I joined the EFEO I didn't stint on my efforts, and I set to work to study the Chinese characters for several years. (1923:194)

This capacity for working hard was also a characteristic of many others such as Nguyễn Văn Tố, Nguyễn Văn Vĩnh, and Đào Duy Anh, who were motivated by their questioning of Vietnamese society and culture.

These scholars were able to self-teach so much thanks to the multitude of research tools available, in particular, the museums and libraries. Although only a small number have access to the EFEO library, municipal libraries and those of the learned societies are much more accessible. At the EFEO, Vietnamese staff (secretaries, scholars, artists) participated in the different stages of research, which enabled them to familiarize themselves with and absorb both scientific knowledge and methods (Nguyen Phuong Ngoc 2012:45–47). Although books and manuscripts had an important place, the works of Western scholars played an essential role in enabling Vietnamese authors to construct their own *problematiques* and to define themselves.

Direct contact with French scholars also played its part, whether through the EFEO or in the learned societies. Not much information on this subject is available, but by charting the personal contacts between Vietnamese and French, we can map the networks that supported the exchange and diffusion of scientific knowledge. The rather informal style of this cooperation helped research and publication to occur in a spirit of amicableness. On the institutional side, the EFEO (after the status of assistant was created in 1929) and, even more so, the IIEH, encouraged collaborative works jointly signed by Vietnamese and French authors.

A look at the contents of Vietnamese cultural reviews shows that research skills were also gained through articles and conferences. The case of the Société d'Enseignement Mutuel du Tonkin (SEM, 1892–1945) stands out because of its patient labor over half a century (Nguyen Phuong Ngoc 2009). In the minutes of Trần Văn Giáp's conference on the Thiên Mụ pagoda at Hue, we can see how the editors emphasize the necessary scientific attitude:

It is impressive to see how a scholar trained at the French Orientalist school, breaking away from Chinese science, will set himself to study an Annamite pagoda: with a spirit devoid of preconceptions or prejudice, he will form an opinion on the controversies that certain inscriptions may have engendered and express himself in a free and direct fashion without ever hiding his uncertainties or letting his personal judgement be intimidated. A scholar of former times, undertaking this same task of retracing the history of a religious edifice, would have adopted a cowed attitude and composed a few pages of respectful and vague description, hurrying on to other matters.

Mr. Trần Văn Giáp, on the other hand, attacked this element of his task with great honesty. (Trần Văn Giáp 1936:130)

Scientific thinking and methods were also introduced into the curriculum at private schools. During the French *resident* of Tonkin's visit to the SEM, the society's president explained its commitment to teaching pupils scientific rigor. Referring to the Chinese class run by Trần Hàm Tấn, who worked in the EFEO, the president said:

In our view, Mr. Tấn's vocabulary is distinctly superior to most of those used in schools. First, he distinguishes clearly between the different meanings of a word and classifies his examples in groups according to the different senses; thus, the passages that he teaches illuminate each other, so we are no longer dealing with a series of expressions that seem strung together haphazardly by their authors—as is the case with certain Sino-Annamite vocabularies. Second, Mr. Tấn was careful to briefly outline to his pupils which sources he took his texts from. With this measure, he introduced some order into the chaos that can otherwise prevail when Chinese phrases are set alongside each other, given that the texts spread over a period of more than three thousand years. It can be very useful to know whether a particular value attributed to a term originates in a book from antiquity or, conversely, in a book recently published in Canton or Shanghai. (Trần Văn Giáp 1936:189)

The same applied to lessons in French and English: several teachers taught pupils "how to take and use notes, what [modest] resources were available to them—the society's library, the motifs and sculptures in the pagodas, information of all types." Over and above personal commitment, the president emphasized that "within the society you'll find something more modern, a concern with precision and with accurate documentation, right through to the pupils' modern exercises" (Trần Văn Giáp 1936:189).

Scientific Thinking and Methods

Since the publication of Michel Foucault's *Les mots et les choses* (*The Order of Things*) there has been a consensus that all knowledge is embedded within the context of all its contemporaneous discourses and ideas, "*episteme*, which defines the conditions of the possibilities for knowing everything" (1966:179). The primary characteristic of our era is the scientific spirit. Nguyễn Văn Vĩnh, who was a proponent of self-knowledge distinct from morality, affirmed that "an intelligent man . . . must recognize the science of analysis from all these corners of the human soul" (1913). Several authors call for respect for the scientific attitude, not to adopt a position or assign a meaning to something a priori but to describe it as fully and objectively as possible.

Specifically, accuracy and precision with regard to facts, terms, and references are essential to learn. Nguyễn Văn Tố, assistant at EFEO and editor of several reviews (notably *Đông Thanh*, the BSEM, *Tri Tân*), was in the position of intermediary between the Vietnamese scientific, intellectual, and cultural milieus. As such, he is undoubtedly the one who made the most effort to inculcate the scientific spirit and conduct into the Vietnamese public. For instance, he explained that, contrary to learned tradition, no one should henceforth believe in a thing simply because it was written; it must be proven, which was why it was so important to give precise references and sources. In his numerous accounts, he made a point of correcting errors in titles, biographies, translations of Chinese terms, and so on. These labors demanded enormous conviction and patience in the face of others' reactions; for example, Ngô Tất Tố, a scholar turned journalist and writer of a book on ancient literature, wrote "with regard to a book that was already reduced to ashes a thousand years ago, it is not necessary to know that it consisted of two volumes." The pedagogue Nguyễn Văn Tố responded by explaining the scientific procedure: "Mr. Ngô Tất Tố is wrong. On the contrary, with regard to lost books written in Chinese characters, it is important to accurately record the title and the number of volumes in order to be able to locate them again. The EFEO's success in discovering some compositions from the Trần period is due to the fact that we had the exact name of the author, the title and the number of volumes" (1942).

Nguyễn Văn Tố also endeavored to provide guidance to beginners on how to carry out their personal research, as in the case of the reader who wished to compile a collection of proverbs and popular songs.

Elsewhere, he explained how to compare source materials in the case of an ancient text or the methods of a modern archaeological excavation:

Before translating an ancient text, one must assemble the copies and reprints (from the EFEO and Bao Dai [in Hue] libraries, etc.). When one has decided that the number of versions is sufficient, one compares them to see which one is the most complete, which is the closest to the original; only then can one begin to translate, taking care to mention different variations—which must be clearly annotated and precisely referenced. The reader must have enough information to be able to judge for himself. (Nguyễn Văn Tố 1942)

To obtain precise information, one must make several excavations, but methodically. Until now, the people who sell antiquities in the *quartier* Quần Ngựa performed digs at random and didn't respect the method outlined in the *Manual of Techniques for Archaeological Excavations* . . . published in Paris in 1939. . . .

When lovers of antiquities are present at a site where ancient objects are being uncovered, they should record the depth of the excavations and what objects have been found in the same place (e.g., coins—in the *quartier* Quần Ngựa a lot of coins from the Song dynasty [960–1127] have been discovered). In fact, these ancient objects should be kept, even if they are broken, for they might serve as a record, as opposed to written texts. (Nguyễn Văn Tố 1943)

Since, in Nguyễn Văn Tố's estimation, Vietnamese studies were in a state of "immaturity," he established—notably through the magazines *Đông Thanh*, *Thanh Nghị*, and *Tri Tân*—a communal concern for finding and collecting ancient Vietnamese works and critiquing their sources. These sources vary enormously in status, provenance, and nature. Alongside texts written by Confucian scholars, sources included popular songs, "realist" poems, family and village registers, stamps of stelae, oral sources, and tangible remains.

Many authors were engaged in another important project: the definition of scientific terms and concepts. In fact, the Vietnamese language and the Romanized script, *quốc ngữ*, only came into use for intellectual endeavors at the beginning of the twentieth century. In parallel with the task of coming to grips with the scientific attitude and methods, scholars had to create the right words to describe things clearly and accurately. Hoàng Xuân Hãn, author of the well-known *Vocabulaire scientifique*, published in 1942, put it like this in an interview in 1991: "People can't acquire . . . any scientific competence or spirit unless they have a scientific language. Already in 1930, when I entered the Polytechnic, I got this; I was still very young, I was already aware of the lack of scientific language among us, we weren't able to express things clearly, precisely, or in a modern fashion" (Trinh Van Thao 1997:108).

So it is that vocabularies and dictionaries play a particularly important role in the history of social sciences in Vietnam. New terms appeared and were disseminated through cultural reviews, notably *Nam Phong*. Written Vietnamese was decisively cataloged in the dictionary published in volumes (1931–37) by the Association pour la Formation Intellectuelle et Morale des Annamites (AFIMA), but Vietnamese readers learned the new terms and new ideas (particularly about Marxism) in the Chinese-Vietnamese and French-Vietnamese dictionaries compiled by Đào Duy Anh (1932 and 1936, respectively).

Acquiring the scientific mindset, learning the methods and techniques of social sciences and the humanities, translating and creating words to express new ideas and realities: these were the undertakings of Vietnamese scholars and intellectuals in the first half of the twentieth century. This journey was also one of discovery: new knowledge about humankind and society awaited them.

DISCOVERING THE "OTHER" AND ONE'S SELF

In assailing the Confucian belief system, colonialism set off whole new ways of thinking about people and society among the Vietnamese. A combination of factors—the failure of armed resistance; the decline of the monarchy's power; China's evolution; and most importantly, the example of Japan after its victory over "White" Russia in 1905—led to radical criticism of Confucianism and a call among some educated people, Phan Chu Trinh (1872–1926) chief amongst them, for fundamental changes in Vietnamese society to be instituted within the legal framework of colonialism. Manifold actions were undertaken aimed at disseminating knowledge by means of widespread education, modernization of customs, and development of the economy. These achievements are well known, even though further study needs to be done at the grassroots level to appreciate the concrete deeds of groups and individuals.

Here we are concerned with what modern scholars brought to anthropological thinking. If a large part of the population starts to believe that things need to change, and if this modernizing agenda is being propelled by fresh graduates and leaders, then these new thinkers are in fact the principal drivers of a genuine cultural revolution. Their aim was to overcome the ethnocentrism of society in Vietnam and the wider region generally, as explained in *Văn minh tân học sách* (Book of new studies of civilization, 1904). The people resoundingly endorsed this publication's condemnation of the established Confucian institutions. These critics of the existing order were equally scathing about what they considered the defects of the Vietnamese mentality: lack of honesty and irresponsibility. They judged these to have a negative impact on social relations.

At the same time, the new thinkers sought to gain knowledge of contemporary society, not only in the West but also in Japan, in order to modernize Vietnamese society. In this context, the *Quốc dân độc bản* (Reading book for the people) is a precious document: it introduced new concepts such as "citizen" and "the people" with social relations connecting them, political regimes, and the workings of the state and also outlines the structure of a modern economy with components such as private property, salaries, capital, the division of labor, the exploitation of machines, commerce and finance (banking, modern methods of payment, etc.).

Here an analysis of society was under way in order to better understand its workings and, for the first time, intervene in a conscious manner. In contrast to the Confucian tradition, the point of interest is now how people are living in current society, rather than an ideal and idealized society in ancient China. This makes space for a whole new way of thinking about human diversity: the "Other" and the self.

With colonialism, actual contact (administrative, commercial, tourism) between the populations increased and contributed to a gradual change in the way the Other was viewed. Vietnamese newspapers and magazines from before 1945 carried a large number of articles on the world and the local region, and some reviews such as *Đông Thanh* and *Tri Tan* even had a regular column. As an example of the level of significance accorded to neighboring contemporary societies by *Đông Thanh*, for instance, issue no. 21 carried an article about Thailand's provisional Constitution of 1932. The review *Nam Phong* developed a specific genre, *du ký* (relation of travels), which seemed particularly appropriate for reflecting on human differences and resemblances. From a cursory count, around a thousand pages of this review were devoted to travel: whether it was a journey to a distant place (France, China, etc.), a neighboring country (Laos, Cambodia, etc.), or a local region, these reports by staff and readers highlight some hitherto unsuspected aspect of the culture that the traveler discovered.

During the colonial period, the Vietnamese displayed strong curiosity about other societies—and this was mirrored by their interest in their own culture. We have to bear in mind that Vietnamese society evolved in the shadow of China and was greatly defined by this relationship. From declarations of independence in the distant past—such as Lý Thường Kiệt's famous eleventh-century poem or that of Nguyễn Trãi in the fifteenth century—up until the 1930s debate about *quốc học* (national studies), the relationship between Vietnam and China has been very complex, yet hardly studied. During the colonial period, yet another player joined the mix—France. Although at the beginning of the twentieth century, modernist scholars distanced themselves from the Confucian tradition, the common ancestry of Chinese and Vietnamese culture was clear—indeed, the very existence of these scholars was a manifestation of it: they thought and wrote in Chinese characters, even when they were calling for the adoption of the new Roman script invented by Westerners. In the space of one generation, the situation has altered radically, and some people even claim that books written in Chinese characters by Vietnamese authors belong not to Vietnam but to China. Thus without either books or traditions, Vietnamese intellectuals of the 1930s were free to define and build their own culture. As the poet Lưu Trọng Lư bitterly stated, "We borrowed everything from our neighbor, from a simple poetical construction to a wise philosophy. Before, we were Chinese; recently, we have become Western; but we have never been Vietnamese" (1939).

It is clear that how Vietnam was viewed by the West and by France in particular has had a great bearing here. In fact, the Orientalists saw Vietnam as some sort of copy of China. In 1933, in relation to some Vietnamese documents written in Chinese characters, a member of the SEI wrote, "All experts on China ... are close to denying any literary originality in Indochina" (BSEI 1933, no. 4, p. 7). A discussion of this "Chinese paradigm" doesn't fall within the scope of this chapter; however, for intellectuals trained within the Franco-indigenous school, the question of the validity of Vietnam's civilization became fundamental, since they were familiar with the views of the French and other Orientalists. Nguyễn Mạnh Tường (doctor of law and humanities at the University of Montpellier, 1932) wrote of how Nguyễn Văn Huyên, among several others, was responding to this question: "The crucial question addressed here by Mr. Huyen, which he answers in his subsequent works, is this: Is there such a thing in Annam as an 'Annamite' civilization, by which I mean an original civilization which is not merely a reflection of the Chinese? This is not a purely personal question; it is the issue that preoccupies all the men of our generation" (undated article).

This effort to gain self-knowledge, motivated by a desire to define a Vietnamese identity, spurred the production of an abundance of texts. Alongside learned articles, university research, and scientific papers on specific aspects of the question, books were compiled that sought to give a holistic depiction of the reality of Vietnamese culture, for example, *Précis of Vietnamese Civilization* (Đào Duy Anh 1938), *Annamite Civilisation* (Nguyễn Văn Huyên 1944), and *Vietnamese Society* (Lương Đức Thiệp 1944).

This trend also made visible people who up until then were hardly known to exist. Traditionally, there were four social classes (scholar, peasant, craftsman, merchant), but now scientific investigations, journalistic inquiry, and literary creation sought out both men and women, old and young, peasants and factory workers, even those living on the margins. Even the scholars themselves became objects for research (Trần Văn Giáp 1940–41; Ngô Tất Tố 1941).

It was discovered that the artificial borders created by the colonizers didn't only enclose the Việt (or Kinh, inhabitants of the plain) people but also other ethnic groups living at altitude. These other groups were now the subject of intense interest, having previously been considered "barbarians" by the Confucian Vietnamese. The novels of Thế Lữ and Lan Khai describe encounters between Viets and people from elsewhere, in the wilderness. Huỳnh Thị Bảo Hòa published in Vietnamese *Chiêm thành lược khảo* (A summary study of the Champa, 1936), collating French research within the framework of his own observations. The brothers Nguyễn Kinh Chi and Nguyễn Đổng Chi made a study of the Bahnar and Djarai peoples of the central plateaus in 1937. Nguyễn Văn Huyên studied ethnic groups from Southeast Asia and North Vietnam. The interest that these minority ethnic groups attracted led them to be considered part of a big family—Vietnam. This country did not yet exist officially: the territories of the future Vietnam were Annam, Tonkin, and Cochinchine. Yet several authors used the word in their Vietnamese writings, as we have seen in the titles mentioned above.

Evidently, a consciousness of the country of Vietnam now existed, taking account of the existence of different ethnicities. In an account of a tour organized by the review *Thanh Nghị*, the writer, discovering similarities between the Việt and the Mường of Thanh Hoa province (about two hundred kilometers from Hanoi), expresses his feelings by saying, "This young girl looks like my cousin in the village" (Nguyễn Thiệu Lâu 1943). This is also explained by the strong interest in forming a state and a nation of Vietnam; *Thanh Nghị* was spearheading a research project on the establishment of Vietnam, particularly on the Viets' march south and the mingling of populations. This was also one of Nguyễn Văn Huyên's research themes through his studies of demographics, historic regions, and the ethnic groups of northern Vietnam.

What we are seeing, then, is the Confucian organizational model— with civilization at the center and barbarians at the margins—being replaced with a nascent new model of a multiethnic and multicultural Vietnam (Couvreur 1999:87–88). Thus, colonization provided the Viets with an unrivaled opportunity for openness to other cultures.

In Vietnam, anthropology—in the sense of the study of humankind and society—is a Western importation. It emerged and developed as a result of learning scientific thinking and methods. This process occurred at the crossroads of French and Western research with the knowledge of the scholarly tradition and within a specific historical context that was linked to the colonial situation and that stimulated reflection on self and the Other. In the 1930s research went from being a hobby to becoming a professional endeavor at the heart of the EFEO and the IIEH. The successful trajectory of Nguyễn Văn Huyên, the only Vietnamese scientific member of the EFEO and one of the founders of the IIEH, epitomizes this development and the conquest of the scientific domain by Vietnamese authors.

TRANSLATION BY HELENE TAMMIK

REFERENCES

Bezacier, Louis. 1959. Relevés des monuments anciens du Nord Viêt-Nam. Paris: EFEO.

Bourdieu, Pierre. 1980. Questions de sociologie. Paris: Minuit.

———. 1998. Les règles de l'art: Genèse et structure du champ littéraire. Paris: Seuil.

Clémentin-Ojha, Catherine, and Pierre-Yves Manguin. 2001. Un siècle pour l'Asie (L'Ecole Française d'Extrême-Orient, 1898–2000). Paris: Les Éditions du Pacifique—EFEO.

Coèdes, Georges. 1944. Preface. In Le culte des immortels, by Nguyễn Văn Huyên. Pp. v–vii. Hanoi: IDEO.

Couvreur, Séraphin. 1999. Chou King, livre de l'histoire. Paris: Librairie de You-Feng.

Đặng Thai Mai. 1997. Đặng Thai Mai toàn tập. Hanoi: Van Hoc.

Đào Duy Anh. 1989. Nhớ nghĩ chiều hôm. Hochiminh City: Ed. Tre.

———. 1938. Việt nam văn hóa sử cương. Huế: Quan Hải tùng thư.

Dartigues, L. 2001. Les représentations françaises du monde social vietnamien à travers les textes savants, 1860–1940. PhD dissertation, EHESS, Marseille.

Foucault, Michel. 1966. Les mots et les choses: Une archéologie des sciences humaines. Paris: Gallimard.

Goscha, Christopher E. 1996. Récits de voyage viêtnamien et prise de conscience indochinoise (c. 1920–c. 1945). In Récits de voyage des Asiatiques: Genres, mentalités, conception de l'espace. Claudine Salmon, ed. Pp. 253–279. Paris: EFEO.

Gourou, Pierre. 1936. Les paysans du delta tonkinois. Paris: Les Éditions d'Art et d'Histoire.

Gresle, Fr., M. Panoff, M. Perrin, and P. Tripier. 1994. Dictionnaire des sciences humaines (anthropologie–sociologie). Paris: Nathan.

Huỳnh Thị Bảo Hòa. 1936. Chiêm thành lược khảo. Hanoi: Impr. Dông-Tây. Review by Nguyễn Văn Tố in EFEO. Pp. 506–507.

Kleinen, J. 2005. Tropicality and Topicality: Pierre Gourou and the Genealogy of French Colonial Scholarship on Rural Vietnam. Singapore Journal of Tropical Geography 26(November):339–358.

Kleinen, J., Nguyễn Văn Khoan (1890–1975). 2014. An Odd Man out of Vietnamese Anthropology? Moussons, no. 24:79–90.

Luận về quốc học. 1999. Da Nang: Ed. Da Nang.

Lương Đức Thiệp. 1944. Hanoi: Xã hôi Việt Nam.

Lưu Trọng Lư. 1939. Một nền văn chương Việt Nam. Tao Đàn, no. 2, March 16.

Ngô Tất Tố. 1941. Lều chõng. Hanoi: Mai Linh.

Nguyễn Kinh Chi and Nguyễn Đổng Chi. 1937. Moi Kontum. Hue.

Nguyễn Mạnh Tường. De quelques travaux récents de la jeune science annamite. Undated article, archive of the family of Nguyễn Văn Huyên.

Nguyen Phuong Ngoc. 2006. Paul Mus et les "annamitisants" viêtnamiens de l'École Française d'Extrême-Orient. In L'espace d'un regard: Paul Mus et l'Asie (1902–1969). David Chander and Christopher E. Goscha, eds. Pp. 151–171. Paris: Les Indes Savantes.

———. 2009. La Société d'Enseignement Mutuel du Tonkin (1892–1945). In Vietnam le moment moderniste (1905–1908). Gilles de Gantès and Nguyen Phuong Ngoc, eds. Pp. 223–237. Aix-en-Provence: PUP.

———. 2012. A l'origine de l'anthropologie au Vietnam. PhD dissertation, Aix-en-Provence.

Nguyen The Anh. 1985. L'élite intellectuelle viêtnamienne et le fait colonial dans les premières années du XXe siècle. RFHOM, no. 268:291–307.

———. 1992. Monarchie et fait colonial au Viêt-Nam (1875–1925): Le crépuscule d'un ordre traditionnel. Paris: Harmattan.

Nguyễn Thiệu Lâu. 1943. Người Mường châu Ngọc Lặc. Thanh Nghị, nos. 29–31.

Nguyễn Văn Huyên. 1933. Introduction à l'étude de l'habitation sur pilotis dans l'Asie du Sud-Est. Paris: Librairie Orientaliste Paul Geuthner.

———. 1934. Les chants alternés des garçons et des filles en Annam. Paris: Librairie Orientaliste Paul Geuthner.

———. 1941. Recueil des chants de mariage Thổ de Lang Son et de Cao Bang. Hanoi: EFEO.

———. 1942. Lược khảo về khoa thi Hội Quý Sửu (1913). Thanh Nghị, nos. 12, 13, 15.

———. 1944. La civilisation annamite. Hanoi: Direction de l'Instruction publique de l'Indochine.

———. 1995. Góp phần nghiên cứu văn hóa Việt Nam. 2 vols. Hanoi: Khoa Hoc Xa Hoi.

———. 2000–2005. Nguyễn Văn Huyên tòan tập—Văn hóa và giáo dục Việt Nam. 3 vols. Hanoi: Giao Duc.

Nguyen Van Ky. 1995. La société vietnamienne face à la modernité (Le Tonkin de la fin du XIXe siècle à la Seconde Guerre Mondiale). Paris: Harmattan.

Nguyen Van Phong. 1971. La société viêtnamienne de 1882 à 1902. Paris: PUF.

Nguyễn Văn Tố. 1942. Văn học đời Lý của Ngô Tất Tố. Tri Tân, no. 60.

———. 1943. Vết tích thành Đại La. Tri Tân, nos. 85–88.

Nguyễn Văn Vĩnh. 1913. Xét tật mình. Đông Dương tạp chí, no. 6, June 19.

———. 1936. Một tháng với những người đi tìm vàng. Annam Nouveau, no. 528–538.

Papin, Philippe. 1999. Viêt-Nam, parcours d'une nation. Paris: La Documentation Française.

Phạm Quỳnh. 1923. Pháp du hành trình nhật ký. Nam Phong, no. 75(September):193–196.

———. 1930. Le paysan tonkinois à travers le parler populaire. Hanoi: Đông kinh ấn quán.

Pham Thi Ngoan. 1972. Introduction au Nam Phong. BSEI, nos. 2–3.

Said, W. Edward. 1978. Orientalism. New York: Pantheon Books.

Salmon, Claudine, ed. 1996. Récit de voyage des Asiatiques: Genres, mentalités, conception de l'espace. Paris: EFEO.

Singaravelou, Pierre. 1999. L'École Française d'Extrême-Orient ou l'institution des marges (1898–1956): Essai d'histoire sociale et politique de la science coloniale. Paris: L'Harmattan.

Trần Văn Giáp. 1936. Cổ tích của người Việt Nam ở Huế: Chùa Thiên Mụ. BSEM, January–June, 97–109.

———. 1940–41. Lược khảo về khoa cử Việt Nam từ khởi thủy đến khóa Mậu Ngọ (1918). Bafima, 41–92.

Trinh Van Thao. 1990. Vietnam du confucianisme au communisme. Paris: Harmattan.

———. 1997. Hoàng Xuân Hãn: Essai d'un itinéraire intellectuel. Approche Asie, no. 15:105–111.

———. 2004. Les compagnons de route de Hồ Chi Minh: Histoire d'un engagement intellectuel au Viêt-nam. Karthala.

Văn thơ Đông kinh nghĩa thục. 1997. Hanoi: EFEO, Ed. Van Hoa.

Vu Cong Hoe. 1937. Du suicide dans la société annamite. Thesis, Hanoi.

11

Life in Hanoi in the State Subsidy Period

Questions Raised in Social Criticism
and Social Reminiscences

The important exhibition *Life in Hanoi in the State Subsidy Period, 1975–1986* closed at the Vietnam Museum of Ethnology (VME) in the middle of 2007. The exhibition had been extended six months past the original plan to stay open one year, from June 2006 to June 2007. The public regretted the closing of the exhibition. Their regret not only surfaced at that time but continues even now whenever that period of time or the Vietnam Museum of Ethnology is mentioned, as the exhibition had increased the reputation of the VME. As the former director of the Vietnam Museum of Ethnology who chaired the exhibition, I felt distressed and upset when I could find no way to extend the exhibition or move it to another place to meet the needs of visitors who wanted to return or of those who had not yet had a chance to visit the exhibition. Yet when the new VME director made this decision, I had retired already. I knew the exhibition had "hit home," meeting the needs of Hanoians in particular and Vietnamese in general, because it provided them with a chance to reminisce about a past in which it was unthinkable that they could not only survive but also live "innocently." The exhibit and what it stimulated was really a phenomenon rarely seen in Vietnam. Five years have passed. It is now the right time to look back at this unique exhibition.

This chapter, written by an insider, will present the context of the exhibition, clarifying the representation of the conflicting ideology and conflicting people: suffering and the desire to escape such suffering, constraint, and hardship during that state subsidy period while aspiring to hold that time as a nostalgic and good memory. These are two sides of the same coin that are difficult to clearly separate. Thus, the chapter tries to explain that the social psychology reflected by social criticism in the exhibition is characterized by both bringing together many conflicting emotions and memories and satisfying legitimate reminiscence by the owners of the cultural heritage of the state subsidy period.

THE SOCIOECONOMIC CONTEXT AT THE TIME OF THE EXHIBITION

In the first decade of the twenty-first century, Vietnam's socioeconomic situation saw many changes. Its economic face was completely different from that of the past. Its society was more vibrant and dynamic. Economic activities were transitional, from the centralized economy to the market economy, with many unique characteristics seen by some people as an "accumulating period or a primitive capitalist accumulation." The lives of people of all strata greatly improved, social stratification began and expanded, the gap between the rich and the poor widened, and rich and middle classes were formed in society, which was unimaginable in the period prior to Đổi mới (Renovation).

The Vietnam Museum of Ethnology was then in a mature stage, adopting a new approach following a number of exhibitions and demonstrations, meeting the needs of the public. These exhibitions included *Vietnam's Family Annals from Tradition to Modernity* (2001) and *100 Years of Vietnamese Weddings* (2005), which directly involved the community; and *The World through H'mong Children's Eyes* (2003), *Bronze Casting from Dai Bai Village, Bac Ninh* (2003), and *Traditional Weaving of the Lao in Na Sang, Dien Bien* (2003), which invited and involved community participation by providing people with cameras for their photovoice. In particular, the exhibition *Tu Chi—an Ethnologist* (2005) suggested for the VME a new way of looking straight at social problems that were ignored in the past. The VME accumulated certain experiences; most notable was the community approach and curatorship, reflecting daily social life and focusing on contemporary society. This has become a trend to orient the VME's continuous development.

Preparations for every exhibition at the Vietnam Museum of Ethnology often take a rather long time, one exhibition after another, and several exhibitions can be prepared by different working groups at the same time. During the curatorship for the exhibition *Tu Chi—an Ethnol-*

ogist, we had accessed his life history, particularly his life stories during the difficult years after 1975 in Hanoi. Tu Chi, with his symbolic image clad in Cham dress, carried a fabric bag with a container full of food for his lunch. Tu Chi's works included a self-criticism paper delivered at the party cell that stated his position in which he only focused on professional learning, as well as a request for an early payment of his translation fee in which he intentionally added the words "too hungry." These works show both reality and ironic heartrending pain. Dr. Truong Huyen Chi, a young North American–trained anthropologist, had regular discussions with me during the curatorship of the exhibition on Tu Chi. We discussed the exhibition's documentation and messages. I still remember that in such a context, Dr. Truong Huyen Chi more than once mentioned to me that in anticipation of the upcoming twentieth anniversary of Renovation, the VME should do something to exhibit the modern, everyday life of the Vietnamese. If on that occasion the VME failed to do so, we would be blamed by history. She and I often spoke openly in such a way to each other. I listened to Dr. Truong without saying a word and tried to focus on the exhibition on Tu Chi, desiring to make it an interesting and lively exhibition, because it was the first time the VME held an exhibition on the life of a scientist, and the topic of this exhibition was considered by many as not relevant to the Museum of Ethnology. People often think the VME should focus on ethnic minority groups, customs and traditions, costumes and houses, not on the history of a human life.

The second workshop, on ethnological/anthropological films, was sponsored by the Vietnam Museum of Ethnology and funded by the Ford Foundation; it was held on July 7–8, 2005.[1] Dr. Michael DiGrigorio (Ford Foundation) especially encouraged the VME to develop a classic and modern approach to anthropological films through this film festival. He assisted the VME to invite a team of filmmakers from Yunnan, China, to introduce the Yunnan Film Festival, titled *Festival on Images of Cultural Diversity*, held several months earlier in March 2005. He also recommended us to Wendy Erd, an American working for a museum in Alaska, to help the VME filmmaking team to have a new look at anthropological films that were made using a community-based approach. I was attracted by the power of community films and a number of films brought to the workshop from the Yunnan Film Festival. Films such as *Drifting Specks of Dust* (Yi Sicheng, postgraduate student at Kiel University, Federal Republic of Germany), *Boy Not at Home* (He Yuan, Yunnan Social Sciences Institute, coordinator of Yunnan Festival Project), and *Christmas Eve in Cizong* (Zhang Xhongyun, Yunnan Social Sciences Institute), among others, reflect society truly and vividly. In particular, these films did not ignore the pressing issues of society. I was awakened by the socially profound counterarguments made by the filmmakers. Most of them were young but very courageous. That feeling and perception filled my heart during the film festival. A number of questions appeared in my mind. Why can't the museum assume its task of social counterarguments like these filmmakers? Why could our Chinese friends make such films with a new approach, but not Vietnamese filmmakers? Could we do it if we had good facilities and skills? I was urged by my heart to do something for my museum like what my colleagues from Yunnan had done.

I discussed this feeling with some of my colleagues. Once again, Dr. Truong reminded me of the twentieth anniversary of Renovation. I suddenly woke up and found what I needed to do. I was determined to do something very quickly and decisively. There were many things to do on this occasion, but two options for an exhibition came very clearly to my mind. One was to directly represent life in the first years of Đổi mới, with toddling steps, sometimes very silly and doing business in a "snatching" way. Relating to this option, I remembered that in 2001–2 I saw that Dr. Frank Proschan, an expert from the Smithsonian Institute who often worked with the VME, kept a coffee container with the brand name "MeHiCo." I recognized this as a type of advertisement the Vietnamese used in the first years of Đổi mới. Another thing that harassed me for some time in the past was why Vietnam television, when running ads, did not dare to say "advertisement slot" but used the rhetoric "economic information" instead? The other exhibit option was to represent everyday life in Hanoi before Đổi mới, which was suggested by the objects and documents from the exhibition on Tu Chi.

I knew that the Vietnam Institute of Social Sciences had been implementing a project funded by the United Nations Development Programme (UNDP) to review the twenty years of Đổi mới. This was a major political project whose director was Prof. Do Hoai Nam, president of the Vietnam Academy of Social Sciences (VASS). The project, implemented since 2004, involved many institutions, mostly in the fields of economics, legislation, sociology, history, and international studies rather than other scientific and humanities fields such as literature, linguistics, and anthropology. Of course, museums such as the Vietnam Museum of Ethnology were not the subject of this project. However, with long-standing experience in museum work, which can help assume the functions of social criticism, and being strongly urged by the vision of contemporary society after watching the films shown during the Yunnan Film Festival, I took the initiative to see the project secretariat to learn more about what they were doing and their expectations. I knew the project was in the final phase, focusing mainly on the review and successful lessons of the twenty years of Renovation. The project was mainly to praise the achievements of the Renovation process. I immediately realized one thing that was rarely mentioned or not really of interest, which was the root cause that led to Đổi mới. If it was ever mentioned, it was only mentioned theoretically, not from a human aspect and specific issues of everyday life. I made a quick decision to seize the opportunity of the review of twenty years of Renovation to organize an exhibition with social criticism through analyzing the reasons and root causes leading to Renovation. If we could make use of any opportunity from the *Project Support of the Review of 20 Years of Renovation*, this would be a wonderful opportunity to present some issues possibly considered sensitive that had never been openly made public and were absolutely without precedent. I also made a very quick decision on the second option on curatorship for the exhibition on the life of Hanoi people before Renovation as suggested by the documents from the exhibition on Tu Chi. This option was more unique than the first one because it was a gap that had rarely been mentioned and was of interest to researchers and politicians at that time. Moreover, what happened before the Đổi mới became recent history. Criticism of the past and of what was already overcome is somehow easier than criticism of what presently exists. The first option, presenting current life, has too many sensitive issues; thus, criticism could hurt anyone or any policy. Concerning this selection, I immediately looked back on the lesson learned by ethnologist Nguyen Van Huyen, which I had often thought of. In 1942, in the newspaper *Thanh Nghi*, there was a half-finished article, which was never completed, by Nguyen Van Huyen on the examination in the Year of the Ox (1913). He was fascinated by his analysis near the end of the article of the essays of the examinees, but he suddenly realized that the examination was held not very long ago, less than thirty years ago, so his analysis would touch "personal issues relating to legal and ethical aspects" (Nguyen Van Huyen 2000). He then decided to stop writing. The lesson I learned about sensitive issues helped me to focus the exhibition on a period rather long ago to be on the safe side when dealing with many sensitive issues of society.

I also want to mention another point. Without talking about this point, it is impossible to see why the exhibition was possible. When we were thinking of a plan for the organization of an exhibition on the occasion of the twentieth anniversary of Renovation, we realized the Vietnam Museum of Ethnology had no funds. We hoped that by taking part in the *Project Support of the Review of 20 Years of Renovation*, funded by the UNDP, we could access some funding for the exhibition. It was lucky that our exhibition proposal on the state subsidy period was accepted by the president of the Vietnam Institute of Social Sciences as an additional stakeholder of the *Project Support of the Review of 20 Years of Renovation*.[2] Moreover, for many years now, the VME had been a credible partner of Ford Foundation. Since 1996 the VME had received financial assistance from the Ford Foundation, so when we presented our idea on an exhibition on the period of state subsidies to Dr. Michael DiGrigorio, he accepted it immediately and supported us to make a project proposal on the production of a film on this period. Without funding from the *Project Support of the Review of 20 Years of Renovation* and the Ford Foundation, it was impossible for us to implement the exhibition on the life of the Hanoians on the eve of Renovation.

DISCUSSIONS AND DECISIONS ON THE EXHIBITION

To be successful, the exhibition *Life in Hanoi in the State Subsidy Period, 1975–1986* had to overcome many challenges from its initial to its final curatorship. Many issues were raised, and in this chapter I only want to present some of the most important issues.

The first and most important issue for us was how to gain consensus from the leadership of the Vietnam Institute of Social Sciences (currently the Vietnam Academy of Social Sciences), the line agency of VME, on the exhibition plan. Under the VME operational regulations, the director is responsible before the institute president for all of his professional decisions. Different from other foreign museums, it is the museum director, not the curators (exhibition directors), who makes decisions on the exhibition plan, ideological content, and content and art of representation. The museum director is the general director-commander of all curators. Anticipating the sensitivity of this exhibition, I had to hide in the shadow of the project or make use of the opportunity of the review of the twenty years of Renovation to ensure that the exhibition would not face any difficulties in terms of policy or guidelines so that it would not be misunderstood. I met Mr. Ha Huy Thanh, director of the project secretariat, Mrs. Tran Thi Lan Anh, secretary of the institute president, and members of the secretariat of the *Project Support of the Review of 20 Years of Renovation* to see whether we could squeeze into the project. After listening to my explanation, they advised me to see the institute president in person. The institute president realized this was a very interesting issue but asked me to send an official letter and a draft outline of the exhibition, possibly seeing some sensitive issues that needed to be evaluated by the advisory council as a ministerial-level task.

I had completed all the requests from the institute president by the end of July 2005. In a short time, the advisory council met to discuss the idea for an exhibition on life in Hanoi in the period of state subsidies. The outline of the exhibition, titled "The Life of Hanoians: Transition from State Subsidies to Market Economy," was sent to all council members. Present at the consultative meeting, chaired by Prof. Do Hoai Nam on the afternoon of August 12, 2005, were famous figures who had political or scientific authority: Mr. Nguyen Khanh, former secretary of the Party Central Committee and former deputy prime minister; Mr. Vu Quoc Tuan, former secretary to Prime Minister Vo Van Kiet; Prof. Dr. Pham Xuan Nam, historian and former deputy director of the National Research Centre for Social Sciences; Mr. Dang Phong, researcher in history and economics; Mr. Nguyen

Vinh Phuc, a Hanoi researcher; Prof. Dr. Ngo Duc Thinh, director of the Institute on Cultural Studies; and Dr. Ha Huy Thanh, director of the project secretariat.

Following the opening speech by Prof. Do Hoai Nam summarizing the outline of the exhibition, I waited with anxiety for comments from the council members, knowing that they were very valuable for a decision on the future of the exhibition. The meeting took place very favorably. There were no mixed opinions. All participants showed their consensus and support for the idea to organize the exhibition.

Mr. Pham Xuan Nam was the first to speak. He supported the exhibition, saying that through the museum language, the exhibition would contribute to reviewing the twenty years of Renovation. He recommended adding a subtitle, *Collection, Exhibition at Vietnam Museum of Ethnology*, so that this exhibition would not be confused with other research projects. He drew attention to collecting historical documents such as directives, resolutions, and particularly circulars on food distribution in Hanoi, for example, the distribution of bicycle chains and freewheels. A poster with the phrase "Bowls of Noodles without Meat" could be mocked up or reproduced, and objects such as books could be printed on dark paper. Attention should also be paid to moving images such as documentary films taken from the Central Documentary Film Studio showing scenes of people queuing up to buy goods. Prof. Pham Xuan Nam said that the first important thing was that the exhibition should stick to museum language. Social aspects were very important to understand the shift from the state subsidy period to the market economy period. Giving autonomy to the people and evoking their dynamism and sense of mastery have changed society. Hanoi was full of things and issues from the period of state subsidies.

Mr. Nguyen Khanh considered the exhibition project interesting. He said this project was significant for two reasons: first, it deals with renovation, from changes in the way of life and living standards to a description of the Renovation policy and freedom; second, it is of pure historical significance, like the Musée de l'Homme in France, which does not compare but just tells the historical truth. In the Musée de l'Homme, there were about twenty types of Vietnamese palm-leaf raincoats. He also stressed:

What is created today will be heritage in the future. Thus the exhibition should reflect the real life of Hanoi people twenty years ago. During the collection, not too much effort is needed to select objects. In that period, people wore narrow pants and flared trousers, short and long hair. What would the exhibition deal with? What about the improvement in people's living standards in quantity? Or changes that need some comparison? Attention should also be paid to cultural life, not only food and clothing. It should deal with changes in the perception of life, life style, and the perception of enjoyment and criticize a society of consumption, luxuries, and hedonism. On the impact of changes in cultural life in Hanoi, it should mention both positive and negative impacts. The content would likely be controversial.

Mention should also be made to the special characters of the Hanoians. Who are they? Are they Vietnamese, are they Northerners? There should be an introduction of Hanoi. International cooperation could be sought, with the Musée de l'Homme, for example. On collecting objects, attention should be paid to how to collect documents. What is the intention to exhibit them? The exhibition should show the increasingly rich and healthy life of the people. The party always cares for people's life, but is there contradiction between ideology, aspirations, and shortcomings in mechanism and management? (Notes from the meeting)

Mr. Nguyen Khanh also raised the following issue for discussion: "When did the period of state subsidies start?" He reminded us: "Criticism in the exhibition should be considered. Does the young generation ignore the past, and are they used to enjoyment? It is difficult to say what should be forgotten and what should be remembered. What was positive and what was negative? Negativity in the mechanism resulted in inequality, such as the saying 'Ton Dan belongs to kings and mandarins, Nha Tho is of flattering middlemen, and pavements are for heroic people.' It is difficult to praise and also to criticize, thus careful considerations should be made" (notes from the meeting).

Hanoi researcher Nguyen Vinh Phuc agreed with Prof. Pham Xuan Nam's opinion to add a subtitle to the exhibition: *Research, Collection, Exhibition . . .* He commented that the topic did not deal with the period of the market economy, only the period of state subsidies, not talking about Renovation but just starting with "breaking regulations." When discussing the educational program to accompany the exhibition, he said that education was difficult, and contacts should be made with the Hanoi Department of Education to get its support. He also wanted the VME to cooperate with Hanoi museums and the Hanoi Photographers' Association, as they would have related documents and objects. He also noted the use of two films: *Decent Story* and *Hanoi in Others' Eyes* by Tran Trong Thuy. He questioned: Is there a difference in the personality of the Hanoians and people from other regions? Is there any difference in terms of coupons?

For his part, Mr. Vu Quoc Tuan said that the idea of this exhibition project was very interesting, that life in Hanoi symbolized the whole country, and Hanoi was the center of the whole country to be introduced to the world. He added:

> The exhibition, using museum language, should mainly display objects. Texts are just partially needed, not the writings by noted figures; visitors have no time to read everything. The exhibition on culture should clarify culture in economics, culture in good conduct and behaviors between man and man. Cultural activities and cultural life such as those in Ton Dan and Nha Tho, a type of goods distribution shops should be eliminated. The necessity of these models should be made clear, as such models were necessary in wartime. The exhibition should be honest but not critical; careful collection of objects should be conducted, and more objects are better.

Mr. Dang Phong talked about the need to have the exhibition and appreciated the idea for the exhibition but said that this was rather late. He laid special stress on the collection of objects, saying that there is a lack of many objects for the exhibition topics. He suggested a number of typical objects of the period of state subsidies, such as three-pocket shirts; painted wooden clogs; elephant-ear and mouse-ear electric fans; Russian-made sewing machines; Saratov fridges; Neptune TV sets; tin and enamel ovens; wooden furniture such as tables and chairs and sun-shaped beds; motor bikes 102, 103, and 104; goldfish motor bikes; Commanca, Volga, and Muscovite cars; postal stamps and wedding cards; and cartoons, such as a collection of cartoons recorded in discs telling an economic history, including gasoline purchases and queuing up. Intershop is typical of the transitional period, as well as long queues. How can we acquire objects and understand them? The fund of 148 million VND allocated for the exhibition as proposed was too little. Additional funds would be needed because of the need to purchase many objects.

Prof. Ngo Duc Thinh highly appreciated the idea for the exhibition, saying that it was a unique idea. The exhibition outline was just an initial one and needed to be expanded, and attention should be paid to Hanoi. He worried about how the VME could present the transition in its museum language. In the 1975 transition—before Renovation—we struggled painfully to change our vision and our way of thinking. This shift was really great. How could the exhibition show this? How could it reflect the social face of Vietnam in that period of time? The shift could be made clear in our mind but was difficult to represent with objects.

He worried that the present time (1986 to today) was rather blurred in the exhibition outline. How could the exhibition present the gradual change in this period? Without films and objects, we have to revive artifacts. He worried about the words "still haunting" in the exhibition outline ("A not-long-ago past, still haunting the minds of many elderly people, yet for the young generation, it was too strange to them") and said such words should not be used. He also said we should be proud of it, telling two stories that were engraved in his mind from this time. They are memories of the first royalty he got, which was so big that he could buy a quilted blanket, and another memory about queuing up to buy rice, which was a famous story that later on I quoted in the exhibition: "After successfully buying the rice ration, I took a handful of rice to smell. If it had no moldy smell, I would feel excited for the whole day" (Vietnam Museum of Ethnology 2007). In short, Prof. Ngo Duc Thinh thought that the exhibition should reflect the nature of the transition, which was most important but difficult for the museum to do.

The meeting was rather quick and short, lasting for just two hours. Prof. Do Hoai Nam concluded by focusing on the following points:

The exhibition should focus on the topic of life of the Hanoians in the twenty years of Renovation, actually thirty years. They can be divided into subperiods: 1976–86, 1986–2000, 2001 until now.

Economic, social, and cultural life should be closely connected, and the most typical things of each period should be represented.

The exhibition should be associated with the development of Hanoi people supported by the UNDP project *The Cause of Renovation and Human Development in Vietnam*. Message: human development (UNDP).

The exhibition should focus on the collection and exhibition of artifacts. Separate scenarios should be developed for each subperiod: What was life like between 1976 and 1986? What were the most typical economic, social, and cultural aspects of this period? What about 1986–2000? The most typical thing was to create opportunities and build capacity for Hanoi people to develop.

The exhibition should let visitors make their own conclusions. The exhibition should not exhibit too many resolutions and circulars. Text panels should be lively.

The Communist Party had good intentions, but its strategy was poor. How could the exhibition avoid misunderstanding? Careful considerations should be made without criticism.

Prof. Do Hoai Nam concluded the approval of the exhibition project, and the exhibition outline should be further finalized for final submission.

Following the conclusion by Prof. Do Hoai Nam, Prof. Pham Xuan Nam added and fixed the title of the exhibition project, deleting the word "transition." The final title was *Life of the Hanoians before and during the Period of Renovation—Collection and Exhibition at the Vietnam Museum of Ethnology*. He asserted that through the museum language, the exhibition would contribute to reviewing the twenty years of Renovation. For his part, Mr. Dang Phong added the last words before the meeting closing, saying that the exhibition should only focus on the 1976–86 period. This exhibition would serve as the basis for an evaluation of the Renovation.

I sighed with relief, discharging all worries, listening to comments by each participant. I used two final comments made by Prof. Pham Xuan Nam and Dang Phong to revise the exhibition outline as a ministerial-level task.

I have experienced that with difficult issues the Vietnam Institute of Social Sciences often had similar consultative meetings. I still remember that when establishing the Vietnam Museum of Ethnology, the ethnologists in the institute were divided following a long struggle, forcing it to take a group of researchers from the Institute of Anthropology to found a new institution—the Museum of Ethnology. So the approval of the VME idea and the complete exhibition outline would face difficulty. Prof. Dr. Nguyen Duy Quy, director of the National Centre for Social Science and Humanity, said that if ethnologists from the museum and the Institute of Anthropology sat together, they would never come to an agreement on the scientific aspects of the exhibition; therefore, he had decided to approve the exhibition outline at a meeting of the advisory council, which was comprised of some leading professors, the institute director, and two French consultants, Christine Hemmet and Veronique Dolfus, who were working with the VME in 1996. That was the first time the Vietnam Museum of Ethnology had to submit an exhibition idea to the institute leadership. The second time, ten years later (2005), was the approval of an exhibition outline by the council meeting. That meeting went very well, with all politicians and scientists absolutely supporting the outline. This consultation was a guarantee, just like a pass and a permit for the exhibition, and it was valuable not only for the VME director but also for the institute president. After the exhibition was inaugurated, in addition to high praise for the exhibition content and the courage and straightforwardness of the museum in presenting a critical view of the issues of the period of state subsidies, there were also other public views. Some criticized the exhibition for praising the period of state subsidies at this time. Others had contrary views, saying that the exhibition was too harsh and even too merciless when looking back at the past and giving a very dull picture of society.

The exhibition *Life in Hanoi in the State Subsidy Period* was funded by the *Project Support of the Review of 20 Years of Renovation* with 397 million VND and also with additional funding by the Ford Foundation for the exhibition curatorship, organization, and production and for making two films on the period of state subsidies, among other things. The exhibition catalog was not mentioned in the project funded by the Ford Foundation; therefore, we had to ask for additional funding from UNDP through the *Project Support of the Review of 20 Years of Renovation*. One thing worried me. As UNDP is an agency of the United Nations, the funding contract does not allow any publications funded by it to be sold. Therefore, the exhibition catalog was only printed with the amount of copies as mentioned in the funding contract. It was not reprinted for copyright reasons and the initial binding contract, although it was much in demand by the public.

The exhibition was announced to be held jointly by two institutions, the Vietnam Museum of Ethnology and Vietnam Museum of Revolution. Many people questioned why the Vietnam Museum of Revolution took part in this exhibition. What was its role in the exhibition? It was true that the Vietnam Museum of Revolution did not join from the beginning, when initial curatorship was done, but was only involved in the last phase of curatorship and the collection of documents and artifacts for the exhibition. After launching a movement for the public donation of objects from the period of state subsidies to the Vietnam Museum of Ethnology and after a time of curatorship and collection, we realized that it would be a great shortcoming if we could not present completely the system of coupons in the period of state subsidies in the exhibition.[3] Objects were collected, but they were few and fragmented. This was the reason why we approached the Vietnam Museum of Revolution.

However, there was another reason. The Vietnam Museum of Ethnology could ask the Vietnam Museum of Revolution if it could borrow its artifacts. Borrowing objects is a normal practice between museums and was not difficult. But pure borrowing has little meaning. We realized that the topic of this exhibition was very interesting and relevant to the target groups that visited the Vietnam Museum of Revolution. It was more reasonable for the Vietnam Museum of Revolution to have done this exhibition. But for a long time now the Vietnam Museum of Revolution has often held short and simple special exhibitions on occasions such as the "celebrations of major anniversaries," humorously and ironically called by Vietnam's museum circle "exhibitions on death anniversaries." Our intention was to involve our colleagues from the Vietnam Museum of Revolution in the exhibition so that they would learn a new way of making an exhibition, not only praising or reporting achievements, as they often did, but telling everyday life stories with social criticism. We wanted our colleagues from the Vietnam Museum of Revolution, through joining us in this exhibition, to learn a new approach in exhibition preparations and curatorship. This goal was not just with the Vietnam Museum of Revolution alone but was the daily way of thinking about the community responsibility of the Vietnam Museum of Ethnology. For many years now, the Vietnam Museum of Ethnology has run training courses for its staff and colleagues from other museums. The Vietnam Museum of Ethnology had an initiative to organize an annual summer school for advanced training and to raise awareness for museum staff throughout the country.

The last reason associated with the big leap of the Vietnam Museum of Ethnology and the context of this exhibition was that this was the first time the Vietnam Museum of Ethnology implemented a major exhibition specializing in the everyday life of Hanoi people and about the residents of a city, the capital city. There were two clear challenges for us. First, the previously held exhibition, *100 Years of Vietnamese Weddings*, implemented by the Vietnam Museum of Ethnology, was a trial run. This exhibition was bigger in size and scale because the Vietnam Museum of Ethnology targeted not only the Viet but also urban residents—a target group not very familiar to many when thinking about ethnology. This was the first time the VME returned and made a firm and undeniable approach to its target group—the Viet and urban residents. Previously, the VME was only entitled to discuss issues relating to ethnic minority groups. This story is proof of the academic distribution map in social sciences in Vietnam, which has been affected by the evolutionary thinking in which ethnic minority groups were considered to have no history (this was the theoretical point of Eric Wolf, a Marxist historian). Second, the exhibition dealt with a politically sensitive issue in an attempt to explain why the Renovation was needed; that is, it talked about a dark night before the dawn and about society and people who had been driven to the wall, the crisis finally forcing the embarkation to the Renovation. A historical and anthropological approach is a way of explaining the root cause of the Renovation. The Vietnam Museum of Revolution and Vietnam Museum of Ethnology, playing their own social and political roles, would support each other in this exhibition approach.

With those thoughts, I came to see Trieu Hien, director of the Vietnam Museum of Revolution, to discuss cooperation. He accepted my proposal immediately and asked the Preservation Division to prepare a list of artifacts related to the period of state subsidies for selection to be presented at the exhibition. This list of artifacts did not stop at different types of coupons, which the Vietnam Museum of Revolution was strong in, but included other artifacts reflecting the life in the period of state subsidies. Some staff of the exhibition and the Preservation Divisions of the Vietnam Museum of Revolution were appointed by the director to work on the exhibition. While working with the exhibition team, these staff members were surprised again and again by the methods of the Vietnam Museum of Ethnology, which were completely different from what they did in their museum. During discussions of the curatorship, they could see group work by exhibition designers, curators, artifact preservation staff, and filmmakers involved in hot discussions, with everyone giving his or her own ideas, rejecting one idea, and agreeing on others. Later on, they told me that that democratic way was very useful, but their museum did not do similarly. Normally, exhibition ideas were given from the top down, and museum staff just did whatever they were told to do in their own responsibility without group work. They had never done any interviews with the subjects to find quotations, and personal stories were not used in the exhibitions. The museum staff had never made any community-based films by themselves. Community-based films have recently been favored because this method helps reflect the voices of the subjects, the owners of their own cultural heritage. Our colleagues from the Vietnam Museum of Revolution had learned new approaches, but back at their museum, how to apply them was another story. It depends on their own need, whether they really want to make a change in their museum, and it depends on the perception and determination of the museum from the director to the staff. Before the Vietnam Museum of Revolution was merged into the National Museum of History (2011), after five years of experience with us in the exhibition of the state subsidy period, I saw no exhibition held by this museum that was attractive, interesting, and lively, with a new approach and social counterarguments. This shows how difficult it is to make an exhibition in a fresh way with a new approach.

NAVIGATING AMID TIDAL CURRENTS

As known by everyone, *Life in Hanoi in the State Subsidy Period, 1975– 1986* became the final official title of this exhibition. In fact, during curatorship, some other names were proposed. As explained earlier, the title in the first exhibition outline presented to the advisory council for approval as a ministerial-level task was *Life of the Hanoians— Transition from State Subsidies to Market Economy* (July 2005). After comments from members of the advisory council, the title given to the exhibition in the revised outline submitted to the president of the Vietnam Institute of Social Sciences for approval in August 2005 was *Life of the Hanoians before and during Renovation*. Actually, the change was made not only to the exhibition's title but also to its content and, to be more precise, its curatorship content, and the exhibition was gradually finalized and became more focused. Both exhibition outlines (July and August 2005) covered the period of state subsidies and the period of the Renovation but focused more on the period of state subsidies. The advisory council was in a divided mind as to the word "transition," fearing that it was difficult for the museum's language to show the transition from state subsidies to a market economy. "Transition is in one's mind, but it is difficult for the exhibition to show it," according to Prof. Ngo Duc Thinh. For this reason, Prof. Pham Xuan Nam, when saying the last words before the meeting closed, recommended deleting the word "transition" in the exhibition title and replacing it with the more direct words "before and during Renovation" (this was the reason for the new title given in the revised exhibition outline in August 2005). Since these two scholars were not museum experts, they could not imagine how a museum exhibition could convey and display the transition from the command economy to the Renovation. The author of the outline wanted the exhibition to only focus on the period of state subsidies. But if the period of Renovation was not dealt with, it would be difficult, if not impossible, to take part in the project. Thus the exhibition outline, in spite of the title *Life of the Hanoians—Transition from State Subsidies to Market Economy*, during the curatorship and collection of artifacts, focused on artifacts from the period of state subsidies. The July 2006 outline stated that the exhibition would build "a special collection of documents and artifacts under the narrow topic of the life of Hanoians in the period of state subsidies" (3). The August 2005 outline repeated that statement and added that the exhibition would build "a special collection of documents and artifacts (including photos, video tapes, pictures, and posters) under the theme 'life of Hanoians in the period of state subsidies'" (4). Both outlines did not identify the research content and artifacts in need of collection on the market economy and Renovation period. Hanoi Researcher Nguyen Vinh Phuc was very sensitive when he commented, "This topic does not deal with the time of market economy, only the period of state subsidies; not Renovation but just the beginning of 'breaking regulations.'"

After the president of the Vietnam Academy of Social Sciences approved the project, we started the curatorship and collection of documents and artifacts. The exhibition content on the period of state subsidies became the main content. The third outline drafted for the working groups was titled "Orientations for the Exhibition *Life in the State Subsidy Period*" (2006). In this outline, to have more time for preparation, we wanted the exhibition to be inaugurated in the third quarter of 2006. But later on, the Secretariat of the Project on Renovation told us that an International Conference on Review of 20 Years of Renovation would be held in Hanoi in the last two weeks of June 2006; thus, the exhibition opted to open before the event so that delegates to the conference could visit it. For this reason, the fourth document, "Outline of the Exhibition *Life in the State Subsidy Period*" (2006), identified the inauguration date of the exhibition as June 15, 2006. So the exhibition was clearly identified with its orientation on the state subsidy period instead of before and during the Renovation. It means that with this identification, the idea of presenting the exhibition in three subperiods (1976–86, 1986–2000, and 2001 until now) as initially commented on by the institute president was eliminated, and the exhibition had only 10 months for preparations before its opening.

When identifying the main content of the exhibition in the orientation document, we clearly determined the period 1975–86/90 for curatorship. The question was raised as to when the period of state subsidies started—1975, or 1976, or before 1975? Actually, the mechanism of state subsidies existed for a long time, much before 1975 and since the anti-French resistance war, particularly since the restoration of peace in 1954 and the anti-U.S. resistance war, and it lasted until the Renovation. Yet this exhibition did not want to deal with the common mechanism of state subsidies but presented the period of the mechanism of state subsidies on the eve of Đổi Mới to explain the reason why the Renovation was needed. The exhibition did not discuss the mechanism of state subsidies and life in the state subsidies regime before 1975. That was a completely different period: the state subsidy period in wartime.

I will always remember the final words said by Dang Phong at the meeting of the advisory council: "Only focus on the 1976–86 period." However, I did not select the landmark of 1976, when consultation was made on the reunification of North and South Vietnam and the establishment of the Socialist Republic of Vietnam. This time was merely administrative and an outer sign. I believe the real landmark of the command economy period, the eve of Đổi Mới, was 1975, when South Vietnam was completely liberated. What about the end of the period of state subsidies? It was difficult to identify a precise landmark for the end of the period of state subsidies because it was a long process. The Sixth National Congress of the Communist Party of Vietnam was held in 1986, but its guidelines had just started. Đổi Mới was, in fact, a gradual process, with a little change in every month and every year. From 1986 to 1990 the Renovation guideline gradually entered into life and really improved the lives of the Hanoi people in particular and the entire Vietnamese people in general. For this reason, when mentioning the end of the period of state subsidies, the exhibition used 1986/1990 to talk about that ending process.

By selecting the life of Hanoi residents in the period of state subsidies as the research subject, the VME created a turning point that surprised many people. Many visitors and researchers wondered whether it was right for the exhibition to be held at the Vietnam Museum of Ethnology and whether it would be better and more reasonable for the exhibition to be held at the Vietnam Museum of Revolution or the Vietnam Museum of History. The subject of the exhibition identified right from the beginning was the lives of Hanoi residents, mainly urban residents. This selection of subject was a major change in the perception of the Vietnam Museum of Ethnology, because so far ethnology had only been seen as a discipline specializing in research on ethnic minority groups. In the last several decades, the strength of ethnology in Vietnam has been its research on ethnic minority groups and mountainous areas. If there was any research project on the Kinh-Vietnamese group, it was only done in rural areas and on the lives of farmers. Urban areas are not the traditional research subjects of Vietnam's ethnology. Since early 2000 the Vietnam Museum of Ethnology step by step has moved toward anthropological research, with a focus on research on contemporary life, and it has expanded its subjects of research to include urban residents. This exhibition was the largest in size and scope on the contemporary life of urban residents.

When the exhibition was inaugurated, there were mixed opinions. Some people questioned, Why did the museum praise the regime of state subsidies, which made many people suffer? This regime was dead; why revive it? Others had contrary opinions: The regime of state subsidies was good; without it we could not win over the United States; why was the museum criticizing it? For what purpose did the museum make this exhibition? Actually, each of these opinions was partially reasonable. At the meeting of the advisory council to approve the exhibition proposal, some members and the chairman of the council had forewarned that "it was difficult to both praise and criticize. . . . The exhibition should not show a critical attitude." They explained that "the Party always wanted to do good things for the people. Its idea was good, but its mechanism was not good, leading to mistakes. . . . The exhibition should take it into considerations to avoid misunderstanding." We always bore these comments in mind during the process of exhibition curatorship, but we also realized some conflicting issues here. Without social criticism, how can we explain the reasons and root cause for the Renovation? How about people's lives and the mechanism that led to the necessity for Đổi Mới? Without explaining the reasons and root cause of Đổi Mới, that is, that the society was driven to an overall crisis, the exhibition would be of no significance. In "Orientation for the Exhibition *Life in the State Subsidy Period*" we had already identified the objective of the exhibition, which was to "help visitors understand the life in the period of state subsidies, its historical context, ways of operations, and why Đổi mới was needed." Thus social criticism should certainly be done, but the question was, By what way could we make visitors accept it without being offended and shocked? We carried the concern for these issues and questions throughout the process of preparation for the exhibition, particularly in the final phase, when panel texts were developed and the exhibition was produced. We thought that the critical attitude of an anthropological exhibition lies in the true reflection of social life. This is relevant to the comments made by Mr. Nguyen Khanh at the meeting of the advisory council: "The exhibition should reflect the real lives of the Hanoians twenty years ago." This was the approach that we wished to use in the exhibition. We felt fully at ease when reflecting truly the social life and the spiritual life of the people on the eve of the Renovation. The final issue was the way of representation and display of events.

After twenty years of oblivion, one of the most outstanding events in the exhibition was the return of the poem "Remembering Uncle in Springtime." Here are a few sentences from the poem:

Spring returns, and I miss dear Uncle
The sound of firecrackers at New Year's Eve we recall those spring
    days when Uncle still gave us Tet wishes
. . . .
Springtime in our country
We miss Uncle Ho forever
We are still awaiting the fulfillment of your ideals
(Bodemer 2010:243–244)

The author of the poem, Ms. Pham Thi Xuan Khai, was invited to the inauguration of the exhibition and interactive activities as an honorable guest. It is still remembered that before the Sixth National Party Congress, the social atmosphere, for different reasons, was very tense and strangled. The poem "Remembering Uncle in Springtime" was published in the newspaper *Tiền Phong* (Vanguard) in March 1986 and was warmly accepted by the public. All copies of this issue of the newspaper were sold out immediately after coming off the press. At that time, photocopying machines were rare. People copied the poem by hand and passed it from one person to another, as the poem reflected social concerns. The poem was like a trumpet urging renovation with the call, "Whoever is empathetic! And who has to make corrections?" Yet the poem was then considered "problematic."

> Some people working in the cultural sector or in the leading agency of Nghia Binh Province (the native province of the poet) criticized the poem and the editorial board of *Tiền Phong* newspaper for allowing the poem to be published, saying that the content of the poem was counterrevolutionary and unconstructive, implying and causing disunity! It was sometimes so tense that Xuan Khai, the author of the poem, was supposed to be arrested. After her graduation, she could not return to her native province of Binh Dinh but had to stay in Hanoi City as a "nomad," suffering difficulties in trying to find a suitable path. Since she had graduated, she no longer had a scholarship, she had no job and no shelter, and thus suffered great hardship, earning her living in Hanoi for more than ten years, not to mention her efforts to support her family members, which made her life even more difficult.[4]

Whoever lived in Hanoi during that period thought that it would be a mistake to talk about the Renovation and the period of state subsidies without mentioning this poem. The poem itself and its fate, and later on the disclosure of the hard life of its author, were typical for the period of state subsidies. The poem was available, but how could we acquire its story? To our surprise, in early April 2006, about two months before the opening of the exhibition, Dr. Mai Thanh Son, secretary of the exhibition project, met the editorial board secretary of *Tiền Phong*, who had been criticized for publishing the poem. Fortunately, he had kept all the documents relating to this story. Dr. Mai Thanh Son also met the poet, Xuan Khai, and learned more about her hardship and difficulties throughout the past twenty years since the first publication of her poem. We were not hesitant in our decision to include the story in the exhibition. Yet a number of great concerns were raised: Will it be problematic to tell this story? What do the insiders think about this issue? Are cultural and arts managers still critical about this issue, as they have been in the past? To what extent is the poem sensitive if it is included in the exhibition? How will we tell this story? The success of the exhibition was storytelling. Our solution for sensitive issues in the exhibition was to observe the principle of no direct criticism or criticism in words, but let the artifacts speak for themselves, and let visitors feel and think for themselves when seeing the artifacts. Criticism means social reflection in an honest way. In this case, we had six objects and documents, but we decided to exhibit only three of them: the original manuscript of the poem, which was already blurred; a criticism paper of the editorial board sent to Mr. Vu Mao, then first secretary of the Youth Union Central Committee; and a paper verifying the antecedents, status, and conduct of the poem's author, who was then a student at Hanoi National University, signed by the university rector, Prof. Phan Huu Dat, and sent to the editor-in-chief of *Tiền Phong*. (Three documents that were not exhibited were a draft official letter of the Management of the Faculty of Philology sent to the university rector on the antecedents of the author and the artistic ideology of the poem, signed by Le Van Niem, secretary of the party cell and deputy dean of the faculty; a draft letter of the editor-in-chief of *Tiền Phong* sent to Mr. Le Duc Tho and Mr. Vu Mao asking for permission to publish an article about the author of the poem in the next issue on March 8, 1986; and a draft article titled "Meeting the Author of the Poem 'Spring in Memory of Uncle Ho,'" written by Le Van Ba, secretary of the editorial board, and a photo taken of Ms. Khai by Mai Ngu.) These three documents are very typical and tell the whole story. The first object was the original manuscript of the poem. The second one was the criticism paper telling the attitude of the authorities toward the poem, when a newspaper editor-in-chief was criticized for lacking political sensitivity in allowing the release of the poem to the newspaper. This criticism paper was addressed directly to Mr. Vu Mao, first secretary of the Ho Chi Minh Communist Youth Union Central Committee, now chairman of the National Assembly Office. The third object was the verification of the antecedents and status of the author of the poem, saying that she had no political problems. This was a common method of handling things whenever someone was suspected of having political problems. Together with the objects and a quotation of the interview, we used a verse from the poem as a conclusion of this section of the exhibition on the eve of the Renovation as a stake in the drama. The verse is "Whoever is empathetic! And who has to make corrections?" It was after this verse that the exhibition led to the section on the Renovation, which is also the concluding section of the exhibition, with the image of the Sixth National Party Congress, setting out guidelines for the Renovation.

The story of the poem was the most sensitive point in this exhibition because it was directly related to an ideological problem that had already been handled and to people who held important positions. Does the fact that this issue was made public mean exposing the childish truth of the past (using the power to handle what was related to a socially conscious poem written by a naive student) in which responsible persons never dared to admit their mistakes and then correct them and return justice to the victims?

After inaugurating the exhibition we received a warm response from the public and the media, yet we "held our breath" waiting for reactions from the authorities, particularly those from the ideological and cultural sector. We really sighed with relief when Mr. Vu Mao himself visited the exhibition. He was very happy to reminiscence about the past.

REMINISCENCES AND/OR SOCIAL CRITICISM?

During the curatorship and inauguration of the exhibition, we never thought it would be so attractive and draw such a large number of visitors, especially people from Hanoi and Vietnamese people in general. Although the Vietnam Museum of Ethnology has drawn lots of visitors, those who visited the exhibition were completely different. They included people of all strata, from poor and ordinary people to state employees and officials and rich business people. Many drove their private cars to the museum, bringing the entire family to the exhibition. It was the greatest surprise for us. We wondered what it was about the exhibition that was most attractive to them. Was it the content of the exhibition, or was it the design or techniques of the exhibition? We were very proud of the clear and logical road map of the exhibition, its good design and beautiful graphics, and its sophisticated lighting. All these elements contributed to the success of the exhibition. Yet they are not the reasons why people visited the exhibition. What were the reasons?

We observed visitors and found that all of them concentrated on each artifact, carefully reading the texts and quotes on the walls or in the panels. Parents discussed items with their children and grandparents shared with their grandchildren, explaining to them the objects and their stories. Those visitors who did not know each other stood together, contemplating the mockup of people queuing in front of a food shop, sharing with each other their memories and their stories relating to their queuing experiences in the past. We watched the visitors standing at the back of the last mannequin, one after another, smiling and talking to each other, sharing their memories of moldy rice, sorghum grains, and dried cassava sold together with rice. They shared with each other and told stories in a happy and humorous way. We did not see any angry faces. Visitors were happy finding a stone inscribed with the name Mai Hai, a staff person from the Research Institute of Nom Characters. The stone had been placed in the queue for him because the queue was too long, and it took a very long time to get into the museum. Visitors explained to each other how to use similar stones, bricks, or baskets to replace themselves in the queue, which sometimes formed in the early hours of the morning. A Vnexpress.net reporter wrote: "Mr. Vu Tran Cuong and his wife, who live in the new urban development area of Dinh Cong, heard about the exhibition yesterday and decided to visit it this morning by all means. Seeing 'the stone in a queue,' very small in the show case, named Mai Hai, No. 127 (the number of the book for purchasing goods), Mr. Cuong said he had two buckets used for the same purpose" (Viet Phong and Ha Vy 2006). The exhibition was really attractive to them, we realized, because they had a chance to reminisce about a past they had experienced.

The exhibition's book of visitors' autographs helped us understand more. The diary books of the exhibition had to be replaced, one after another, very quickly because so many visitors wanted to express their opinions and comments about the exhibition. In the exhibition diary on July 7, 2006, a visitor named Linh wrote, "Visiting the museum exhibition on the state subsidy period, many memories rushed back to me. I had the shivers standing in front of a former apartment in the period of state subsidies in the past. It was just like mine, with the same table and cupboard, a larder and a pig at the back of the house! I stood there silently for a long time. The only thing different is that my house was much narrower than this one at the museum." We had reproduced the apartment and the real story of the family of Ms. Tran Thi Lan Anh, a friend of ours and secretary of the project on the Renovation. While listening to the discussion at the meeting of the advisory council, Ms. Lan Anh told me about her husband family's apartment, no. 307 in Trung Tu Living Quarter, where she lived during the 1970s and 1980s. Eight persons belonging to four generations, including three married couples, lived in this twenty-eight-square-meter apartment. Her family raised a pig in the toilet. I realized that this was a typical apartment that would fit well into the exhibition, so I appointed staff to interview her family members and collect objects to accurately reproduce the whole life during the 1980s of that family. The true reconstruction of the apartment, from the wedding photo and bed of the newlyweds to the kitchen cupboard and even the pig squealing, made many visitors shiver, with many memories of their own circumstances rushing back. Most of the visitors to the exhibition shared this feeling. The hardship and difficulties of that period did not make them angry or resentful; on the contrary, it helped them love more what they experienced and to feel proud of the fact that they had successfully overcome such trials. They thought of that time and imagined that if they had to live again in that period, they could not have overcome such hardship and difficulties. This was the feeling of most Hanoi visitors to the exhibition who had undergone the period of state subsidies. The exhibition was not aimed to praise but explain that it was the destitute life in the period of state subsidies that led to the Renovation. Hanoi visitors to the exhibition felt proud that they had endured that period. Hanoi residents thought of the humane values and human sentiments they had shared with each other, although sometimes they had envied each other, and their creativeness, strength, and resilience. True life with great hardship was reflected by the exhibition, and the story of the tiny apartment in the Trung Tu Living Quarter was told without hiding the poverty, hardship, and stagnation. The conflicting feeling of Hanoi visitors to the exhibition lay balanced between the harsh and poor life, which was sometimes so painful that one wanted to get rid of it, and their reminiscences of that past full of hardship but also of pride. This was possibly the success of the exhibition. It was this reason and this contradiction that drew a large number of visitors to the exhibition. This finding was a great surprise to us.

Was this contradiction the reflexive thinking of Hanoians? This thinking signals a more profound and critical society looking back openly and directly facing their own past and delivering that message to other people, including the next generation of the period of state subsidies. This was the first step in establishing the public in Vietnam, and in this sense, the public is understood as not passively but critically enjoying things, or, to be more precise, the public is always critical, yet in the past it only existed at the margins (in modern folk song, ridiculing music, and jokes, etc.) and only cartoons existed in the form of printing, and everything else melted in everyday life. This exhibition was for the first time social criticism openly presented and exposed to the public for its enjoyment and feedback (as seen in visitors' written impressions and the sudden increase in quantity and quality of visitors' comments).

DISCUSSION

In the spring of 2010 I had a chance to visit Boston, Massachusetts. Prof. Hue-Tam Ho Tai, Harvard University, had on many occasions told me about Yin Yu Tang, a Chinese house in Salem, Massachusetts, because she wanted us to learn from its experiences and write a book about a one-hundred-year-old Vietnamese house, a witness of modern Vietnamese history at the Vietnam Museum of Ethnology.[5] This time, Prof. Hue-Tam Ho Tai again recommended that I visit the Chinese house. Her recommendation was good: I could learn a lot from that Chinese house. When visiting rooms in that family house on the second floor, I related it immediately to the apartment of Mr. Pham Trang in Trung Tu Living Quarter in our exhibition. The approach to the exhibition was completely the same. In that Chinese house, there are rooms reflecting the life of the Chinese in the time of the Cultural Revolution in the 1960s and 1970s. The exhibition of the house is careful, honest, and detailed, helping visitors to perceive that the life of the Chinese at that time was extremely difficult and hard. Everything, from the table, chairs, and household utensils to the newspapers and magazines stuck on the walls, reflects the breath of life. Each object has its own context and story told in audio through a system of earphones. History was reproduced truly through artifacts and their stories. This is what I felt was similar between the stories about life in the time of the Chinese Cultural Revolution and that in the period of state subsidies in Vietnam. Such perception, reminiscences, or criticism of society depend on the outlook and experience of each visitor.

In late 2010 I visited Prague, capital of the Czech Republic. By chance, while I was walking on a main thoroughfare of this capital city, I saw a very strange billboard in the shape of a Petruska in familiar colors, a symbol of former Soviet culture, hanging on a lamppost. What surprised me was that this Petruska had horribly bared pointed teeth, and under it was this line: Museum of Communism. This billboard led me to see the exhibition, as I immediately related it to our exhibition. The exhibition was held after the fall of the Soviet Union and the founding of the Czech Republic. The exhibition displayed everyday objects and life in Czechoslovakia from 1948 to 1990, but the message in this exhibition was to denounce the barbarous and brutal state of Czechoslovakia under the influence of the Soviet regime. The people's stuffy lives were described inside barbed-wire fences. High walls and statues of Lenin, Stalin, and other Czech leaders were scattered on the floor without any base, just like discarded objects. The exhibition showed visitors the attitude of decisively giving up Communism and the former way of life at that time. In this exhibition, I saw no reminiscence of the Czech people like that of the Hanoians but only the attitude of hatred and anger, breaking with the past.

The attitude of the Hanoians is completely different from that of the people of Prague. Reminiscences about the period of state subsidies by the Hanoians and visitors were expressed not only during the exhibition but afterward. What happened after the exhibition closed? In January 2007 the book *Spring in Memory of Uncle Ho—Narrative by the Author* by Pham Thi Xuan Khai was published. It has 386 pages, a very large number of pages for a book. *Tiền Phong* wrote: "The book *Spring in*

Memory of Uncle Ho—Narrative by the Author, published by the News Agency Publishing House, is to help readers understand more about the context of the poem, perception and thoughts of a young generation in the period full of difficulties and hardship of the nation. Many documents related to the event of the poem 'Spring in Memory of Uncle Ho' are for the first time made public to readers" (Tien Phong 2007). Next, the News Agency Publishing House, quickly capturing readers' needs, consecutively published two other books, *Memories of the State Subsidy Period*, a collection of writings and articles from different authors (various authors 2007). Many printing and online newspapers and blogs had special columns on the period of state subsidies, calling for readers to tell their memories of that difficult time or to produce pictures, paintings, and video clips related to the period of state subsidies. The themes also included stories of economic activities and household utensils in the state subsidy period. And there were also discussions about foods in the state subsidy period. A blogger wrote on March 10, 2012:

> It can be said that the state subsidy period only remains in the minds of those who were born before the 1970s and not those who were born since 1986. Without a clear and profound understanding of the hard time of our parents and grandparents, it is difficult to understand deeply the values of the Renovation today. A meal during the period of state subsidies with cakes made of sorghum powder, rice mixed with sweet potatoes, and loaches cooked with brine and *trám* (*Canarium odontophyllum*) fruit from an outskirt restaurant in Nguyen Gia Thieu Street, Hanoi, etc. can partially retrace a corner of what is called that "period of state subsidies." Dishes of foods that create nostalgia for those who once lived in that period of state subsidies can be a sharing experience to help younger generations understand more about yesterday to perceive all the values of today. Amidst the chilly weather at the end of autumn, in a space that's reminiscent of memorable city outskirts, it is very significant sitting with friends and enjoying foods of that hard and miserable time. (Yume 2012)

When I was writing this essay, an article by Mai Quynh Anh was released on the Internet about the memories of watching films in the period of state subsidies.

I still remember the outdoor area where films were screened, remember the whole family going to see a film during summer vacation in which my mother sat hand fanning us children while father carried me on his back after the film show to return home, remember the loudspeakers informing us about a new film to be screened. All of them became part of my childhood memories, very beautiful of the past time. . . . In the years in the middle and late 1980s, when no families in my area had a TV set, the greatest pleasure for us children was to go to watch film shows. My home was half a kilometer away from the film show area in the provincial town. Every afternoon, some of my friends pedaled their bikes to see whether there was any information about new film shows. If yes, they rushed back and shouted loudly in the living quarter, informing us about the new film to be screened that night, its country of origin, and the opening time. From time to time, a Watt car with loudspeakers on its top ran around the provincial town to advertise a new film. Then everyone in my village went to see the film, had dinner earlier than usual so as to go to the film show area early to get good seats. (Mai 2012)

In such reminiscences of the past, criticism was implied. This is possibly the reason why the reporter from Vnexpres.vn gave his article the title "State Subsidy Period Economy: Watching While Tears Rain Down" (Viet Phong and Ha Vy 2006). Critic Vuong Tri Nhan has this comment on the period of state subsidies:

If wanting to smile, many of us had to hide our tears. Yes, how could we hold back our tears when thinking of the "initiatives" in that period of time? Raising pigs inside a twenty-square-meter apartment; mending a shirt collar by turning it inside out; "padding" the parts of the trousers that were easily torn; collecting used films to make hand baskets; collecting used ball-point pens to be refilled; and reusing a used envelope by turning it inside out, etc. It is right if we call them potential creativeness. Yet I feel pity for the term "creativeness." A risky creativeness and a forced creativeness etc. and other names can be given to such "initiatives" by using different painful terms. (Vuong 2012)

Our exhibition suggested to visitors that they could reflect on and reveal the truth of the past, present, and future. The purpose of reminiscences in Vietnam in the first decade of the twenty-first century is not only to remember and reassert things as a way to be critical and self-critical of the past but also to view the present with a vision full of hope for the future. Mr. Nguyen Thanh Kien wrote in the exhibition diary on July 7, 2006, "I already came here [to the exhibition]! But I visited it again, this time with one of my nieces. I want young children to further learn about life in the past, particularly in the period of state subsidies. I wish them to understand that to have a plentiful life as it is today, their parents and their grandparents had to undergo hard circumstances. I want my niece to understand better and love the current life better." And this is what Nguyen Viet Toan, a 12th grader from Le Qui Don Upper Secondary School, wrote: "I myself realize that I have to live a life more responsible to society, to everyone around me" (exhibition diary, August 18, 2006). Such words by Mr. Kien and Toan are shared by many visitors to the exhibition.

CONCLUSION

The exhibition has gone into history, becoming an event of Hanoi history in the first decade of the twenty-first century. Kim Ninh, director of the Asia Foundation Vietnam Office, wrote in the *Wall Street Journal* in July 2006: "The entire Capital of Vietnam was in tumult about an abnormal show: an exhibition organized to strongly criticize the socialist past of this country" (2006).

The exhibition marked a new stage of development of the Vietnam Museum of Ethnology, moving strongly from ethnology to anthropology. The exhibition stemmed from the internal need of the VME to be involved in modern social life. It wished to explain to visitors the social context of Vietnam before the Renovation, to help them understand why Vietnam had to embark on Đổi Mới. This step of progress is also the step of development of anthropology being formed in Vietnam.

The exhibition drew great public attention and had good results. This can be explained as a hypothesis because the Hanoi people had integrated their reminiscences of the past and self-reflection and their sense of criticism. Reminiscences and criticism do not rule each other out, yet they are the two sides of an entity. Isn't that entity the personality of the people of Hanoi and their psychology in the first decade of the twenty-first century?

NOTES

1. Reference documents from the Second Festival of Ethnological/ Anthropological Films, Hanoi, July 2005.
2. Contract and supplementary contract on the *Project Support of the Review of 20 Years of Renovation*; 397 million VND were allocated for the exhibition on the subsidies period.
3. See the release of VME on the movement on donation of objects of the state subsidies period to the Vietnam Museum of Ethnology on its website.
4. Cited from the forum http://www.lyso.vn/diendan/viewtopic.php?f= 42&t=16685, accessed on April 5, 2013.
5. Yin Yu Tang, a two-hundred-year-old Chinese house, was brought to America and reassembled at the Peabody Essex Museum.

REFERENCES

Anonymous. 1999. Research Projects of the Vietnam Museum of Ethnology [Các công trình nghiên cứu của Bảo tàng Dân tộc học Việt Nam]. Vol. 1. Hanoi: Social Sciences Publishing House.
———. 2001. Research Projects of the Vietnam Museum of Ethnology [Các công trình nghiên cứu của Bảo tàng Dân tộc học Việt Nam]. Vol. 2. Hanoi: Social Sciences Publishing House.
———. 2002. Research Projects of the Vietnam Museum of Ethnology [Các công trình nghiên cứu của Bảo tàng Dân tộc học Việt Nam]. Vol. 3. Hanoi: Social Sciences Publishing House.
———. 2004. Research Projects of the Vietnam Museum of Ethnology [Các công trình nghiên cứu của Bảo tàng Dân tộc học Việt Nam]. Vol. 4. Hanoi: Social Sciences Publishing House.
———. 2005. Research Projects of the Vietnam Museum of Ethnology [Các công trình nghiên cứu của Bảo tàng Dân tộc học Việt Nam]. Vol. 5. Hanoi: Social Sciences Publishing House.
———. 2008. Research Projects of the Vietnam Museum of Ethnology [Các công trình nghiên cứu của Bảo tàng Dân tộc học Việt Nam]. Vol. 6. Hanoi: Social Sciences Publishing House.

———. 2011. Research Projects of the Vietnam Museum of Ethnology [Các công trình nghiên cứu của Bảo tàng Dân tộc học Việt Nam]. Vol. 7. Hanoi: Social Sciences Publishing House.

Bodemer, Margaret Barnhill. 2010. Museums, Ethnology and the Politics of Culture in Contemporary Vietnam. PhD dissertation, Department of Anthropology, University of Hawai'i.

Mai, Quynh Anh. 2012. Ký ức thời bao cấp: Chuyện xem phim bãi. http://toithichdoc.blogspot.com/2012/04/ky-uc-thoi-bao-cap-chuyen-xem-phim-bai.html, accessed on March 16, 2016.

Nguyen, Van Huy. 2010. Vietnam Museum of Ethnology: The Making of a National Museum for Communities. On Museums series, Common Ground Publishing.

Nguyen, Van Huyen. 2000. Nguyen Van Huyen Collection [Nguyễn Văn Huyên toàn tập]. Vol. 1. Hanoi: Education Publishing House.

Ninh, Kim. 2006. Home Trusts in Hanoi. Wall Street Journal Online, July 7, cited by Nguyen-Vo Thu Huong on http//www.Talawas.org/?p=6524.

Tien Phong. 2007. Mùa xuân nhớ Bác—Tự sự của tác giả [Spring in memory of Uncle Ho]. Tien Phong News, http://www.tienphong.vn/van-nghe/mua-xuan-nho-bac-tu-su-cua-tac-gia-73839.tpo, accessed on April 15, 2010.

Various authors. 2007. Memories of the State Subsidy Period [Chuyện thời bao cấp]. Hanoi: Vietnam News Agency Publishing House.

Vietnam Museum of Ethnology. 2007. Hanoi Life under the Subsidy Economy, 1975–1986. Hanoi: The Gioi Publisher. Exhibition catalog.

Viet Phong and Ha Vy. 2006. State Subsidy Period Economy: Watching While Tears Rain Down. http://vietbao.vn/Kinh-te/Kinh-te-bao-cap-Vua-xem-vua-chay-nuoc-mat/10963906/87/, accessed on May 16, 2016.

Vuong, Tri Nhan. 2012. Con người và tư tưởng thời bao cấp [People and ideas in the subsidy period]. http://www.viet-studies.info/VTNhan/VTNhan_ThoiBaoCap.htm, accessed on May 15, 2013.

Yume. 2012. Ẩm thực Việt Nam thời bao cấp [Vietnamese food in the subsidy period]. http://yume.vn/am-thuc-viet-nam-thoi-bao-cap-35a97d1d.html, accessed on February 2, 2015.

12

Between Ethnos and Nation

Genealogies of Dân Tộc *in Vietnamese Contexts*

The Vietnamese term *dân tộc* evades easy translation. Variously rendered as "nation," "nationality," or "ethnicity," *dân tộc* connects historical and contemporary Vietnamese discourses of ethnic difference and national belonging to two intellectual projects. The first, most closely associated with reformers in Meiji Japan (1868–1912), involved the rendering of European philosophical terminology into the logographic script common to Japanese, Chinese, Korean, and Vietnamese. The second, which occurred after the Meiji period and during French colonial rule in Southeast Asia, engaged directly with the notions of *nation* and *gens* in the work of Rousseau and Montesquieu. By the 1950s, with political authority over Vietnam contested by competing states, *dân tộc* appeared in a new Marxist-Leninist context. It remains an element of both the political grammar of "nationness" and the exclusionary language of ethnicity, a word with multiple meanings in official discourse and everyday speech.

This essay examines the historical career and contemporary life of *dân tộc* in Vietnam. Across the twentieth century and into the twenty-first, the often contested nature of *dân tộc* animates anticolonial activism, postcolonial revolution, and everyday speech. Although historians have located the discourse of peoplehood and nationness surrounding *dân tộc* within the scholarly debates of the 1920s, this Vietnamese term continues to hold a shifting place on the conceptual plane between ethnicity and nation, sometimes meaning one, at times the other, often both at once. In the following pages, I will consider the meanings of nationness and ethnicity in historical contexts and in contemporary Vietnam.

The etymological history of *dân tộc* connected Vietnam to Japan. When Meiji scholars translated European philosophy, they brought the major works of the Enlightenment to an East Asian literary audience (Howland 2002:122–149). As would later Chinese intellectuals such as Liang Qichao, Meiji scholars rendered key European terms into logographic script (漢字, Japanese, kanji), which made concepts such as "society" (社會, Vietnamese, *xã hội*), "sovereignty" (主權, Vietnamese, *chủ quyển*), and "politics" (政治, Vietnamese, *chính trị*) legible for members of the classical ecumene. Brought into Romanized Vietnamese (Quốc Ngữ), these neologisms became familiar to those Vietnamese speakers not educated in the classical script.

Included in these newly rendered terms was "nation" or *Volk* (民族, *dân tộc*). Although it originated as a component of the Meiji intellectual project to establish a new philosophical vocabulary, one that would both challenge European dominance and serve a new Japanese Empire (Howland 2002), *dân tộc* would recur in very different contexts in twentieth-century Vietnam.

In English, the language of this essay, "nation" is no less complex. Etymologically, it denotes birth. In *Leviathan*, Thomas Hobbes (1985) proposed that "nation," which he adapted from its earlier use in English translations of the Old Testament, refers to a group of subjects united by a sovereign. By the eighteenth century, Jean-Jacques Rousseau would give "the people" sovereign status, a philosophical inversion of Hobbes later continued by the Abbé Sieyès, whose famous speech during the French Revolution connected Rousseau's notion of popular sovereignty with the French term "nation" (Baker ed. 1987:155–179). In 1882 Ernest Renan's deceptively simple characterization of the nation as a "spiritual principle" suggested that nations have destinies beyond political projects, even as political communities or states might reflect the influence of people acting on behalf of the nation (Bhabha 2000:8–22).

The sense of nation as an ethnic identity or nationality also connects this nineteenth-century neologism to the intellectual traditions of ancient Greece. For Thucydides, *ethnos* or *ethnē* signified people beyond the reach of the polis, people "over there" (McInerney 2001:54–59).

In the case of Vietnam, *dân tộc* as nation and its twin, ethnos, coexist into the early twenty-first century.

Despite the efforts of Meiji translators, *dân tộc* did not appear in the works of Phan Châu Trinh and Phan Bội Châu, two of the most prominent Vietnamese political intellectuals of the early twentieth century. Although both maintained a close relationship to Japanese activists such as Fukuzawa Yukichi and viewed the Meiji Restoration as a potential ally against French colonialism, neither formulated his position on the future of Vietnam in terms of *dân tộc* (Trần 2005). However, they both engaged with questions of nationness, a task that, for Phan Châu Trinh, led to a new synthesis of East Asian and European philosophical concepts.

In 1925, when Phan Châu Trinh gave a public address in Saigon upon his return from France, he blended eighteenth-century European philosophy with the works of Confucius and Mencius. Later republished, his speech "Đạo đức và Luân lý Đông Tây" (Morality and ethics East and West) explained that notions of democracy and popular sovereignty found in Montesquieu and Rousseau smoothly harmonized with East Asian ideals. The European Enlightenment, he contended, was a filter that separated the corrosion of imperial Chinese history, namely, the Qin Empire during the third century BCE, from the deep truths of Confucian tradition (Vinh 2009).

In European Enlightenment philosophy, Phan Châu Trinh encountered what he believed was a fundamental and essential universal truth. In the two peoples (*dân*) of Europe and Asia, the nearest inheritors of Rousseau and Mencius, Phan Châu Trinh saw two very different "spirits" (民氣, Vietnamese, *dân khí*). His term for these spirits combined a word with civic undertones (民, Vietnamese, *dân*, or "people," in the sense of *Volk*) with the basic spirit-life stuff that animates everything under heaven (氣, Vietnamese, *khí*). His remarks recalled Herder's and Savigny's concept of the *Volksgeist* and Montesquieu's *l'esprit des gens*, each of which claims that natural groups have an essential distinctive quality (Berlin 1976; Ergang 1966; Wells 1959). As a description of difference, Phan Châu Trinh's *dân khí* was hybridity itself, a blend of

Enlightenment philosophy and Confucian ideals in a dialectical defense of Vietnamese society.

Phan Châu Trinh's narrative of Vietnam's plight contrasted with that of his intellectual rival, Phan Bội Châu. Two years after Phan Châu Trinh's speech, Phan Bội Châu wrote about the *dân* of "Nam Quốc" (the southern country, referencing Vietnam in relation to China). Deploring the condition of Vietnamese people as French colonial subjects, Phan Bội Châu, who often advocated violent struggle, referred not to the distinctive spirit of the Vietnamese people but to the "people of the South" (南人, Vietnamese, Nam Nhân) (Phan 1978). Phan Bội Châu's own intellectual orientation was squarely in the Confucian tradition, absent any meaningful study of Enlightenment philosophy. He represented the traditional response to French colonialism, one that offered no conceptual compromise between Europe and East Asia.

Although he never used the Vietnamese term *dân tộc* in his address, Phan Châu Trinh had begun to redefine the dominant political metaphor in French colonial Vietnam. When *dân tộc* did appear more widely in the 1940s, it would signify both the synthesis of Phan Châu Trinh's *dân khí* and the dual, mutual significance of nation and ethnos.

Although the first mention of *dân tộc* is rather difficult to locate, one possible source is Hoàng Xuân Hãn, an intellectual active during the 1940s who translated scientific terminology into Vietnamese. A close colleague of Trần Đức Thảo, the Continental phenomenologist and a student of Husserl, Hoàng Xuân Hãn compiled a scientific dictionary that included key social scientific vocabulary. He also "imported" anthropological terminology into Vietnamese, including the language of nation and ethnos, although the question of whether concepts can be lifted from one context to another without some kind of transformation remains open (Nguyen 2012:39–40). Hoàng Xuân Hãn introduced translations of European terminology independently of both Phan Châu Trình's efforts and the Meiji translations.

Dân tộc's usage might begin in the 1940s, but its lingering absence marked the strength of more traditional notions. Trần Trọng Kim's *Việt Nam Sử Lược*, for instance, contains no reference to a *dân tộc*, despite frequent mention of the Vietnamese people (*người*) and country (*quốc gia* and *nước*). A classically trained scholar who wrote a major work on

Confucian philosophy, Trần Trọng Kim served in the occupation government established by the Imperial Army of Japan before the end of World War II (Taylor 2002). His intellectual defense of the Confucian tradition, itself an act closely tied to his own career, put Trần Trọng Kim between the conceptual worlds of Phan Bội Châu and Phan Châu Trinh. Following the surrender of Japan, Trần Trọng Kim faded from the political scene. As a new discourse emerged in the wake of World War II, *dân tộc* entered the Vietnamese political vocabulary through revolutionary Marxist-Leninism.

THE DEMOCRATIC REPUBLIC AND STALINIST VOCABULARY

After 1945 *dân tộc* simultaneously signified membership in a revolutionary transformative community and, with the qualifier "minority" (*thiểu số*), the secondary nationalities therein. Through inclusion in the Vietnamese political project, nationalities could transform themselves (*hóa*) into members of a national socialist community (Ninh 2002; Pelley 2002). Under the Democratic Republic of Vietnam, which accepted the abdication of the last Nguyễn emperor, *dân tộc* connected a Vietnamese state to the language of global Marxist-Leninism. Stalin's definition of the nation, explained first in "Marxism and the National Question" and elaborated in "The National Question and Leninism," provided a blueprint for DRV policy, despite the fact that the question of a distinction between nation and country, and nation and ethnos, was never fully resolved.

Stalin's definition of a nation shares certain similarities with those of Ernest Renan from the nineteenth century and of Karl Kautsky, the German Marxist socialist famously reviled by Vladimir Lenin. It was this definition that the editors of the *Concise Philosophical Dictionary*, published in Hanoi in 1987, chose for the term *dân tộc*: "khối người cộng đồng ổn định thành lập trong lịch sử, dựa trên cơ sở cộng đồng về tiếng nói, về lãnh thổ, về sinh hoạt kinh tế và về hình thành tâm lý, biểu hiện trong cộng đồng văn hoá (Stalin)" [a mass of people with a historically established, settled community based upon a common language, territory, economic practices, and psychological makeup all reflected in a common culture].

This definition was hierarchical. In 1929, responding to unnamed critics in the form of a pamphlet, Stalin dismissed concerns about the need for each "nation" to have an independent state, a pressing concern, given the situation in the Soviet Union at the time. He reminded his critics that two types of nations exist: bourgeois nations and new Soviet nations. Bourgeois nations emerged as "a historical category belonging to a definite epoch, the epoch of rising capitalism." Bourgeois nationalism, therefore, as an ideology tethered to a discrete stage of human history, would not survive the induced and, for Stalin, historically inevitable march of dialectical progress.

For the leadership of the DRV, their *dân tộc* was a revolutionary socialist formation. However, bringing the revolutionary nation into being, a political priority for the DRV in the 1950s, exposed serious fissures as social realities failed to match theoretical expectations.

One Vietnamese political leader, Trường Chinh, articulated a unique understanding of the national question. At a meeting that marked the birth of the Vietnamese Workers Party, which formally assumed control of the Vietnam wing of the former Indochinese Communist Party in 1951, Trường Chinh, as party secretary, issued a statement that claimed to resolve Vietnam's own "national question." "Vietnam," he argued, "includes many *dân tộc.*" For Trường Chinh, *quốc gia* indicated the political apparati of the DRV, the hierarchical state governed by the Marxist-Leninist Vietnamese Workers Party. In fact, his 1951 statement included a section titled "Giải quyết vấn đề dân tộc" (Resolving the national question), an obvious reference to earlier writings on the subject by Lenin and Stalin, the theoretical forebears of Trường Chinh.

Writing about Trường Chinh, Christian C. Lentz describes a "slippage" between the terms *quốc gia* and *dân tộc,* a slippage that reflects, or creates, a sense of ambiguity about the terms of the DRV state project. Trường Chinh's justification for "autonomy" (*tự trị*), a form of self-rule assigned to particular non-Việt groups such as the Thái, Hmông, Yao, and Rade, finds him further qualifying the political nature of these concepts. He echoes Stalin's later clarification of the "national question," perhaps better described, for the purposes of this essay, as the "nation question." Describing the collective unity of all *dân tộc* in the struggle against foreign aggression under the leadership of the revolution, Trường Chinh writes: "Dân tộc Việt Nam, đa số và thiếu số, tự giác và tự nguyện đoàn kết chặt chẽ thành một quốc gia để bảo vệ quyền đó" [Vietnamese Nations (*ethnē*; or nations/*ethnē* in Vietnam), majority and minority, have consciously and voluntarily united to form one country to protect sovereignty]. Trường Chinh's statement could be rendered in a variety of ways, each of which broadcasts shades of political anxiety. Does he mean the Vietnamese nation, all the ethnic groups within the territory claimed by the DRV? Does the majority group (Việt or Kinh) have a responsibility to minority groups in their voluntary unity? These questions continued to occupy the architects of state socialism in Vietnam, particularly in areas such as the Northwest, where "autonomous zones," often led by traditional Tai elites, reflected a hybrid approach to local political economy into the 1970s.

Trường Chinh was one in a long list of intellectuals who grappled with the difficulties of articulating nationness and its relationship to political authority. Writing about the national tradition of historical thought in Germany, Georg Iggers remarked that Wilhelm von Humboldt, in the early nineteenth century (before the founding of the German Empire), posed the essential unity of "nation, state, and people." Humboldt, influenced by Herder, saw the nation and state as "interwoven," with the nation as a "metaphysical reality" of the state (Iggers 1983:53).

THE REPUBLIC AND NATIONAL LIBERATION FRONT: *ĐỒNG BÀO* AND *DÂN TỘC*

Rendering metaphysical nations into territorial states also occupied southern Vietnamese intellectuals during the twentieth century. During the Second Indochina War, often referred to as the "Vietnam War" in the United States, the life of *dân tộc* followed the dissonant directions that characterized Vietnamese political cultures. The government of the Republic of Vietnam, the name adopted by the former Associated State of Vietnam, based in Saigon, published official works on national ethnic minorities in the late 1950s. Compared with the work of Trường Chinh, official publications on ethnic groups and nationalities from the Saigon government used a very different conceptual vocabulary, one entirely devoid of any reference to *dân tộc*.

In 1959 the President's Office for Upland Societies, a task force linked with the republic's struggle against hostile forces in the south, published a manual on the cultural practices of ethnic groups in the central highlands. Unsurprisingly, this book eschewed the Stalinist language favored by Trường Chinh. Rather than addressing ethnicity in terms of nationness and *dân tộc*, the manual referenced an older notion of common ancestry.

Its title, *Phong-Tục Tập-Quán Đồng Bào Thượng* (Habits and customs of our upland cousins), includes a term, *đồng bào*, that literally means "from the same egg." The people at high altitudes, including the Bahnar, the Jarai, and the Rhade, are "people" (*người*) or "lineal descendants" (*giòng* or *dòng*). According to the manual, uplanders (*người Thượng*) have society (*xã hội*), rich cultural traditions, and a good chance to progress under the leadership of the Republic of Vietnam. In this text, they are not described as *dân tộc*. Neither, for that matter, is anyone else. Although the text features several terms for the RVN administration, including a reference to a Vietnamese state (*nước Việt*), *dân tộc* remains absent. The complexities of a multiethnic nation posed no problem for a state based in Saigon that viewed itself as the steward of the great ancestral ovum.

The manual closes with a vague reference to a looming enemy of the republic. "Việt Cộng," it states, "along with the forces of colonialism and feudalism, must be smashed" (Nha Công-tác 1959:122). Since the National Liberation Front was not organized until 1960, "Việt Cộng" indicates anyone espousing revolutionary Communist ideas, enemies of the Saigon government.

The NLF itself, properly known as the Mặt Trận Dân Tộc Giải Phóng Miền Nam Việt Nam, referred to the national struggle, the struggle for the *dân tộc*. The complexities inherent in this nomenclature were apparent during the war. As Ralph Smith remarked in 1971, "Interestingly, the word for 'nation' here is not *quốc gia*, which means literally 'nation-family,' but *dân tộc*, whose meaning is more akin to 'race' or 'people'" (162). The terms "race" (*chủng tộc*) and "people" (*nhân dân*), for Smith, blend with *dân tộc*. Superficially, there is a resemblance between these terms, despite the lack of a connection either in terms of documentary evidence or etymologically. Smith's comments may seem from another time; given the fact that he published his thoughts on the name of the

NLF in 1971, they most certainly are. However, the bemused tone of his observation belies the ideological ties of *dân tộc* to an alternate revolutionary vision for southern Vietnam.

DÂN TỘC AS INDEX: NORMS AND FORMS OF ETHNOPOLITICAL DISCOURSE

The contemporary contours of *dân tộc* in the Socialist Republic of Vietnam blend the pragmatic anxieties of the 1950s with the useful ambiguities of a term that seems to mean both "nation" and "ethnos." We can find these shades of meaning in official discourse and popular speech, in the careful language of the state project, and in the everyday forms of deliberating, negotiating, and deriding official efforts to delineate *dân tộc*.

Political changes within the Vietnamese state and within the Vietnamese Communist Party (founded in 1976 on the basis of the Vietnamese Workers Party) contributed to an enhanced openness about multiculturalism and ethnic pluralism. Following the landmark ratification of Decision 121 in 1979, the Vietnamese government modified those ethnonyms, terms of address for other ethnic groups, that carried insulting connotations (Khong Dien 2002). "Mèo" became "Hmong" or "Hơ Mông," reflecting the self-referential term for speakers of Hmong languages. "Man," a term meaning "wild or savage," no longer referred to the speakers of Mien, who now became Dao, although often pronounced as "Yao" by Mien speakers. These and other changes provided minority ethnic groups (*dân tộc thiểu số*) with names supposedly cleansed of derision, names that captured a sense of self-reference.

In contemporary Vietnam, in official discourse and in everyday speech, the term *dân tộc* conveys several meanings, a fact that underscores the relationship between ethnicity and nationness. In 1998 the Council on Folk Art in Hanoi published an edited volume on "protecting and promoting the cultural assets or wealth" of ethnic minorities in mountainous regions of Vietnam (Hội Văn Nghệ Dân Gian Việt Nam 1998). The title in Vietnamese, *Tài Sản Văn Hoá các Dân Tộc ở Tây Bắc và Tây Nguyên*, includes a pluralizer (*các*). Multiple *dân tộc* mean, in this context, ethnicities within the nation.

Within this volume, academics at Vietnamese universities and cadre from Cultural Information Offices (Sở Văn Hóa) offer their thoughts on ethnic cultural heritage in contemporary Vietnam. In his introductory essay, Tô Ngọc Thanh, the secretary of the Folklore Association, explains the concept of "ethnic culture" (*văn hóa dân tộc*), identifying the Northwest of Vietnam and the central highlands as two distinct "cultural zones" (*vùng văn hóa*). That these two particular areas also contain a historically small population of Vietnamese speakers reminds us of the dynamic interplay between notions of minority ethnicity and the normative claim of nationness. The same volume's chapter on folk dances notes that the ethnicities located in the Northwest or even, in a curious compression of the phrase, Northwest Ethnicities (*dân tộc Tây Bắc*), maintain cultural practices that reflect their productive relationships to the land. Even an appreciation of ethnic pluralism within the Vietnamese nation, evident in the dozens of ethnic groups represented, albeit as subject matter, in publications such as this one, relies on materialist notions of culture as an echo of livelihood.

A second official source, from 2005, focuses on strengthening cultural exchange in uplands ethnic minority areas ("giao lưu văn hóa vùng dân tộc thiểu số-miền núi"). The result of a policy conference hosted by the Ministry of Culture and the Committee for "văn hóa dân tộc," this volume explicitly addresses the role of state authorities, cultural authorities, in mitigating the possible deleterious effects of tourism on ethnic cultural traditions while also encouraging the development of tourist industries under the authority of the proper authorities (Bộ Văn Hoá Thông Tin and Vụ Văn Hoá Dân Tộc 2005). Trịnh Thị Thủy, from the leadership of the Ministry of Culture, reminds readers that a central government decision in 1998, just months after the publication of the book on cultural zones, called for the construction and development of a vanguard Vietnamese culture ("nền Văn Hóa Việt Nam tiên tiến") that "cherishes ethnic identity" ("đậm đà bản cắc dân tộc") (Bộ Văn Hóa Thông Tin and Vụ Văn Hóa Dân Tộc 2005:42). Another essay provides details about traditional singing festivals, which, in step with the opening of the economy in the age of reform (after 1986), have increased annually (Bộ Văn Hoá Thông Tin and Vụ Văn Hoá Dân Tộc 2005:105–122). However, most of the essays reflect a concern for "cultural identity" ("bản sắc văn hóa các dân tộc"), casting a somewhat gentler frame around the vexing issue of nation and ethnicity that confronted Trường Chinh in the 1940s.

Official policy regarding cultural work and ethnicity, vital tasks in the context of contemporary Vietnam whether or not one embraces the notion of a "vanguard Vietnamese culture," inspires volumes, workshops, projects, papers delivered at Asian studies conferences, and so on. However, this official multiculturalism does not necessarily filter down to everyday speech.

From 2007 to 2012 I worked as a field advisor for a project that I had cofounded with colleagues in Vietnam and France. Concerned mostly with the writing traditions of the Yao (Dao) ethnic community in the province of Lào Cai, our project managed the distribution of funds to village schools and sought the help of Yao elders in the creation of a digital archive of texts. During the course of this work, I became acquainted with the various meanings of *dân tộc* in everyday speech, especially in a multiethnic location like Lào Cai.

One afternoon, a colleague and I stopped for lunch in Lào Cai city. We had been on motorbikes all morning, and the threat of rain forced us to cut our visits to villages short, so we returned for lunch in town. At the restaurant, the owner, who was ethnically Vietnamese from Nam Định but had moved to Lào Cai years ago, greeted us as he had many times before. This time, though, he looked a little concerned. "So," he began, "not too busy right now. Only one cook, though, and he's ethnic [người dân tộc], so maybe lunch takes a little longer." My colleague shot back: "Ethnic? Which ethnicity? [Người dân tộc gì đấy?] Is he Tày like me or Việt like you? [Dân Tộc Tày như tớ hay Kinh như cậu?]" After a few tense seconds, some apologies, and a few complimentary bottles of Hanoi Beer, the awkward exchange seemed forgotten.

My Tày colleague would recall this episode weeks later during a workshop on indexing texts in Lào Cai. At a large table, around which sat a dozen young cultural cadres, he expressed his concerns that his young children were growing up without learning to speak Tày, just as many Yao might not appreciate their own traditions if not for the work of the Office of Culture. For my colleague, the insult of the restaurant owner notwithstanding, nonmajority ethnicities have equal footing with the dominant, "vanguard" Vietnamese culture, even as the basis of that footing, namely, cultural preservation, supports the political leadership of the cultural authorities.

CONCLUSION

In the multicultural ideal of postsocialist Vietnam, a hierarchical understanding of nationness and ethnicity, the double idea of *dân tộc*, yields to the rich and diverse ethnic traditions of the communities within the country. While the discourse of nationness and ethnicity links Vietnam to larger intellectual trends, both the nineteenth-century Meiji project to translate new words from Europe and the twentieth-century Stalinist project to place nations into a revolutionary ranking, the negotiation of *dân tộc* at different times highlights its contested status.

During the twentieth century, the inherent tensions of *dân tộc* as a term that marks both inclusion into the revolutionary struggle and exclusion from the putative ethnic norm (Vietnamese) yielded to official policies that, on the surface, accounted for and celebrated cultural diversity. However, changes to official categories do not necessarily force a change in popular behavior. In its official and everyday careers, *dân tộc* remains firmly between nation and ethnos in contemporary Vietnam.

REFERENCES

Baker, Keith Michael, ed. 1987. The Old Regime and the French Revolution. Chicago: University of Chicago Press.

Berlin, Isaiah. 1976. Vico and Herder: Two Studies in the History of Ideas. New York: Viking Press.

Bhabha, Homi K., ed. 1990. Nation and Narration. London: Routledge.

Bộ Văn Hoá Thông Tin and Vụ Văn Hoá Dân Tộc. 2005. Tăng Cường Hoạt Động Giao Lưu Văn Hoá vùng Dân Tộc Thiểu Số-Miền Núi. Hanoi: Nhà Xuất Bản Văn Hoá-Thông Tin.

Ergang, Robert Reinhold. 1966. Herder and the Foundations of German Nationalism. New York: Octagon Books.

Hobbes, Thomas. 1985. Leviathan. New York: Penguin Books.

Hội Văn Nghệ Dân Gian Việt Nam. 1998. Giữ Gìn và Phát Huy Tài Sản Văn Hoá các Dân Tộc ở Tây Bắc và Tây Nguyên. Hanoi: Nhà Xuất Bản Khoa Học Xã Hội.

Howland, Douglas. 2002. Translating the West: Language and Political Reason in 19th Century Japan. Honolulu: University of Hawai'i Press.

Hữu Ngọc, Dương Phú Hiệp, and Lê Hữu Tầng, eds. 1987. Từ Điển Triết Học Giản Yếu. Hanoi: NXB Đại Học và Trung Học Chuyên Nghiệp.

Iggers, Georg. 1983. The German Conception of History: The National Tradition of Historical Thought from Herder to the Present. Middletown CT: Wesleyan University Press.

Khong Dien. 2002. Population and Ethno-demography in Vietnam. Chiang Mai: Silkworm.

Kim Ninh. 2002. A World Transformed: The Politics of Culture in Revolutionary Vietnam, 1945–1965. Ann Arbor: University of Michigan Press.

McInerney, Jeremy. 2001. Ethnos and Ethnicity in Early Greece. In Ancient Perceptions of Greek Ethnicity. I. Malkin, ed. Pp. 51–73. Cambridge MA: Harvard University Press.

Nguyen Phuong Ngoc. 2012. À l'origine de l'anthropologie au Viet-Nam: Recherche sur les auteurs de la première moitié du XXe siècle. Aix-en-Provence: Presse Universitaire de Provence.

Nha Công-tác Xã-Hội miền Thượng Phủ Tổng-Thống. 1959. Phong-Tục Tập-Quán Đồng-Bào Thượng. Saigon.

Pelley, Patricia. 2002. Postcolonial Vietnam: New Histories of the National Past. Durham NC: Duke University Press.

Phan Bội Châu. 1978. Thiên Hồ! Để Hồ! Hanoi: Nhà Xuất Bản Khoa Học Xã Hội.

Smith, Ralph. 1971. Viet-Nam and the West. Ithaca NY: Cornell University Press.

Taylor, Keith W. 2002. Vietnamese Confucian Narratives. In Rethinking Confucianism: Past and Present in China, Japan, Korea, and Vietnam. Benjamin Elman, John Duncan, and Herman Ooms, eds. Pp. 337–369. Asian Pacific Monograph Series. Los Angeles: UCLA.

Trần Trọng Tân. 2005. Phong Trào Đông Du và Phan Bội Châu. Vinh: Nhà Xuất Bản Nghệ An.

Vinh Sinh. 2009. Phan Chau Trinh and His Political Writings. Ithaca NY: Cornell SEAP Publications.

Wells, G. A. 1959. Herder and After: A Study in the Development of Sociology. The Hague: Mouton and Company.

13

Arthur Nole (1940–2015)

Tahltan Elder, Raconteur, and Friend

Arthur Nole, Tahltan Indigenous elder and storyteller, died on January 3, 2015, after breaking his leg while chopping wood. He lived a life indicative of the complexities of Indigenous lives and, particularly, the meshing of traditional activities and wage work. He was a dedicated moose hunter and passionate hunting guide, and he was tremendously interested in the telling and recording of Tahltan history. His later life was dominated by family activities and motivated by teaching young people the traditional skills of camping, hunting, and life on the land.

Arthur was born on July 21, 1940, at Telegraph Creek, British Columbia, to Ester Quock and Bell Nole and was one of sixteen siblings. He was a member of the Tsesk'iye (Crow) Clan.[1] Arthur had several Tahltan names. He was Natēyah (Traveler), a name received from the ancestors in a dream, and also Iłdūk (no translation), the name used by Kishkoosh, Bell Nole's stepfather. His nickname was Kazūne (Otter), from his grandfather Leon Dennis. Arthur met his future wife, Nancy Louie, in August 1958. At a dance at Telegraph Creek, he bought Nancy a slice of pie, and their relationship began. They were married soon after they started dating, in January 1959, because they did not want to live in a common-law relationship. Arthur and Nancy had five sons and five daughters, and at the time of his death there were thirty grandchildren and twenty-two great-grandchildren. Arthur lived to see one great-great-grandchild. Nancy died after an illness in 1992. After Nancy's passing, Arthur refused to consider remarrying, saying, "There'll never be another Nancy."

In recent years, Arthur came to accept the role of family record-keeper and, more generally, raconteur of the history of the Tahltan Athapaskans who lived at Iskut Village, British Columbia. In conversations with Arthur, I learned that he saw himself as an example of someone who, like many in northern Canada, lived through the rapid transition from sustenance food harvesting to wage work. He embraced both positions on that economic spectrum, enjoying hard work of any sort and chastising children who were lazy, particularly at camp and on the hunt. A self-described "true Tahltan," he asserted his Indigeneity by speaking the Tahltan language and was particularly fond of place-names and their etymology. He relished time on the land as a hunter and hunting guide. His hunting camps and cabins dotted the landscape near Iskut Village and into the Tl'abāne (open grass flats) region to the south of Iskut.[2] Within the context of land claims and Aboriginal rights, which have dominated Tahltan politics for the past decade, Arthur was firm in his insistence that outsiders understand that Tahltan rights were not predicated solely on unchanging cultural practices. For him, the pairing of wage work and what he called "traditional" practices infused his political outlook, as well as the wide range of activities that preoccupied him during his life. I offer, then, this account of Arthur's life in the spirit of friendship and admiration for a generous man whose interest in local history was intensely personal and yet highly revealing of the intricacies of Indigenous lives in Canada.

EARLY LIFE AND TEACHERS

Arthur was raised at Telegraph Creek, a small community on the Stikine River in northwestern British Columbia. Some of his childhood was spent on the lands set aside for the Iskut people on the south side of the Stikine River, opposite the homes of non-Native residents and the Telegraph Creek Tahltans. During his early life, he also lived at various camps and villages along the sixty-five-mile trail (one hundred kilometers) that stretches between Telegraph Creek and Łuwechōn Menh (Kluachon Lake), where Iskut Village is located. Arthur and Nancy raised their family in Iskut Village, and he lived there until his death.

Arthur offered no memories of his life before the age of six. He insisted that after six he was old enough to carry himself when his family traveled and implied that his memories were grounded in that burgeoning independence. He attended day school in Telegraph Creek and was spared the trauma of moving away and attending a residential school as a young child. But he was nevertheless at odds with the priests who taught him and who resorted to corporal punishment for misbehavior. He stopped attending school after grade 4, motivated by a conversation with his father. "He gave me a choice," said Arthur. "'What you wanna do?' he say. 'Learn our culture,' he say, 'or you wanna go to school?' First choice I take. Didn't want to go to school." Despite an antipathy toward formal schooling, Arthur left Telegraph Creek in 1954 to live for a year in a boarding school at Miller Bay, British Columbia, near Prince Rupert. There, he pursued general studies and, proudly, moved between grade levels quickly. He completed grade 7 by correspondence with the assistance of the Telegraph Creek school principal. Arthur confessed to me that he wished he had completed more formal education because he felt it would have helped him to be a better leader for the Iskut people.

Arthur grew up surrounded by Tahltan mentors. His father, Bell Nole, taught him to hunt. His early hunts, like most hunts throughout his life, were for sustenance. Arthur shot his first caribou at nine years old at a lake near Iskut Village after the elders in his camp asked him to do so. With that success, the elders told him he was already a man. Arthur participated in his first beaver hunt with his father when he was ten years old. He estimated that he shot almost two hundred moose and countless caribou over sixty-five years of hunting. Throughout his life, Arthur was committed to distributing meat to family and friends, hinting always that respect for animals was expressed by sharing what you have. His hunting belied, in fact, a suggestion I heard that the arrival of electric freezers in northern communities ruined sharing networks. I believe that because Arthur had a freezer he hunted more and shared more. He was able to provide hunted food to family and community members who had taken paid work in the band office or at a local mine and, thus, were hunting less often.

Arthur talked endlessly about hunting episodes in which a moose, caribou, or other animals were pursued (see, e.g., McIlwraith 2008). Shared often within earshot of young grandchildren, these accounts are instructive of the central role hunting played in Arthur's identity and, more generally, of the factual tone and brief content of colloquial and casual conversations in Iskut Village. In this example, presumably from his teenage years, Arthur explained that moose were taken for food when the need arose. A freezer is part of the story:

> Yeah, we had no choice when we lived in Telegraph Creek. Sometimes they see cow moose at time when season open, eh. But we don't have any choice. Anytime we see moose, we shoot it. 'Cause there is no deep freeze, no power. So we just have to go and get a moose every once in a while. And we have good timing in winter because we go past Buckley Lake sometimes, right to 40 Mile Flat to get a moose or caribou.[3] That's a long walk . . . two days from there to Telegraph.

Without missing a beat, Arthur moved to the next story:

> One time we hunt in December. Walter [brother-in-law] and me and Loveman [brother] and my Uncle Paul Reed. Loveman shot two cow and Walter shot one. Only moose hang around there too. We went to get our moose, me and Walter. I put hole through on the dog sled [because there was] hardly any snow. We go right down to bare ground. I have to help with the dogs, push the sleigh. Put it into our camp. The others bring their own. I end up cooking it. I have to cook. After supper I go out and haul that meat out of them bone. Strip them and smoke. I look around. I make pole [to hang the meat]. "When you gonna quit working?" they say. "When I'm finished." I finished everything. Then I cut wood.

These accounts are representative of the stories Arthur told about everyday life on the land. They are limited in their elaboration of details such as location and date. They prioritize the camaraderie of family relations. And, for Arthur, they were statements of work ethic. As he said, as if to address any thought that his was an impoverished life, "Yeah, we used to live a good life. I don't remember starving. Since I learn how to shoot, I always hunt chicken or rabbit. Sometimes I make fire I cook chicken or rabbit."

Arthur was a spiritual man and intensely proud of living close to the land. Consistent with the Tahltan understanding of reincarnation

(Emmons 1911:108; Teit 1956), Arthur explained that he was reborn from his brother Thomas, who died shortly after birth. He walked all over Tahltan territory, coming to know particularly the river corridors of the mountainous Spatsizi Plateau and Stikine and Skeena River headwaters. Throughout his life he traveled the trail between Łuwechōn Menh and Telegraph Creek, past the Mount Edziza volcano, and he knew the names of places all along these trails. Some places were descriptive and given in the Tahltan language; others, like those that marked the trails in miles, evoked the gold rush and big game guiding eras. As he spoke, he blended the two easily, and to sit with him when he recounted the names was to listen as he walked the trails in his mind:

> From Telegraph [Creek] we go to 2 Mile to camp or go another mile up to 3 Mile. Then we move on to 10 Mile, where we stay about three or four days. Then they get moose. Then we move on. When we do that, moving out in the evening, me and my dad always set rabbit snare. We get to 10 Mile, after we have supper we walk up the trail to set snare.... From 10 Mile we go to Stinky Lake. I understand now there's gas under that lake and that's why it get so stink after ice freeze over. When you cut through you hear sssssssss. Then we go right down to that River Bend Lake, River Bend Camp. Hotālīn [they call it]. Used to be nice spot. My favorite place. It kind of grown in since we never use it. In there too I think we stayed a couple of days. Then we move on.... From Dāsghā' Łuwe (Hair on Trees Fish, or Canyon Lake) to Haven Point, that's where they camp. Elders always ask, "You get tired?" I say no.

Arthur's knowledge of the local landscape was a result of frequent hunting, to be sure. But it was also an indication of a close relationship with the spirits of the elders who helped and traveled with him. They gave Arthur the Tahltan names of places once he encountered them. "I want the name and they tell me," Arthur said. He elaborated briefly: "Things I want to learn, I just think about it." Where place-names were concerned, the landscape reflected names, and the elders simply made them audible to Arthur. In a brief example drawn from a guiding trip on the Spatsizi Plateau, he explained how he came to know Tehodenī, a name that refers to a slide that went into a lake:

[It's called on the map] Tuaton Lake. But it is Tehodenī. As I went round that lake I wondered, "What's the name of this in our language?" As we go along with pack train we hit this slide around the lake. It goes from the top right to the lake. So I sit on my horse and I wonder how they say it, and that Tehodenī got in mind before we get to camp. It just comes naturally. So I ask Old Tom. He's living in Tehodenī. He said, "How do you know, Tehodenī?"

It wasn't that Arthur made up the names. He was, rather, imagining names that already existed. The names were confirmed by others, after all.

Arthur spoke further about his connections to the spirits of the elders. He described himself one time as a doctor but not a healer. He understood how to make and use plant medicines, but his doctoring was associated with knowledge of the land. It was established in close and personal associations with animals, like camp robbers (the gray jay, *Perisoreus canadensis*), who would lead Arthur to moose and success in the hunt (McIlwraith 2012b:72). "Every time I go out I get a moose," explained Arthur. "My birds never tell me [where to go], those camp robbers. [But] if they come around, they whistle. It means 'I'm going to get moose.' I'm somehow gonna get moose." This was what he called *mela'o'tīn*, or "luck." It was a cherished relationship of respect with animals that helped Arthur be successful as a provider for his family and community. It kept him safe from bears when he traveled and camped.

Arthur commanded a small repertoire of traditional stories or what are sometimes called *sa'e* (long time ago) stories. These stories frequently involved groundhogs whose actions served as metaphors for human foibles and failures. He also shared accounts of lost families and abandoned women who were forced to survive a winter on their own. He was particularly fond of situating an interview session with the history of the fighting between Tahltans and the Nisga'a or Gitksan peoples, neighbors to the south. These stories, many of which were old and taught to him by his father, are *bahi* (war) stories (McIlwraith 2012b:23).[4] One story in particular, that of Stādegah and his brothers Tsēgentah and Engahtah, prefaced Arthur's modern orientation to Tahltan territorial integrity. He also liked to talk about the follies of a disrespectful hunter who was turned to stone at a place called Deneka'ladiyah (Person Who Walked into a Spear). Set on the Spatsizi River at a specific bluff where the actions described in the story take place, Dene-ka'ladiyah evokes traditional values related to respecting animals and other people through appropriate and thoughtful treatment. The result of the story, a man and his dog punished for disrespecting a goat by being turned to stone, is a powerful reminder of the covenant between hunter and prey (Teit 1919:241–242; McIlwraith 2012b:118–120).

Most importantly to his family, Arthur devoted his life to teaching young people about hunting and fishing. His home with Nancy and their hunting and fishing camps in the Tl'abāne at Morchuea Lake, at Kon'sūl (Fire under Rocks), and near Telegraph Creek on the Stikine River at Kuwegānh Tū'e (Deer Creek, 5 Mile) were open to anyone who wanted to visit, learn, and share a meal. Arthur and Nancy took young people hunting, sometimes in large groups, and children were known to ask Arthur if they could travel and camp with him. My under-standing of Iskut traditions is due in part to Arthur accepting me just as he did any other young person. Arthur and Nancy often took chil-dren into their home when they had nowhere else to go. They raised some of those children too. Arthur was concerned that children learn old stories and the values of hard work and commitment to family that were so frequently embedded in them. He stated: "Computers aren't our traditional life!" But, not one to forget contemporary and practical realities of wage work and employment, he elaborated, saying: "You're supposed to first learn about our traditional life and then get education to fight or work with government." Indeed, he indicated to me that a perfect tribute to his interests would be the publication of a govern-ment topographical map labeled with Tahltan language place-names.

WAGE WORK AND CHANGING CONTEXTS

Arthur's commitment to hard work and physical labor was evident in his participation in the northern wage economy. Beginning in 1959 and continuing until 1964, he worked as a guide, wrangler, and cook for renowned outfitter Tommy Walker at Hok'ats Łuwe Menh (Cold Fish Lake) (Walker 1976).[5] He found working for Walker largely pleasur-able, and he described good relations with Walker. In his book, Walker (1976:236, 240) called Arthur a "first class wrangler" and told how he was inseparable from a horse named Albert. Arthur talks fondly of receiving a raise from Walker on account of his hard work. He was known as an excellent cook—pancakes may well have been his signature item—and was very skilled at shoeing horses. He enjoyed traveling with client hunters from Germany and the United States, although he noted with some annoyance their lack of preparedness for the bush. Still, it rankled Arthur, as it does many at Iskut Village today, that Walker's characterization of the Tahltan laborers was less than charitable. Walker (e.g., 1976:9) wrote that he saved Iskut people from starvation by providing them with food and work.[6] Walker (1976:236) also called Arthur an Indigenous Sekani person, which contradicts Arthur's view of himself as a Tahltan. In Arthur's case, the Sekani label is erroneous, as his primary family connections are to Tahltans at Telegraph Creek and, farther back, to Gitksan people to the south.[7] The Iskut people who worked for Walker were also mentioned in the published travel diary of American essayist Edward Hoagland (1969), who visited northern British Columbia in 1966. Arthur is not named by Hoagland, although the Iskut people and their peripatetic history is told, and in unflattering terms. Arthur did not seem comfortable with his place or that of his family and friends in these books by notable outsiders. He told me that Hoagland's book made him "mad." I have wondered if the observations of Walker and Hoagland inspired Arthur, at least in part, to tell his own story in his own words. That said, Arthur is graciously acknowledged in Bob Henderson's (2006) memoir of guiding on the Spatsizi Plateau and in Wade Davis's (2011) account of the resource conflicts in the Tl'abāne.

Arthur worked in other wage-earning positions. Like others in Iskut, he was a laborer, primarily clearing brush on the construction of British Columbia Highway 37, which, during the 1960s, was built south from the Alaska Highway to Kenes'kani Menh (Kinaskan Lake), twenty-five miles south of Iskut Village.[8] He was content with the changes that came with infrastructure developments like the highway and the construction of a grade for a railway line to Dease Lake.[9] Indeed, he benefited from these access routes and used them frequently to drive his blue pick-up truck or his snowmobile into hunting and trapping areas. For some thirty years, starting in the early 1970s, he also worked as a custodian at the Klappan Independent Day School, run by the Iskut

First Nation in Iskut Village. He served the community on its Band Council at various times in the 1970s and 1980s.

Arthur was a devout Catholic and an altar boy in his youth. He oversaw many of the religious and spiritual activities of Iskut, including directing funerals. He cared for the recently deceased, a role he inherited from his father, and speaks emotionally about the challenges of that work. He believed strongly in church marriages and funerals. He became disillusioned by the behavior of priests, particularly as a result of stern punishment when he was a young student. As a young adult, he was concerned about the political influence wielded by priests. As a result, he did not attend church regularly, although he never abandoned a Christian life. I struggled to understand the relationship in Arthur's life between his Catholicism and his traditional beliefs in an animated landscape. I asked Arthur how, after a moose kill, he gave thanks to the spirit of the moose for its sacrifice. He replied succinctly: "I pray to the Lord." In another instance he explained: "One day I hunt and I talk to our Lord. 'Lord, your birthday coming up. I'm trying to get a moose for my family.' It worked. I go about a mile and there's a moose. I shot it. I say, 'Thank God.'" For Arthur, there was no conflict between Christianity and the traditional aspects of a hunting relationship. Such blending seems only to confuse visitors like me.

COMMUNITY AND RESEARCH

Arthur was a quiet, subtle man who rarely made a fuss publicly about his position, his knowledge, or his experience. He cooked for community dinners and coordinated events because someone needed to do so. He went camping without announcement or fanfare at any one of the sites he built across Tahltan territory. He explained to me that *kime* was the Tahltan word for both "camp" and "home," and I was witness to the warmth of family life in the camps on several occasions. Spending time with Arthur at Didini Kime (Young Caribou Camp), for example, showed me the multigenerational education, storytelling, and land-centered activities so central to his personality and passions. Sitting on a high stool near a fire and beside the camp kitchen, he spoke sternly to young grandchildren, both boys and girls, who did not clean their game promptly or left their wet boots too close to the fire. He insisted that all children (and anthropologists) take turns collecting wood, maintaining the fire, and getting water from a nearby creek. He was an amazing camp cook. His breakfast dishes were known widely by names like Spatsizi Slam and Klabona Special, labels that drew inspiration from local place-names, Denny's restaurant, and laboring as a hunting guide. He once owned eight horses, and his camps still have corrals. He was sometimes competitive, with a penchant for gambling, and card games were central to camp life. Away from camp and when he was a younger man, he played baseball and tried downhill skiing and skating—and did so with varying amounts of success:

> In 1948 we did a lot of skiing at Telegraph Creek. I don't know how many times I go down that hill. It was no problem, but one time I just got cut off. I hit the bottom with my legs too stiff. I pile up. Boy, just hit that ground. I sit up, kick it out, and walk away. "Look that ski. You left your ski," the other kids say. "I'm done," I yelled back. It was the same thing with skating. I fell and quit. I just left my skates right on the ice. But baseball, they can't beat me in baseball.

I first met Arthur in the late 1990s when I was involved in a land use and occupancy study with the Tahltan government. He was a key informant and a frequent tour guide on that study. Despite his bad knee, I could barely maintain his speed on the trails near Buckley Lake, and keeping up with his stories of how moose hide stretchers worked and the genealogies of the Buckley Lake families was almost impossible. During my dissertation fieldwork in Iskut Village in 2002–3, Arthur permitted me to camp with him and with his extended family. As nervous as I was when I asked to spend time with him, he was pleased with my interest and supportive of my efforts to learn about his life and demeanor. It was Arthur who showed me that even in the most mundane encounters with moose, moose were sentient (McIlwraith 2008, 2012b). His participation in research activities was understated, but his voice grew louder as relatives and friends passed on. Late in his life, social space opened for him to take on the role of record keeper and local historian. Young people and researchers alike sought out Arthur as an expert on local history and the Tahltan language.

Arthur understood politics, particularly around Indigenous identity and territorial control. He recognized, for example, that recent conflicts between Iskut community members and resource companies like Shell Oil, Fortune Minerals, and Imperial Metals over the exploitation of the Tl'abāne region were only the most recent provocations by outsiders (Davis 2011; Paulson 2006). When historical disputes with neighboring Indigenous groups or the Hudson's Bay Company are considered, such challenges had been going on for generations. In his reflections on contemporary political events, Arthur noted the spiritual assurances provided by the ancestors: "[The ancestors] told me too about this area here. That they [the outsiders] not gonna win. Twice they told me that. They're not gonna win. It's our land." At the height of conflicts with Shell and Fortune Minerals, Arthur and I prepared an essay explaining why hunting camps, *kime*, as he preferred to call them, could not be moved away from resource extraction activities. It was simple: camps were homes (McIlwraith 2012a). Arthur never judged community and family members who chose to work with mining companies, but he was staunchly opposed to unlimited development or development without compensation. Like his interest in the history of intercommunity raiding and his disdain for the impolite behavior of non-Indigenous hunters who stole from his camps, Arthur's perspectives on contemporary resource development were couched in contemporary views about private property and its ownership.

CONCLUSION

Arthur's life and his presentations of it show a skillful commitment to both hunting and wage work, and those activities overlapped and intertwined in intriguing ways. Wage work complemented his hunting activities, literally as he hunted for a wage while working with Tommy Walker and, later in life, as a family and community hunter whose camping was supported financially by his work in the school. His camping, from the canvas wall-tents to the insistence on camp hygiene, revealed what he learned and the jobs he did while guiding. I suspect his commitment to family, wage work, and traditional history and practices—his life lived during a time of significant economic and cultural change—is unexceptional and visible in the experiences of many Indigenous peoples in Canada.

At the time of his unexpected death, Arthur was recording his life story, and I was helping to write it down. In the course of that work, he rebelled against the consent process and, particularly, against the signing of the consent forms I had brought with me. "I don't need a lawyer to tell my own story," he exclaimed. Together, we ripped up the forms, and in their place I was cautioned to "just do my best." Arthur's historical presentations are reminiscences and anecdotes of a life lived. Rather than be offered chronologically, his accounts flow in relation to a moment or a place or a lesson that needs telling. He recorded his story as if he was speaking to his grandchildren, in short bursts that sometimes include a moral or a lesson. This is "told-to" history (McCall 2011:2), and I have had the good fortune to be the scribe. Arthur's desire to document his own life history in writing reminds me that all communities have historians. In the context of land claims and resource politics, Arthur knew that it is sensible to tell both community history and personal narratives. In the case of Iskut Village, a diverse community comprised of several families, shared and divergent histories are important markers of local identity. His accounts are part of that community story even if they do not always line up with the accounts of others from Iskut. This is a basic reality of local Indigenous history even if outsiders seek or expect a single and homogeneous Indigenous worldview.

An academic obituary might easily ignore Arthur's family roles, how he raised grandchildren compassionately, and how he welcomed friends and strangers alike. At his funeral, Arthur's children and grandchildren reflected on Arthur's generosity and his hospitality. There was always room for friends and guests at Arthur's table and in his hunting camp—even if we visitors failed to wash the dishes properly! Attention to and care of family and community was Arthur's work too. It merits a central place in his story.

Arthur's knowledge of Tahltan lands, the names of places, and historical events must not be forgotten. I was honored when he asked me to help him write his life story. It is a project that continues and now engages members of Arthur's family more directly than he might have initially envisioned. But Arthur meant far more to me as a friend and companion than as a research subject, informant, or collaborator. He taught me to listen to the quieter voices and to be aware of the spirits of moose. My work with Arthur is unfinished. His interest in his own story and sharing it with his family, his community, and a wider world has passed with him. But my lingering sadness is mostly for the death of my friend, a gentle and generous man who saw the goodness and humor in life all while showing the importance of local and personal history to both Indigenous and non-Indigenous peoples.

ACKNOWLEDGMENTS

This obituary is a lengthy elaboration of the eulogy I wrote for Arthur's funeral. I was assisted in writing that obituary by Jodi Nole-Payne, Arthur's granddaughter. At the funeral, I was pleased to meet Karla Henyu Gibson and Denise Nole, both granddaughters, who shared their memories of Arthur with me. I thank Arthur's siblings, particularly Jim Nole and Regina Louie, for sharing their reflections on Arthur's life. And I thank Arthur's children and their spouses for their friendship, hospitality, and continuing interest in completing the biography. Thanks to Douglas Hudson (University of the Fraser Valley) for useful questions and editorial suggestions. My father, Thomas F. McIlwraith (University of Toronto), helped greatly with format, style, and tone. I am grateful to David W. Dinwoodie (University of New Mexico) for continuing to talk with me about this work. A version of this essay was presented at the annual meetings of the American Anthropological Association in Denver, Colorado, in November 2015. The biographical work with Arthur was supported financially with a Phillips Fund grant from the American Philosophical Society (2014). All interpretations of the events in Arthur Nole's life are my own.

NOTES

1. All Tahltan words are written using the Tahltan practical orthography developed by Colin Carter (Carter, Carlick, and Carlick 1994; replicated in McIlwraith 2012b).
2. The Tl'abāne name is Anglicized as Klappan or Klabona. The region is now known popularly as the Sacred Headwaters in recognition of the sources of the Stikine River, the Nass River, and the Skeena River found there (see Davis 2011).
3. Iskut families, including Arthur's, lived for a brief period in the early 1950s at a village site on the shore of Buckley Lake. It is located on the

south side of the Stikine River, on the trail between Telegraph Creek and Łuwechōn Menh (Kluachon Lake, Iskut Village). Forty Mile Flat is a small collection of cabins on British Columbia Highway 37, three miles (five kilometers) north of Iskut Village.

4. Sterritt and colleagues (1998:35–41) indicate that these clashes were largely over food and date them to perhaps two hundred or three hundred years ago. The work of Sterritt and his collaborators (1998:24–28) suggests a long history of movements throughout the headwaters of the Stikine, Skeena, and Nass Rivers (see also Dawson 1887:184; Emmons 1911:115).

5. *Hok'ats* means "cold," *łuwe* is "fish," and *menh* is "lake." Hok'ats Łuwe Menh is located centrally in the Spatsizi Plateau Wilderness Park. It is a significant place for sports fishing and the location of an outpost established by Walker and now run by B.C. Parks. Walker ran a guide outfitting business in the lands around Hok'ats Łuwe Menh from 1948 until 1972, a business that routinely employed Tahltans. He lobbied for the creation of the Spatsizi Plateau Wilderness Park and other regional parks in Tahltan territory in the 1970s (Walker 1976).

6. Walker's characterization of Iskut people is noted by other writers, including Hoagland (1969:84, 104, 164), Janice Sheppard (1983:29–30), Bob Henderson (2006:22), and me (McIlwraith 2012b).

7. The Sekani are Athapaskans to the east of Tahltan territory. Their territory is in the Rocky Mountain Trench, and some Iskut people trace their ancestry to Sekani families. The Gitksan speak a Tsimshian language and live along the Skeena River.

8. *Kenes'kani* means "raft across," in reference to an older means of travel through the area. Highway 37 now connects British Columbia Highway 16 (the Yellowhead Highway) with the Alaska Highway. Highway construction began in 1953, and the road was built incrementally over a twenty-one-year period. The final piece, constructed in 1974, was a bridge over the Stikine River (Sheppard 1983:241–246).

9. That line was graded but never laid with rails, and trains never ran. Iskut people continue to use the rail grade as a road to access hunting areas in Tl'abāne. Resource extraction companies and non-Indigenous hunters use the grade too (Sheppard 1983:246–250).

REFERENCES

Carter, Colin, Patrick Carlick, and Edith Carlick. 1994. Tahltan Children's Illustrated Dictionary. Dease Lake: Tahltan Tribal Council. Prepared in collaboration with Patrick Carlick (Telegraph Creek), Angela Dennis and Regina Louie (Iskut), Susie Tashoots and Myra Blackburn (Dease Lake), Freddie Quock, and Edith Carlick.

Davis, Wade. 2011. The Sacred Headwaters: The Fight to Save the Stikine, Skeena, and Nass. Vancouver: D&M Publishers.

Dawson, George M. 1887. Notes on the Indian Tribes of the Yukon District and Adjacent Northern Portion of British Columbia. *In* Annual Report of the Geological Survey of Canada, 1887. Ottawa: Geological Survey of Canada.

Emmons, G. T. 1911. The Tahltan Indians. Philadelphia: University of Pennsylvania Press.

Henderson, Bob. 2006. In the Land of the Red Goat. Smithers BC: Creekstone Press.

Hoagland, Edward. 1969. Notes from the Century Before: A Journal from British Columbia. New York: Random House.

McCall, Sophie. 2011. First Person Plural: Aboriginal Storytelling and the Ethics of Collaborative Authorship. Vancouver: University of British Columbia Press.

McIlwraith, Thomas. 2008. "The Bloody Moose Got Up and Took Off": Talking Carefully about Food Animals in a Northern Athabaskan Village. Anthropological Linguistics 50(2):125–147.

———. 2012a. A Camp Is a Home and Other Reasons Why Indigenous Hunting Camps Can't Be Moved Out of the Way of Resource Developments. Northern Review 36(2):97–126.

———. 2012b. "We Are Still Didene": Stories of Hunting and History from Northern British Columbia. Toronto: University of Toronto Press.

Paulson, Monte. 2006. A Gentle Revolution. Walrus 2(10):64–75.

Sheppard, Janice R. 1983. The History and Values of a Northern Athapaskan Indian Village. PhD dissertation, University of Wisconsin.

Sterritt, Neil J., et al. 1998. Tribal Boundaries in the Nass Watershed. Vancouver: University of British Columbia Press.

Teit, James A. 1919. Tahltan Tales. Journal of American Folklore 32(124):198–250.

———. 1956. Field Notes on the Tahltan and Kaska Indians, 1912–15. Anthropologica 3(1):40–171.

Walker, T. A. (Tommy). 1976. Spatsizi. Smithers BC: Harbour Publishing.

CONTRIBUTORS

EVELYN J. BOWERS, Department of Anthropology, Ball State University (emerita)

REGNA DARNELL, Department of Anthropology, University of Western Ontario; email: rdarnell@uwo.ca

BRADLEY CAMP DAVIS, Department of History, Eastern Connecticut State University; email: bcampdvs@uw.edu

DAVID W. DINWOODIE, Department of Anthropology, University of New Mexico; email: ddinwood@unm.edu

FREDERIC W. GLEACH, Department of Anthropology, Cornell University; email: f.gleach@cornell.edu

OLGA GLINSKII, Department of Anthropology, University of New Mexico; email: glinskii@unm.edu

MICHAEL E. HARKIN, Department of Anthropology, University of Wyoming; email: harkin@uwyo.edu

ANDREW P. LYONS, Department of Anthropology, Wilfrid Laurier University (emeritus); email: andrewpaullyons@gmail.com

THOMAS MCILWRAITH, Department of Sociology and Anthropology, University of Guelph; email: tmcilwra@uoguelph.ca

NGUYEN PHUONG NGOC, Institut de recherches asiatiques, Aix Marseille Université; email: nguyenpngoc@yahoo.fr

NGUYEN VAN HUY, Nguyen Van Huyen Museum, Hanoi; email: huy.nguyen@nguyenvanhuyen.org.vn

JAMES M. NYCE, Department of Anthropology, Ball State University (emeritus); email: jnyce@bsu.edu

FRANK A. SALAMONE, Department of Sociology, Iona College (emeritus); email: fsalamone@iona.edu

ROBERT C. ULIN, Department of Sociology and Anthropology, Rochester Institute of Technology; email: rcugla@rit.edu

www.ingramcontent.com/pod-product-compliance
Lightning Source LLC
Chambersburg PA
CBHW032345280326
41935CB00008B/455